Corporate
Financial
Management
Second edition

CORPORATE FINANCIAL MANAGEMENT
SECOND EDITION

Julian R. Franks
and
Harry H. Scholefield

Gower Press

First edition published in Great Britain by Gower Press 1974
Reprinted 1977 by Teakfield Limited

This edition published by Gower Press, Teakfield Limited,
1 Westmead, Farnborough, Hants., England

Reprinted 1979

ISBN 0566 02054 8 Cased edition
ISBN 0566 02055 6 Limp edition

British Library Cataloguing in Publication Data

Franks, Julian Ralph
  Corporate financial management.—2nd ed.
  1. Corporations—Finance
  I. Title   II. Scholefield, Harry Houchen
  658.1'5   HG4026

Printed in Great Britain by Biddles Ltd, Guildford, Surrey

7055238

Contents

PART THREE   CAPITAL STRUCTURE

PART FIVE   GLOSSARY AND APPENDICES

Preface

This book examines the financial problems confronting management, and introduces concepts and operational techniques designed to produce effective decisions. In addition, we have tried to place such problems in a logical framework which will form a valuable basis for a coherent corporate financial strategy. We believe the book will interest both the financial manager and the manager who has financial responsibility. In addition, students of finance will find it a comprehensive introduction to corporate finance.

In this second edition, although the underlying structure of the book remains substantially the same, we have introduced some modern capital market theory and evidence as well as updating and simplifying the original text throughout. We have incorporated in Chapter 8 an explanation of the relationship between the stock market and capital project appraisal. Our treatment of inflation, leasing and the valuation of the firm has been significantly altered and that of replacement reduced in complexity.

We wish to thank Dr Jack Broyles of the London Business School, and Professor D. R. Myddelton of the Cranfield School of Management, for their many helpful comments. In addition we are grateful to all the students and colleagues who have pointed out errors and omissions in the first edition.

Appendices 1 and 2 are reproduced, by permission of the authors and publisher, from *The Finance and Analysis of Capital Projects* by A. J. Merrett and Allen Sykes (Longmans, 1963).

June 1977

JRF
HHS

PART ONE
WORKING CAPITAL

1

Cash management

This chapter reviews cash management and suggests methods of achieving an optimum cash balance. Cash is an obvious part of every firm's working capital and is vital to meet a firm's day-to-day obligations. These include wages and salaries, rent and rates, suppliers' invoices and the many other demands on a firm's resources. A firm does not necessarily need actual cash in hand; such obligations can be met, for example, by an overdraft facility, or by utilizing suppliers' credit facilities. Cash management must be thought of in terms of the overall liquidity needs of the firm, specifically its current assets and liabilities.

Current assets represent a firm's most liquid assets, while current liabilities form the short-term claims against the firm. Figure 1:1 presents the format of the balance sheet, which is a statement prepared at a particular point in time summarizing the financial position of the firm. On the left-hand side are the firm's sources of finance, including shares issued and loans outstanding; on the right-hand side are the uses to which that finance has been put – its investment in different classes of assets.

Some current assets can be highly illiquid and require frequent analysis by management to ensure that the operations of the company are not impeded by lack of funds. For example, examination of the debtors account may reveal an unexpected level of debts that are difficult or impossible to collect; or a realistic stock valuation may indicate that some goods are unsaleable.

Figure 1:1   Format of the balance sheet

Sources of funds	Uses of funds
Owners' equity Ordinary shares Retained earnings	*Fixed assets* Buildings and property Machinery Goodwill

Long-term liabilities
Debentures
	Current assets
	Stock – finished goods
	     – work-in-progress
	     – raw materials

Current liabilities Creditors Bank overdraft	Debtors Marketable securities Cash

It is often the lack of marketability of both current and fixed assets that prevents management from realizing their value quickly and from obtaining an accurate estimate of their worth. If the company holds shares in other companies, quoted on the Stock Exchange, it is aware of the value of each investment and is able to realize that value immediately. The machines and the factory are usually less readily marketable and their resale prices are more uncertain in consequence.

The cash balance

A cash balance represents the amount of money a company keeps with a bank on current or deposit account plus any funds the company holds in its own tills. This is the company's most liquid asset and can be used immediately to make payments. Reducing the cash balance by reinvesting in an illiquid asset that gives a higher return may increase the risk that there will be insufficient cash to meet future obligations. Such a shortage of cash may prevent a company discharging its debts, compelling it either to sell off assets rapidly, or call in a 'receiver' to manage its affairs. It is this trade–off between profitability and the risk of running out of cash that will determine the necessary cash balance. Excessive liquidity can lead to a loss of earning power if a company refuses or is unable to finance attractive investments.

In order to increase the cash balance, it is often worth while to clear customers' cheques rapidly. This practice will also save interest on overdrafts and provide more money for reinvestment purposes. It may take up to three days to clear a cheque, but this can be reduced to one day with a 'quick clearance'. If, for example, cheques totalling £100,000 are to be banked, a reduction of two days in clearance would be worth £56, assuming an interest rate of 10 per cent a year (10% x £100,000 x 2/360). If a company receives such sums once a week, the savings would total £2,912 a year. Banks usually charge a small sum for quick clearance, but it is profitable to employ such a facility for large cheques. In addition, this practice prevents a firm from exceeding its agreed overdraft facilities; this can be important at a time of credit shortage.

To establish an appropriate cash balance, a firm's financial manager and analyst must take account of the trading cycle. A toymaking company would be expected to have a low cash balance or a high overdraft before Christmas because customers are invariably allowed to delay payment of their invoices until after the Christmas sales period. The continuance of such high overdrafts after, say, January would signify either a late and inefficient debt-collection policy or low sales.

Measuring liquidity

Before reviewing several measures of efficiency of cash management, it is useful to look at wider measures of liquidity. Two measures commonly used are the current and liquid (quick) ratios. They compare the firm's current assets and liabilities.

$$\text{current ratio} = \frac{\text{current assets}}{\text{current liabilities}}$$

$$\text{quick ratio} = \frac{\text{liquid assets}}{\text{current liabilities}}$$

Current assets are the total balance-sheet value of cash, easily realizable securities, debtors and stocks. *Liquid assets* may be defined more narrowly as current assets less stocks. *Current liabilities* are all outstanding short-term payments due.

Using the quick ratio to measure liquidity is commonly known as applying the 'acid test'. An example is shown in Figure 1:2.

The current ratio informs management whether current assets are sufficient to meet short-term liabilities. Most industrial firms are advised to maintain a current ratio in excess of 1.5:1 because some of the components in current assets might be illiquid. For example, stocks of raw materials could be difficult to return to the supplier, while work-in-progress would probably be of little resale value if the product line was suddenly discontinued. Most companies with a liquidity crisis find that stocks realize much less than their cost or balance-sheet value. Lines Bros, the toy company, found its high stocks of toys and raw materials worth only a fraction of balance-sheet value when it tried unsuccessfully to stave off liquidation. For this reason the 'quick ratio' may be a more useful measure since it excludes stocks; for many companies a ratio of 1:1 is acceptable.

Figure 1:2   Measuring liquidity from short-term balance sheet items

Current liabilities (£'000s)		Current assets (£'000s)	
Creditors	40	Stocks	50
Bank overdraft	10	Debtors	45
		Marketable securities	10
		Cash	5
	—		—
	50		110

$$\text{current ratio} = \frac{\text{current assets}}{\text{current liabilities}} = \frac{110}{50} = 2.2$$

$$\text{quick ratio} = \frac{\text{liquid assets}}{\text{current liabilities}} = \frac{60}{50} = 1.2$$

This ratio must also be treated with care because debtors may contain bad or doubtful debts. In addition, companies that give generous credit terms find that many customers are unable or unwilling to pay immediately just because the vendor is short of cash.

Current and quick ratios are based upon balance-sheet data, which record the asset and liability balances at the date the balance sheet is prepared. Therefore they provide management with only an overall picture of the company's liquidity. Neither ratio gives any indication of the correct level of cash or other current assets to be held; only their existing levels are reflected by the ratios. Finally, balance sheets are usually out of date even before they are published. Clearly, the ratios are of limited use in exposing a problem and must be treated with caution. For cash-management purposes, more detailed information is required.

Measuring the efficiency of cash usage

There are two methods of measuring the efficiency with which cash is being employed:

$$\text{cash in current assets} = \frac{\text{cash balance}}{\text{current assets}}$$

$$\text{turnover of cash in sales} = \frac{\text{sales per period}}{\text{initial cash balance}}$$

The ratio of cash in current assets provides an index of current operations. For example, if a company had an opening cash balance of £25,000 and the current assets totalled £250,000, then the cash in current assets would be ten per cent. Whether such a ratio is high or low can be judged by looking at the individual company's cash needs. Monthly control of cash and an analysis of historical records will give management some indication of trends. An increasing level of cash in current assets could be caused by a reduction in credit given by the company's suppliers or by too high a cash balance. The first may be unavoidable, but the second is not. The ratio can only give an indication of a potential problem; further analysis is required to determine the cause, and only then may action be taken.

If there was one standard for this cash ratio, management's task would be made easier. Unfortunately, there is no one correct value since each industry has its own pattern of cash payments, receipts and requirements. A working guide can be created by comparing average values over time for the ratio of cash to current assets among firms in the same industry. The industry average is only the first step in the process, for an efficient firm should want to do better than the average. Like all ratios, this one can be misleading as it includes all current assets. An increase in stocks without a corresponding increase in the cash level will reduce the ratio and indicate a more efficient use of cash. This would be misleading if the increase in stock levels was caused by decreasing sales. It is important to identify the cause of any change.

The turnover of cash in sales can aid management in monitoring its use of cash. It is a measure of the velocity with which cash moves through a company's operations. For example, if sales for a three-month period are £200,000 and the initial cash balance is £20,000, then the turnover of cash in sales is 10. If the turnover of cash in sales is only 5, then the initial cash balance would be £40,000. The rate of turnover of cash in sales is a measure of efficiency in the use of cash as well as a measure of a company's liquidity. The higher the rate of cash turnover, the greater the efficiency of cash usage.

A company which can increase the velocity of cash passing through its operation can either expand its sales volume without adding extra cash or, if it cannot increase sales, can decrease the amount of cash in hand. However, a higher rate of cash turnover can be produced by enforcing a tighter credit policy so that a lower cash balance is required. This may be beneficial to the company, but it must be a calculated policy. The financial controller may want to reduce trade credit to customers while the sales director will want to increase it in order to encourage higher sales (see Chapter 2). As with the ratio of cash in current assets, there is no universal standard with which to measure turnover of cash in sales. The ratio shows what is happening to the cash balance but not why.

Insolvency

Insolvency suggests an inability to meet payments on demand from existing resources of cash, near cash, or credit. A distinction must be made between technical and legal insolvency.

Technical insolvency [1] occurs when a company has too high a proportion of its assets far removed from cash and is unable to generate cash when required; this is often caused by overtrading. In this situation creditors become apprehensive and will demand immediate payment of their debts. It is a situation where a firm has sufficient assets to meet all its financial obligations, but not enough time to convert those assets into cash.

Legal insolvency is a condition in which there is a permanent cash shortage no matter how much time is provided. The cash that could be released from a firm's assets is less than the immediate demands of its creditors.

The distinction between technical and legal insolvency is often a fine one: a company may have sufficient assets to cover its liabilities – providing it is given sufficient time for conversion. The problem arises when creditors believe they may not be paid and request payment immediately. The company is compelled to convert assets into cash rapidly, which may force sales at prices below real worth. Property and trade investments are considered 'real assets', but if they have to be sold rapidly they will not fetch reasonable prices. In this case, the demands of creditors might convert the company from being technically insolvent to legal insolvency. The end result is harmful to both the company and its creditors, as, given time, all bills could have been met in full and perhaps the company would have been able to continue trading.

A company that finds itself technically insolvent should consider calling in a receiver. A receiver may be appointed by the company, or one of the creditors and he must be a qualified accountant. He is able to continue running the company and is empowered to sell the assets over a reasonable period of time in order to obtain the maximum price for the creditors and the company's shareholders. Such an appointment prevents the company being declared insolvent immediately and its assets sold off too quickly. After the receiver has discharged the company's outstanding liabilities, assuming it is still solvent, the company will be passed back into the control of the management and shareholders.

In 1971 Rolls-Royce Ltd faced a serious cash crisis. If it had been declared insolvent, the company's operations would have ceased immediately and the assets would have been sold forthwith. Such assets as factories and stocks might have been sold at prices substantially below their value, while, if the company's debtors had been pressed for immediate payment, they, too, would have found themselves in a financial crisis. In fact, a receiver was appointed and the operations were kept running with government funds. There is no doubt that creditors received much more under these conditions than they would have done if the company had been declared insolvent and placed into immediate liquidation.

Raising short-term credit

So far it has been assumed that a company must meet all cash payments from its own cash resources. However, it could be wasteful for a company that has attractive investments to maintain a high level of cash, in anticipation of emergencies, when it could use bank overdrafts to meet regular or irregular cash demands.

An overdraft facility can be easily negotiated with one or more commercial (clearing) banks, with rates varying from 2 to 5 per cent a year above the bank's minimum lending or base rate. The interest rate charged will depend on the customer's status, the purpose of the borrowing, its duration and the security offered. Unsecured overdrafts will tend to cost at least 2 per cent a year more than those that are secured.

Overdrafts are an important line of credit invaluable for cash emergencies, but companies tend to consider them as permanent sources of finance. The bank can ask for the overdraft to be repaid at any time, unless a specific credit period has been arranged. It usually costs very little, if anything, to obtain a one-year loan. It is also possible to obtain substantial loans for up to five years, with interest payable only on the amount outstanding. The negotiation of such facilities may require an initial commitment fee of up to 1 per cent of the facility granted, but such potential borrowing can reduce the firm's needs for cash substantially and should be reviewed in the light of the firm's cash-flow forecasts and the prevailing credit situation. Of course, lines of credit should be established when credit conditions are easy. It is at this time that a company is likely to have an excess amount of cash and believe that short-term borrowings are not required. However, during these periods it is possible to make medium-term arrangements with the commercial banks and such facilities will be valuable when credit becomes tight. Such arrangements allow reduced levels of cash to be held, as any emergency can be satisfied by the unused lines of credit.

Depositing receipts

Many firms collect cheques, drafts and other receipts once or twice a week. These receipts are entered in the firm's accounts and then banked.

The cost per day of holding cheques is either an opportunity cost or the real cost of not depositing these cheques. The cost is real if the company has used an overdraft to pay bills which could otherwise have been paid out of receipts. For a company with zero overdraft, failure to deposit cash with the bank does not carry a real cost. However, there is an opportunity cost, which is equivalent to what the cash could have earned if invested, for example, in the short-term money market.

As an example, suppose that overdraft rates and money-market rates are both 10 per cent a year or approximately 0.03 per cent a day ($10/365 = 0.03\% = £0.0003$ per £1). What is the cost to a company of not depositing receipts immediately? The effect is shown in Figure 1:3 for two companies with annual sales of £10 million and £100 million. Assume cash is being banked on Wednesdays and Fridays and daily sales are £40,000. The cost per day of not banking £40,000 is £12 (0.0003 × £40,000). If Monday's cash is not banked until Wednesday, then the loss is £24. If Tuesday's is not banked until Wednesday, then the loss is an additional £12 and Thursday's loss brings the total to £48 per week, or £2,496 a year. This loss or cost increases to £120 per week, or £6,240 a year if the company banks only on the Friday of each week. For a larger company with sales totalling £400,000 per day, the cost of banking only once a week instead of banking daily will be £62,400 a year.

Figure 1:3   Cost of banking once or twice a week compared with daily banking

	£	£
Annual sales	10,000,000	100,000,000
Average daily sales*	40,000	400,000
Cost per day: £0.0003 per £ of receipts	12	120
Interest cost per week of banking only twice a week compared with banking daily	48	480
Interest cost per week of banking only once a week compared with banking daily	120	1,200

*The average daily sales are computed by dividing annual sales by the number of working days (250).

Clearly, a company has to take account of clerical costs in establishing the frequency of deposit.[2] The larger the volume of receipts, the lower the cost per pound of deposit.

For large firms consisting of small autonomous units, a once or twice weekly schedule of deposits may be acceptable. Even in a decentralized company, it is often profitable to centralize the company's bank accounts and bank frequently. Thus individual subsidiaries, for example retail stores, may be permitted to bank at the local branch, but all deposits should be cleared to a central bank account [3] where the overdraft can be minimised or the maximum funds invested. If there is a centralization of accounts, management will appreciate more readily the value of frequent banking. Also, if money is left on premises for several days or more there must be a safe and insurance facilities; frequent banking will reduce such security costs and compel local staff to control their funds more effectively. When subsidiaries of the same company borrow from or lend to the parent, a market rate of interest should be secured. In order to compare divisional profit performance and encourage good cash management, the transfer of funds between subsidiaries or divisions of the same company should be made at market rates of interest.

It has been assumed that a permanent reduction in working capital by more frequent use of banking facilities will either reduce the overdraft outstanding or increase funds for reinvestment. The overdraft and investment rates have been taken at 10 per cent a year on a pre-tax basis. However, if the company is in a position of capital rationing, a permanent increase in funds available might enable the company to invest in additional capital projects with returns greater than the cost of borrowing.

Investing excess cash

There are two important aspects of a company's short-term money flows: the first is to maintain a high level of liquidity with minimum risk and the second is to generate additional income by investing idle funds when they are available or to reduce outstanding loans. Therefore, as a general rule, excess cash above some minimum level[4] should be invested in marketable securities. This rule is subject to the qualification that the interest earned over the expected holding period must more than compensate for transaction and inconvenience costs.[5] If cash projections are reasonably certain, then the transfer between cash and marketable securities can be made efficiently.

Various types of marketable securities are available to smooth out fluctuations in cash flows. They include bills of exchange, certificates of deposit and government securities. Such investments are of varying lives, ranging from overnight to 20 years. Large companies that find they have a cash surplus even for a day can invest in the short-term money market – the minimum amount is about £50,000. An investor may lend such money to an industrial company of the highest repute, a local authority, or to the government. The government issues Treasury bills each week with a maturity of 90 and 180 days and the investor can either buy these securities outright, or purchase them in the market with a maturity of less than the stated term from previous buyers. Companies should be aware that there are a variety of financial instruments that can be purchased in the money market and there are a number of 'money brokers' who advise on the short-term investment of surplus funds.

It should be apparent that in order to achieve the high returns that can be made from investing surplus funds, most companies need centralized banking facilities. Each subsidiary of a company should be allowed its own bank account, but there should be procedures to ensure that a subsidiary's surplus funds are directed towards a central bank account. From here cash balances can be invested or overdrafts of other subsidiaries reduced, with a consequent decrease in interest charges. In a period of high interest costs, such procedures are of particular importance.

Preparing a cash budget

To control a company's cash flows, one requires a plan of the company's operations for the relevant future period. This plan will be based on forecasts of cash receipts from sales and cash disbursements for costs and purchases of equipment etc. It will reveal to the financial manager the timing and amounts of future cash inflows and outflows, enabling him to determine the future cash needs of the company, plan for their financing and exercise control over the company's liquidity. Clearly, the usefulness of the cash budget will depend on the accuracy of the forecasts employed; sensitive variables should be altered to examine their effects upon the firm's sources and uses of funds.

Cash receipts

The key to the accuracy of most cash budgets is the forecast of sales. A forecast of sales is not the same as a forecast of cash receipts if the sales are made on credit, for then only a proportion of the value of a month's sales will be received in that month. Consider an example of a company with a sales forecast for a six-month period (July-December) as outlined in Figure 1:4. A schedule has been established of expected sales receipts based on the assumption that 10 per cent of total sales are cash sales and 90 per cent credit sales, of which 90 per cent are collected after one month and 10 per cent after two months.

Figure 1:4   Projected sales and cash receipts

	May	June	July	Aug	Sept	Oct	Nov	Dec
Total sales (£'000)	63	65	68	81	91	83	89	68
Credit sales (£'000)	56.7	58.5	61.2	72.9	81.9	74.7	80.1	61.2
Collections (£'000):								
1 month (90%)			51.0	52.7	55.1	65.6	73.7	67.2	72.1
2 months (10%)				5.7	5.9	6.1	7.3	8.2	7.5
Total collections (£'000)			58.4	61.0	71.7	81.0	75.4	79.6
Cash sales (£'000)			6.8	8.1	9.1	8.3	8.9	6.8
Total sales receipts (£'000)			65.2	69.1	80.8	89.3	84.3	86.4

From this example it is easy to see the effect of a variation in sales on the magnitude and timing of cash receipts. For simplicity, no account has been taken of potential bad debts. An estimate of the percentage of credit sales which will result in bad debts can easily be incorporated into the cash flow.

Cash disbursements

The next step is to estimate the expenditures required to generate these receipts. A schedule should be drawn up of raw materials, wages, overhead and administrative expenses, to which should be added capital expenditure, interest, dividend and tax payments. There is a time lag between purchases of materials and cash payments. Figure 1:5 is a schedule of expenses associated with the sales forecasts of Figure 1:4 where there is a time lag of one month between purchasing materials and paying for them.

Figure 1:5   Projected expenses

	June	July	Aug	Sept	Oct	Nov	Dec
Purchases (£'000)	36	45	30	24	31	32	24
Cash payments for purchases (£'000)		36	45	30	24	31	32
Wages paid (£'000)		21	25	28	29	27	29
Other expenses (£'000)		13	14	14	15	15	35
Total cash expenses (£'000)		70	84	72	68	73	96

In addition to cash expenses, account must be taken of capital expenditures, all interest, dividend and tax payments. Dividend and interest payments for most companies are paid on specific dates, while tax payments will depend on projected earnings. For simplicity, these additional expenses have been incorporated in the item 'other expenses' in Figure 1:5. In a more detailed analysis these items would have been listed separately.

Net cash flow and cash balance

The final stage is to construct a monthly budget in which the net cash gain or loss is calculated from the projected cash flows. The net cash flow may then be added to the initial cash balance and the projected cash position computed month by month for the period under review. The estimated monthly net cash gains (losses) have been computed from Figures 1:4 and 1:5, and are outlined in Figure 1:6 with the initial and final cash balances. The minimum cash balance is taken to be £10,000, the sum which is always deducted from the final cash balance to yield the total excess or required cash for that month.

In this example the cash budget indicates that the company is able to cover all its cash commitments. The cash budget is part of the master plan for controlling a company's cash flow. If an excess of required cash over cash inflows occurs, then the company must see if disbursements can be delayed, receipts brought forward or overdraft facilities arranged. Indeed, one of the principal purposes of a cash budget is to determine the timing and magnitude of prospective financial needs, so that the most appropriate methods of financing can be arranged. Furthermore, on the basis of a cash budget, a financial manager can plan to invest excess funds in marketable securities. The result is an efficient transfer of funds from cash to marketable securities and back.

Figure 1:6   Net cash increase (reduction)

	July	Aug	Sept	Oct	Nov	Dec
Total receipts (£'000)	65	69	81	89	84	86
Total payments (£'000)	70	84	72	68	73	96
Net cash (£'000)	(5)	(15)	9	21	11	(10)
Initial cash balance (£'000)	30	25	10	19	40	51
Ending cash balance (£'000)	25	10	19	40	51	41
Minimum cash balance (£'000)	10	10	10	10	10	10
Excess (required cash) (£'000)	15	0	9	30	41	31

Variations in cash flows

The usefulness of a cash budget depends on the accuracy of the forecasts on which it is based. However these estimates may have been computed, it is likely that there will be a deviation between actual and estimated cash flows. There are two methods which can help management to improve cash budgeting. The first is to analyse deviations that occur. When the reasons for these deviations can be determined, account should be taken in preparing future cash budgets. The second is to apply a crude risk analysis to the cash budget. In other words, it may be desirable to see how a decline in sales and alteration in the average collection period for debtors would affect the budget for cash receipts and how a change in material prices or wages would affect the budget for cash expenses. A simple sensitivity analysis based on general economic and industry factors should be carried out to see how the firm's expected cash position would alter under different trading conditions. When this is produced, management should work out how the firm could adjust to these situations should they arise. It is far better to provide for a range of possible outcomes[6] than to rely upon a single expected result because this allows the financial manager to reassess the margin of safety provided by the minimum cash balance and to judge the adequacy of financial plans to meet unexpected changes.

Summary

Cash management is an essential factor in the operations of all companies.

A shortage of cash may lead to insolvency. Cash management must aim to reduce the required level of cash, but minimize the risk of being unable to discharge claims against the company as they arise. Cash budgeting and the establishment of credit facilities with banks are important ingredients of successful money management.

Notes

1 J. E. Walter, 'Determination of technical solvency', *Journal of Business*, vol. 30 (January 1959), pp. 30–43.
2 F. W. Searby, 'Use your hidden cash resources', *Harvard Business Review*, vol. 46, no. 2 (March–April 1968), pp. 71–80.
3 F. E. Horn, 'Managing cash', *Journal of Accountancy*, vol. 117 (April 1964), pp. 56–62. Reprinted in *Foundations for Financial Management: A Book of Readings*, edited by J. Van Horne (Homewood, Ill: Irwin, 1966), pp. 25–35.
4 R. F. Calman, *Linear Programming and Cash Management/CASH ALPHA* (Cambridge, Mass: The M.I.T. Press, 1968).
5 D.E. Peterson and R. B. Haydon, *A Quantitative Framework for Financial Management* (Homewood Ill: Richard D. Irwin, 1969), pp. 212–19.
6 G. Donaldson, 'Strategy for financial emergencies', *Harvard Business Review*, vol. 47, no. 6 (November-December 1969), pp. 71–9.

Further reading

C. J. Anderson, 'Managing the corporate "money" position', *Business Review* (Federal Reserve Bank of Philadelphia), March 1961.
S. H. Archer, 'A model for the determination of firm cash balances', *Journal of Financial and Quantitative Analysis*, vol. 1 (March 1966), pp. 1–14.
W. Beranek, *Working Capital Management* (Belmont, Calif: Wadsworth, 1966).
H. Bierman, Jr, and A. K. McAdams, *Management Decisions for Cash and Marketing Securities* (Ithaca, NY: Graduate School of Business, Cornell University, 1962).
M. Churchill and B. Ward 'How BMW computerised cash planning' *Accountancy*, (June, 1976), p. 87.
G. P. E. Clarkson and B. J. Elliott; *Managing Money and Finance* (London: Gower Press, 1969).
R. W. Johnson, *Financial Management*, third edition (Boston, Mass: Allyn and Bacon, 1966).
M. H. Miller and D. Orr, 'An application of control limit models to the management of corporate cash balances', in *Financial Research and Management Decisions*, edited by A. A. Robichek (New York: Wiley, 1967).

M. H. Miller and D. Orr 'The demand for money by firms'. *Quarterly Journal of Economics*, (1966), pp. 80, 413

A. E. Reed, 'Corporate cash management', *Financial Executive*, vol. 31 (October 1963).

S. Robbins, 'Getting more money out of cash', *N.A.A. Bulletin*, vol. 42 (September 1960).

R. I. Robinson, *Money and Capital Markets* (New York: McGraw-Hill, 1964).

G. W. Woodworth, *The Money Market and Monetary Management* (New York: Harper & Row, 1965).

2

Management of debtors and creditors

In this chapter we discuss the interrelationship of cash needs and debtor balances and analyse credit terms and collection procedures in the light of a company's requirements for funds. We also consider the management of creditors.

Factors in credit policy

In the modern commercial environment, most companies find that they have to give credit to customers in accordance with industry practice if they are to achieve a worthwhile sales volume. However, many other factors are involved in setting credit policy besides conventional practice. Before a company decides on a particular set of credit terms it must establish its strategic objectives. It may, for example, wish to alter its credit terms in order to:

1   Raise sales of new and existing products to enable its customers to purchase and stock a wider range of goods. In industries where the buyers have limited capital resources, this may be essential.
2   Create a more even production flow. For example, because of the seasonality of the trade, a dress manufacturer employed a labour force on overtime during the busy season and laid them off during the remainder of the year. This practice increased operating costs because

of the employment of temporary unskilled labour and led to labour troubles. The problem was alleviated by improving credit terms to customers, enabling them to stock the goods in advance of the selling season. The switch of policy resulted in increased sales, reduced stock and improved productions flows.

3 Accept higher-risk credit customers where profits are sufficiently large or a sufficient risk premium can be obtained. The cost of a bad debt is the incremental cost (that is, the variable cost of producing a unit) of the product, not its selling price, for if the customer does not pay, the loss is represented by the cost of the sale rather than by the lost revenue. (This assumes the sale could not have been made without credit terms being granted.) Consequently, the lower the product cost (or the greater the profit margin) the more high-risk credit customers can be accommodated.

The main instruments used to achieve changes in the level of credit will depend upon the particular objective. An expansion may be brought about by increasing customer credit limits or by extending the period of credit. Conversely, in order to reduce credit levels, the firm may grant discounts for early payment, exact a charge on overdue accounts, or enforce more rigorous collection procedures. The credit instruments used will be determined by the firm's ability to meet increased sales, its cash position, the sophistication of the credit department and its importance within the corporation, and, above all, competitive practice in the industry.

Initial analysis of debtors

Debtors are among a firm's most liquid assets, but the expected revenue is only transformed into cash receipts when customers pay. The promptness of payment is important because credit requires financing, which is costly, while lengthening delays in payment are a sign of doubtful or bad debts. One way of assessing such delays in customer payments is to compute the average period of time for which debts have been outstanding('the age of debtors'):

$$\frac{\text{average age}}{\text{of debtors}} = \frac{\text{debtors at end of period}}{\text{credit sales during the period}} \times \frac{\text{number of days in}}{\text{accounting period}}$$

If, at the end of a four-month period (120 days), the debtors balance is £1 million and the total credit sales for the period are £2 million then the average age of debtors is 2 months:

$$\text{average age of debtors} = \frac{\text{£1 million}}{\text{£2 million}} \times 120 \text{ days}$$
$$= 60 \text{ days}$$

If the average age of debtors rises over time, increasing amounts of working capital are tied up in credit. An increasing percentage of bad debts may also be occurring and therefore a more detailed analysis of the age of debtors is required, for a company is not only interested in their average age but also in their quality. This can be found by classifying debtors by date of sale and this concept will be illustrated later in the chapter.

Effect of extending credit terms

In theory a firm should lower its standards for accepting credit accounts as long as the profitability of sales exceeds the costs of increased credit sales. What are the costs associated with a relaxation of credit standards? The costs to be considered initially are those associated with an additional investment in debtors and an increase in their average age.

Assume that a firm's product sells at £10 per unit, of which £6 represents variable costs (including credit-department costs) before taxes. Fixed costs total £1 million. Current sales (all credit sales) are £5 million and it is estimated that by relaxing credit terms to customers who were not previously considered creditworthy, the average age of debtors will increase from 1 to 2 months, and sales revenue will improve by 20 per cent to £6 million. The total cost of £6 million of sales is therefore £4.6 million computed as follows:

	£
Fixed costs	1,000,000
Cost of present sales (500,000 × £6)	3,000,000
Cost of additional sales (100,000 × £6)	600,000
Total costs	4,600,000

The profit from additional sales must now be compared with the increased cost of the investment in debtors. The profit from additional sales is £400,000:

	£
Revenue from additional sales (100,000 units at £10)	1,000,000
Less the variable cost of additional sales (100,000 units at £6)	600,000
Profit from additional sales	400,000

What is the company's increased investment in debtors? First calculate the present investment in debtors. This is £416,667.

Annual sales × selling price × average age of debtors
(expressed as a fraction of one year)
$$= 500{,}000 \times £10 \times \tfrac{1}{12}$$
$$= £416{,}667$$

As the average age of debtors has increased to 2 months on the increased sales volume of 600,000 units, the company's investment in debtors has increased to £1,000,000:

$$600,000 \times £10 \times \tfrac{1}{6} = £1,000,000$$

The increased funds invested in credit sales total £583,333 (£1,000,000–£416,667) and, if the cost of funds is 20 per cent, then the new credit policy will cost £116,667 a year (20% × £583,333). Clearly, the new credit policy is profitable, as the increased profits of £400,000 exceed the increased costs of £116,667.

There are, of course, practical problems in this type of policy as it has been assumed that estimated outcomes are known. However, it is possible to attach a probability distribution to the changes in demand and to the average age of debtors and to compute a range of possible outcomes. Alternatively, management may estimate a range of sales and the average age of debtors at specified sales levels and compute the resulting net profit.

Analysing the risk of default

It is possible that debtors will default and that there will be an increase in the credit collection period. Different credit policies will involve both these factors and will produce various levels of profit or loss. Continuing with the example considered in the previous section, Figure 2:1 outlines the present policy, the revised policy (policy 1) and an alternative, termed policy 2.

Figure 2:1   Three possible credit policies

	Present Policy	Policy 1	Policy 2
Increase in sales	0	20%	30%
Average age of debtors	1 month	2 months	3 months
Percentage of bad debts		2.5%	5%

The cost of additional investment in debtors for policy 1 has already been calculated at £116,667 per year. In the case of policy 2, with sales of 650,000 units and an average age of debtors of 3 months, an additional investment in debtors of £1,208,333 is required.

	£
Total investment in debtors	
(650,000 units × £10 ×)	1,625,000
Less present investment in debtors	416,667
Additional investment in debtors	1,208,333

At the company's borrowing rate of 20 per cent the cost of this additional investment is £241,667 p.a. (20% × £1,208,333).

The additional cost to the company of an increase in bad debts for both policy 1 and policy 2 can now be calculated. Under the present policy, bad debts increase with the level of sales in relative and absolute terms (Figure 2:2).

Figure 2:2   Value of bad debts under different sales policies

Annual sales × variable cost per unit × percentage of bad debts	Present Policy	Policy 1	Policy 2
500,000 × £6 × 0.01	£30,000		
600,000 × £6 × 0.025		£90,000	
650,000 × £6 × 0.05			£195,000

The profitability of each policy is summarized below.

	Policy 1 £	Policy 2 £
Profitability of additional sales	400,000	600,000
Additional bad debts	60,000	165,000
	340,000	435,000
Cost of the additional investment in debtors per year	116,667	241,667
Additional net profits (profits less costs)	223,333	193,333

In these circumstances it is best to pursue policy 1.

In the preceding analysis we have separated the cost of servicing the increased level of debtors and the expected increase in bad debts. This approach postulates that the cost of financing an increase in the level of debtors is equal to a default-free interest rate, such as the government bond rate. Thus, if the average age of debtors is three months the cost of lending should be represented by the three month rate of interest on a government bond. The risk of a debtor defaulting has been costed separately. If the analyst wishes to combine the two costs he requires an interest rate that reflects both the cost of lending to the debtor and the risk of the debtor's default. To calculate this a risk premium should be added to the government's three-month bond rate. How would the analyst obtain such information on the risk premium? He could simply find the interest rate charged by the clearing banks on unsecured loans to customers of that particular risk. One large company has established four risk classes for

debtors with the appropriate costs of finance. The cost of finance for each
risk class differs by the size of the risk premium. The risk premium is found
by comparing the interest rate or average yield received on the unsecured
loan stocks of particular companies traded on the Stock Exchange, with
that of a default free government bond. For example, if the ten-year
unsecured loan stock of Company X yields 20 per cent and a government
bond of the same maturity yields 12 per cent then the risk premium is 8 per
cent. If we assume that the three-month government borrowing rate is 10
per cent then the interest rate to be charged or imputed to a three-month
receivable is 18 per cent. It is essential that the debtor falls within one of the
risk classes that has been constructed and that he is graded accordingly. In
addition, the risk premium has been computed on a ten year loan stock.
Presumably that premium varies with the period of credit that has been
granted. We have assumed a three month credit period. Since additional
goods are frequently delivered prior to payment for the original goods, the
credit period is in fact longer than three months, as there will always be 60
at a balance outstanding. As a rule of thumb we would assume the risk
premium appropriate for a receivable is a long term one; clearly this is only
an approximation.

In the analysis a specific level of bad debts has been assumed; yet that
level is an uncertain one and it is now necessary to examine how an
increasing level of doubtful debts can be monitored. Returning to the
previous example, annual sales have been projected as increasing from £5
million to £6 million and the age classification of debtors for the four-
month sales period (March to June) is as shown in Figure 2:3. For the four-
month period ending June, credit sales total £2 million while the value of
debtors totals £1 million. In column 4, outstanding debtors are classified by
the date of sale and therefore it is easy to see how old the outstanding
debtors are.

Figure 2:3   Estimated age classification of debtors based on forecast sales

Age classification (days)	Month of sale	Monthly credit sales (£'000s)	Value of debtors (£'000s)	Monthly value of debtors as percentage of credit sales (%)
1–30	June	400	360	90
31–60	May	600	360	60
61–90	April	600	180	30
91–120	March	400	40	10
121 +	Earlier	—	60	—
		2,000	1,000	

The forecast average age of debtors is, approximately,[1]

$$\frac{£1 \text{ million}}{£2 \text{ million}} \times 120 \text{ days} = 60 \text{ days}$$

If the actual value of debtors at the end of June is shown in Figure 2:4, what can be said about the success or failure of the credit policy?

Figure 2:4   Age classification of debtors based on actual sales

Age classification (days)	Month of sale	Monthly credit sales (£'000s)	Value of debtors (£'000s)	Monthly value of debtors as percentage of credit sales (%)
1–30	June	400	360	90
31–60	May	600	450	75
61–90	April	600	240	40
91–120	March	400	40	10
121+	Earlier	—	60	—
		2,000	1,150	

The actual average age of debtors is 69 days compared to the estimate of 60 days.

$$\text{average age of debtors} = \frac{£1.15 \text{ million}}{£2.0 \text{ million}} \times 120 \text{ days} = 69 \text{ days}$$

How does this affect the estimate of the profit to be gained from relaxing the credit standards assuming the estimates of bad debts are correct? On the basis of these four months an additional investment of £150,000 is required due to the increase in the average age of debtors from 60 to 69 days.

	£
Actual investment in debtors for sales of £2 million	1,150,000
Estimated investment in debtors for sales of £2 million	1,000,000
Additional annual investment in debtors[2]	150,000

At the company's required rate of return of 20 per cent, the cost of this increase amounts to £30,000 annually. How has this arisen? From Figure 2:3 it may be seen that the estimated monthly profile of debtors as a percentage of credit sales is 90, 60, 30 and 10 per cent for each of the four months. In Figure 2:4 the actual figures are shown to be 90, 75, 40 and 10 per cent. Therefore, the customers who purchased goods in April and May failed to pay within the stipulated credit period. Having highlighted where the difference has occurred it would now be possible to examine these accounts and to consider whether a more stringent credit policy is necessary.

Conversely, sales may prove higher than estimated so that additional profits cover the additional costs of debtors.

An increase in credit must be measured against the net revenue received. However, it is important not only to review the total debtors outstanding, and their age, but also the distribution of credit by customers.

Cost and benefits of a discount policy

Management may be faced with a deteriorating debtors situation, or, as in the previous example, with a difference between actual and estimated debtors. It is most unlikely that a new, more stringent credit policy can be implemented without cost. Thus management hàs to weigh up the benefits of persuading customers to pay their bills earlier against the cost of greater control. One method is to offer a discount to customers if they pay early and measure this cost against the savings from the funds released. This policy may be useful if management wishes to discriminate between those customers who are able to pay cash within ten days and others who require a significant credit period if they are to purchase the company's products. To illustrate, a simple example will be analysed to show the principles involved; this analysis will then be expanded to a more generalized approach.

Assume a company has annual credit sales of £6 million and an average collection period of 2 months (on average £1 million is outstanding). The company is considering an offer of a discount to encourage prompt payment and hence reduce the average age of debtors. Analysing costs first, reduced sales revenue is a function of the discount offered, the number of customers who take up the offer and the sales level. For example, assume the offer of a 2 per cent discount for prompt payment (within 10 days) is taken up by 50 per cent (by sales) of customers; the cost of the offer will be:

$$\text{discount} \times \text{proportion of customers accepting} \times \text{sales (£)}$$
$$= 0.02 \times 0.5 \times £6,000,000$$
$$= £60,000 \text{ per year}$$

The savings are a function of the reduction in the debtors ledger and the cost of those funds. Suppose the average collection period falls from two months to one month; in the short term, cash flow would be increased by the value of one month's sales. If the cost of funds is 20 per cent before tax then the savings resulting from the credit policy are:

opportunity investment rate $\times$ value of sales converted into cash
$$= 0.20 \times £500,000$$
$$= £100,000$$

In this example the cost of funds represents not only the time value of money but also the risk of default of the debtor. It is a risk-adjusted required rate of return. In the present case, savings exceed costs by £40,000 and the policy is judged to be worthwhile. This said, it is virtually impossible to gauge the response rate precisely and this makes the decrease in the average collection period for debtors correspondingly difficult to estimate. However, the uncertainty can be reduced substantially by a more rigorous analysis.

The customer response rate appears to be the most uncertain variable in the above analysis. In fact it is also important to determine which customers respond – in other words the way in which the response affects the average collection period. One assumption which can be made is that for any response rate the respondents to the discount will be drawn proportionally from the entire age distribution of outstanding debtors. So the average collection period for the debtors who do not respond is the same as the average collection period for all debtors before the discount offer was introduced.

For example, if the discount offer is 2 per cent for payment within 10 days and it is taken up by 60 per cent (by value) of customers and the average collection period previously was 2 months, then the collection period will fall to 1 month. It is assumed in the calculations below that everyone who responds pays at the end of the stipulated periods. Then the new average collection period is:

% responding $\times$ discount period + (100% – % responding)

$\qquad\qquad\qquad\qquad\qquad\qquad$ $\times$ previous collection period

$$= 60\% \times \tfrac{1}{3} + 40\% \times 2$$

$\qquad\qquad\qquad\qquad$ (taking 10 days $= \tfrac{1}{3}$ month)

$$= 1 \text{ month}$$

With these assumptions about the way debtors will respond to the discount offer, the change in the average collection period is

$\qquad$ % responding (previous collection period – discount period)

For the example discussed so far, the broken line in Figure 2:5 gives the costs of the discount offer in terms of the response rate, calculated from the following equation,

$\qquad$ cost $=$ % responding $\times$ total sales $\times$ discount rate

Obviously it is a straight line.

The complete line in Figure 2:5 gives the savings from the discount offer,

savings = change in average collection period × total sales
                                    × opportunity investment rate
      = % responding (previous collection period
                              – discount period) × total sales
                                    × opportunity investment rate

Figure 2:5   Costs and savings from a 2 per cent credit discount

Annual sales £6 million; previous average collection period 2 months;
terms of discount offer 2 per cent for payments within 10 days; opportunity
investment rate 20 per cent.

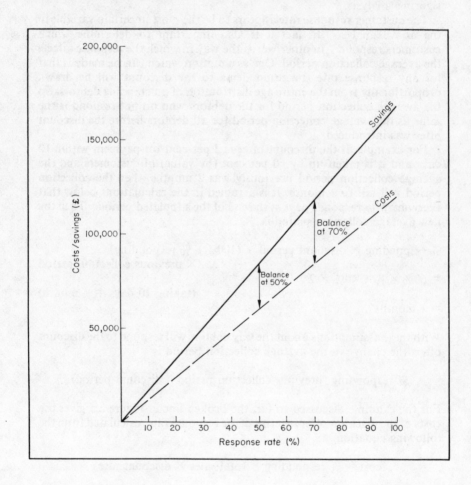

Clearly this is also a straight line. The cost and savings curves intersect at zero.

In fact, with the above assumptions about the way debtors will respond to the discount offer, the scheme will be profitable whatever the response rate. The amount of profit will vary with the response rate and be represented by the vertical line between costs and savings at a particular response rate.

The profit or loss implicit in the credit discount decision will depend on the following factors:

1 The terms offered (discount and period).
2 The opportunity investment rate.
3 The age structure of debtors who do not take advantage of the offer.

Factor 1 is determined by management, 2 is known and attention can now focus on 3. In effect the assumption is that customers who respond to the offer are drawn proportionately from the entire age structure of debtors. In fact, those customers who have paid promptly in the past will be more likely to respond to the offer than those who have frequently delayed making payments and hence the estimate of the reduced average age of debtors may prove optimistic. A sensitivity analysis can be employed, using various combinations of terms, showing the largest non-responding portion of the ledger which the policy could sustain before becoming unprofitable. The managerial decision then rests on an analysis of the effects of the proposed policy on the age structure of debtors.

The analysis may seem complex, but it does provide a useful framework: the outcome of the credit policy decision depends on estimates of the quality of debtor likely to respond, as well as the numbers involved. Careful credit management should permit fairly accurate estimates to be prepared as a basis for prudent decision-making.

Alternative collection procedures

The debtors ledger often represents a substantial investment, usually dictated by market conditions and commercial practice in the industry. The main objective in financing these debtors is to generate the maximum cash inflow at the lowest possible cost. Apart from the approach mentioned above, there are several alternative financial policies which can be used to ensure efficient credit management, but only three will be examined here. They are:

1 Sell all debtors at the end of the month to a commercial factor for cash.
2 Borrow against debtors balance.
3 Develop a credit and collection department to collect own and other firms' debts.

Factoring of debtors

The objective is to sell the entire collection of debtors to a commercial factor. If a satisfactory price is negotiated, the factor takes on the responsibility of collecting all accounts due and accepts the risks of non-payment on a proportion of these accounts. The purchase price is determined on the basis of the net cash value of the debtors balance. Generally an advance payment is made – for example, 90 per cent of the net cash value. The balance after deducting service and financing charges is paid to the company on the average due date of the accounts.

The advantages of this policy are that the firm has no direct collection charges of its own, it receives the cash earlier and carries no risk of bad debts. These advantages have to be weighed against the price paid to a commercial factor, normally in the form of a discount on the total debtors ledger balance.

Borrowing against the debtors balance

An alternative approach is to pledge the debtors balance as collateral for a loan provided by commercial or merchant banks.[3] In this case, the company retains its obligation to collect debts as well as the risk of bad debts. The usual practice is for the commercial bank to lend the firm 70–80 per cent of the net value of the debtors and exact interest and possibly a service charge. Generally the company will reduce the loan as debts are paid; this policy is cheaper than factoring, although the company is still responsible for accounting, ledger control and collection, and of course, the risk of non-collection.

Purchasing of debtors

If a company has a credit department, why not put it to further use? An efficient credit department should find little difficulty in providing a collection service for other companies with similar customers. First of all, management must decide whether this is cheaper than other alternatives, and second, what volume of debtors must be processed to yield maximum efficiency. If management feels that this volume can be attained, it should seriously consider extending the activities of the credit control department to achieve a more efficient utilization of resources.

Setting a policy for payment of creditors

Trade credit is a very useful source of finance, especially for smaller companies. Its control requires different techniques from those for current assets, because the nature of the decision process is different. Within limits (such as the supplier's payment period) a company can choose when to pay its trade bills and problems of ageing and bad debts do not arise. Given the general desirability of deferring payment, a progressive approach can be developed to the problem of deciding exactly when to pay.

Assuming that a discount is offered by the supplier for prompt payment, the first question to decide is whether acceptance will prove worth while. Suppose that the credit terms are '2/10 net 45' – that is, a 2 per cent discount is given if payment is made within 10 days but the full amount must be paid anyway within 45 days. The question to decide is whether a buyer would be better off by paying promptly and taking advantage of the discount, or paying later and using the funds meanwhile. In effect the opportunity of the discount attaches a cost to the funds and this cost can be compared to the investment rate. If advantage is taken of the discount, then payment is made on day 10 (still delayed as long as possible); if not, then payment is made on day 45. Thus, not paying at day 10 gives an extra 35 days credit, the cost of which is the 2 per cent discount that has been lost.

First, the discount of 2 per cent must be compared with the return on investment. If £98 is paid at day 10 the saving is £2, which is equivalent to a return of £2 on an investment of £98. This produces a rate of return of:

$$\frac{2}{98} \times 100\% = 2.04\%$$

This 2.04 per cent return on investment applies for 35 days; it must be multiplied by 365/35 to obtain an equivalent annual rate:

$$\text{equivalent annual rate} = \frac{2.04 \times 365}{35}\%$$

$$= 21\%$$

This 21 per cent is the annual before-tax cost of trade credit for the supplier who has offered the terms. It must be compared with the buyer's investment rate to decide whether he should take the discount. If the buyer can earn more than 21 per cent on a comparable very low-risk investment, it is worth his while to delay payment until the forty-fifth day; if not, it is better for him to pay the bill promptly and take the discount.

The equivalent annual rate is a simple concept which enables management to compare a whole series of different credit terms on a consistent basis. The analyst does not need to know the amount of any bill to be included; all that matters is the discount offered and the difference in collection periods with and without it. Thus it is possible to compare different credit policies very simply. The equivalent annual rate also indicates the precise value of trade credit to the buyer; 2/10 net 45 is a typical example of credit offered to a large number of businesses and yet it means that a buyer must be sure of earning over 21 per cent before taxes on a safe short-term investment before he decides to refuse the discount, because such discounts entail no risk for him.

The next question to decide is whether or not to pay on the due date, assuming no discount is taken. Obviously, if the buyer decides to pay after the due date, he gains an extra period of credit, but may incur intangible costs such as supplier dissatisfaction and a poor credit rating. Financial analysis is of little help in deciding the advantages and disadvantages of such a policy; the benefits can be presented in a similar manner to the above and management must then weigh them against the presumed costs. Often, moderate extensions of trade credit may be in line with industry practice and hence feasible, whereas very long extensions will start to raise doubts amongst suppliers as to the liquidity and solvency of their customer. If management does decide to extend its repayment schedules, the calculations of equivalent annual rate must be reworked to take account of the lengthened period of credit.

Once a firm has decided its repayment policy and has worked out which trade discounts it would like to accept, after careful consideration of the equivalent annual rates, credit repayment is very much a cash-flow problem; the firm must balance its cash inflows against outflows. Short-term borrowing may prove more rewarding than a decision to forgo a discount. For example, it would be to a firm's advantage to arrange a bank overdraft at 10 per cent rather than to forgo a discount worth 21 per cent.

Summary

A planned credit policy can assist in increasing corporate profitability. When considering whether to relax credit terms management must weigh the likely profits from increased sales against the cost of additional investment in debtors. Once a particular credit policy has been decided it is then important to observe where doubtful debts are occurring by analysing the average age of debtors. To reduce doubtful debts, management must pursue a more stringent credit policy or, perhaps, introduce a discount scheme. Finally, in connection with collection procedures management has to decide whether the company should have its own credit control department, or employ a commercial factor.

It is important for a company to weigh the advantages of delaying payment of creditors against the benefits that can be derived from prompt payment and the discount thus available. The equivalent annual rate of the discount terms provided by creditors should be computed and compared with the return the company could obtain on the investment of these funds.

Notes

1   For simplicity of computation it has been assumed that debtors totalling £60,000, classified as being outstanding 121 days or more (Figure 2:4) relate to additional sales made in March.

2   The same answer would ensue if the forecast credit sales for the four-month period were multiplied by the estimated average investment in debtors:

$$£2 \text{ million} \times \frac{60}{120} = £1 \text{ million}$$

$$£2 \text{ million} \times \frac{69}{120} = £1.15 \text{ million}$$

3   R. P. Shay and C. C. Greer, 'Banks move into high-risk commercial financing', *Harvard Business Review*, vol. 46, no. 6 (November–December 1968), pp. 149–61.

Further reading

V. L. Andrews, 'Captive finance companies', *Harvard Business Review*, vol. 42, no. 4 (July–August 1964), pp. 80–92.

T. N. Beckman and R. S. Foster, *Credits and Collections: Management and Theory*, eighth edition (New York: McGraw-Hill, 1969).

H. Benishay, 'Managerial controls of accounts receivable – a deterministic approach', *Journal of Accounting Research*, vol. 3 (Spring 1965), pp. 114–32.

W. Beranek, *Analysis for Financial Decisions* (Homewood, Ill: Irwin, 1963).

S. Friedland, *The Economics of Corporate Finance* (Englewood Cliffs, NJ: Prentice-Hall, 1966).

C. C. Greer, 'The optimal credit acceptance policy', *Journal of Financial and Quantitative Analysis*, vol. 2 (December 1967), pp. 399–415.

T. G. Hutson and J. Butterworth, *Management of Trade Credit*, second edition (Epping: Gower Press, 1974).

R. W. Johnson, 'More scope for credit managers', *Harvard Business Review*, vol. 39, no. 6 (November–December 1961), pp. 109–20. Reprinted in *Foundations for Financial Management: A Book of Readings*, edited by J. Van Horne (Homewood, Ill: Richard D. Irwin, 1966), pp. 49–69.

J. H. Myers and E. W. Forgy, 'The development of numerical credit evaluation systems', *Journal of the American Statistical Association*, vol. 58 (September 1963), pp. 799–806.

R. M. Soldosfsky, 'A model for accounts receivable management', *N.A.A. Bulletin* (January 1966).

J. C. Van Horne, *Financial Management and Policy*. fourth edition (Englewood Cliffs, NJ: Prentice-Hall, 1977).

3

Management and control of stocks

Stocks, like debtors, constitute a large part of current assets. For most companies they include raw materials, work–in–progress and finished goods.

Raw materials and finished goods are relatively easy to value as their costs and prices are known to the company. However, the valuation of work–in–progress is more difficult to measure: in liquidation its components would realize very little, but on conversion to a finished product they become a saleable commodity and consequently increase substantially in value.

In nearly all manufacturing concerns, stocks of raw materials, partly finished and finished goods are required for reasons which include the following:

1   Stocks act as a buffer between supply and demand, which are often out of balance.[1] Thus, a gas reservoir, for example, will slowly fill up during the day as production exceeds demand, and will then be emptied in the evening during peak-period demand; the reservoir or stock enables a smooth production process to meet a highly varying demand rate.

2   Stocks help in the problem of lead time – the interval between ordering and receiving an item. Lead times on manufactured goods are often lengthy and if demand forecasts are even slightly wrong, so that actual

production does not match actual demand, the firm would be unable, in the absence of stocks, to meet orders without lengthy delays.

3 Another advantage in maintaining stocks is the greater flexibility it gives to the production department in planning production runs. Usually a run has a high element of fixed costs which do not vary with the actual amount produced. The larger the production run, the lower the average unit cost, hence producing partly or wholly for stock enables production management to plan longer runs. Obviously there must be a balance between lower average unit costs and increased stockholding costs; techniques for achieving this balance are discussed later.

4 Ordering raw materials for stock and current production may enable management to obtain larger bulk discounts from suppliers.[2]

The advantages of flexibility which occur with increased stock levels have to be weighed against the additional costs involved. Clearly, efficient stock control can reduce a company's working-capital commitment. This chapter will establish the factors which affect stock levels, propose techniques for efficient stock control and outline certain accounting procedures for evaluating a company's stock position.

Objectives of stock-control policy

Stock control is concerned with all aspects of materials management from raw materials to finished goods. Its objective is to minimize total stock costs to the firm, bearing in mind the differing objectives of various departments. For example, the marketing department will tend to want very large stocks of finished goods to enable all demand to be met promptly, whereas the production department may want greater raw-material stocks to allow maximum flexibility in product planning. The finance department will want to minimize stocks to reduce working-capital levels. The stock controller must balance these objectives within a coherent materials policy.

Before discussing specific stock-control techniques, some important variables will be considered.

Lead time

For raw materials lead time is the time between placing an order with a supplier and receiving the goods. For finished goods, it is the time spent manufacturing the item and delivering it to the warehouse.

Obviously, lead times are rarely certain and the possibility that lead time will exceed expectations should always be borne in mind. Manufacturing lead times can often be reduced by expediting orders and the company must have some idea of the relative importance of particular products to be able to take decisions on changing lead times. Clearly, any reduction in the uncertainty of lead time enables lower stocks to be maintained. It is desirable, therefore, that materials management should, where possible, conclude a series of agreements with suppliers to arrange specific lead times for items of stock that are in frequent use and that have substantial value; a reduction in the uncertainty in lead times for such products will enable management to reduce both the level of stock and the possibility of a stockout.

Stockout costs

If stocks of an item fall to zero, this is called a *stockout*. The costs of a stockout vary enormously between products and raw material items. Stockout costs for finished goods may be very low if spare productive capacity exists and goods can be produced quickly. If there is no spare capacity and thus no chance of expediting the order, stockout costs may be very high. However, a company should be able to rank stock items roughly in order of stockout cost. For finished goods there is always the problem of the intangible costs of being unable to meet customers' orders and a company may feel that stockouts of finished goods are very undesirable.

In a refinery warehouse, for example, the importance of understanding stockout costs can be seen at once. A stockout in one item may cause part of the refinery to shut down, while a stockout in others will make little difference providing lead times are not too lengthy. In such situations it is useful to divide stocks into categories in order of importance. For example, in category A, a stockout cannot be tolerated, while in category B, it can be tolerated for up to, say, one week, provided suppliers can assure management that lead times will not exceed this period. In category C longer lead times can be stipulated and a lower level of stocks maintained. Such a categorization should be carried out in conjunction with operating management.

Establishing the cost of stockholding

Too often materials management believes that the cost of stock is the cost of borrowing – about 8 per cent after taxes – but this underestimates the real cost and hence the importance of stock reduction. Stockholding costs may be classified as follows:

1 Cost of borrowing.
2 Storage costs (including insurance) – some question arises whether this is a justifiable cost. If marginal costing is used, storage costs would only be included if there was some alternative use for the space.
3 Obsolescence, deterioration and theft – deterioration can be an important cost, for example, in the storage of particular petroleum products.
4 Handling and clerical costs – the printing of large numbers of orders and their processing through the accounts department can be a significant cost.

Stockholding costs usually vary between 15 and 40 per cent of the cost of goods in stock each year and they must be balanced carefully against the reduced unit costs of reordering in large batches. It is essential that management in marketing, production and stock control appreciates the heavy cost involved. This section discusses specific techniques for deciding when to reorder goods for stock and how large the order should be.[3]

Reorder point

Many systems exist to determine when stocks should be reordered. Two relatively straightforward approaches are the two-bin system and the periodic-inspection system.

With the two-bin system, all items of stock are physically separated into two groups, one large group to meet normal demand and a smaller group to cover the time between reordering an item and receiving it in the warehouse (lead time). Items are supplied from the large group until it becomes exhausted: at this point an order for further stocks is made and existing supply is continued from the smaller group. When the new order arrives, the two groups are replenished.

In the periodic-inspection system, stocks are checked at regular intervals. A reorder is made whenever the level of stocks is unlikely to last until the next inspection, plus the lead time.[4]

Lead times are uncertain and both systems can incorporate a safety factor to reduce the probability of a stockout during the reorder period. Costs of stockouts will vary substantially with each product and management must set safety-stock levels to achieve an approximate balance between stockout costs and the increased cost of holding extra stock.

Reorder size

Having determined when to reorder it is necessary to decide how many units are needed. Several algorithms, or specific analytical methods, have been developed to balance stockholding and manufacturing costs. The economic order quantity (EOQ) and least-unit-cost algorithm are outlined.

Economic order quantity

The economic order quantity (EOQ) is a well-known concept for determining the optimum order size for stocks of raw materials, semi-finished and finished goods, given expected usage, ordering and storage costs. Assume that the usage of a particular item of stock is known and that the fixed costs per order, 0, are the same whatever the size of the order. The total ordering cost for a specified period is therefore the number of orders times the cost per order.

Storage costs per unit per period, S, represent the cost of storage, capital costs, handling and insurance. Assume these costs are constant for this item of stock, per unit of time. Total storage costs are therefore equal to the average number of units of stock for the period multiplied by the storage costs per unit. Assume further that stock orders are filled without delay (this assumption can be relaxed quite easily).

If the usage of this item of stock is steady throughout the period of time, then average stock can be expressed as

$$\text{average stock} = \tfrac{1}{2}Q$$

where Q is the quantity ordered and is assumed to be constant for the period. The average cost of stockholding is therefore $\tfrac{1}{2}SQ$.

The total number of orders for the period of time is the total usage of an item of stock for that period, T, divided by Q. Consequently, the total ordering costs are TO/Q.

Total stock costs, which are holding costs plus ordering costs, are:

$$\frac{SQ}{2} + \frac{TO}{Q}$$

From this equation it can be seen that the larger the order quantity Q the higher the storage costs, but the lower the total ordering costs per unit. The idea of EOQ is to trade off economies of increased order size against the added cost of carrying more stock. From the equation the optimum order quantity Q can be obtained by differentiation:

$$\frac{d}{dQ}\left(\frac{SQ}{2} + \frac{TO}{Q}\right) = \frac{S}{2} - \frac{TO}{Q^2}$$

Therefore, $= 0$ for a minimum

$$Q_{min}^2 = \frac{2TO}{S}$$

$$Q_{min} = \sqrt{\frac{2TO}{S}}$$

This equation is known as the economic lot size formula. To illustrate its use, suppose that the usage of a stock item is 80,000 units during a 90-day period, ordering costs are £100 per order, with storage costs at £1 per unit per 90 days. The most economic order quantity, then, is 4,000 units.

$$Q_{min} = \sqrt{\frac{2 \times 80{,}000 \times 100}{1}} = 4{,}000 \text{ units}$$

With an EOQ of 4,000 units, the firm would reorder 20 times (80,000/4,000) during the 90-day period, or every 4-5 days.

It should be remembered that simplifying assumptions have been made in arriving at the EOQ formula; some of these can be adapted to suit various situations, but others limit the applicability of the method and under certain conditions other analytical approaches must be used.

Least-unit-cost algorithm

The main problem with using an EOQ approach is that it assumes constant and continuous demand. Where demand varies, EOQ is unable to cope adequately with the changing schedule.

In the least-unit-cost approach, the demand schedule over a number of periods is considered and stocks are maintained to meet demand in future periods until unit costs begin to rise. For example, suppose forecast demand over the next 6 periods is as follows:

Period	1	2	3	4	5	6
Demand in units	20	15	15	20	40	40

Fixed costs per order are £100 and the cost of holding one item for one period is £2. If an order is placed now for only one period (so that holding costs are zero), the unit cost can be computed as £5:

$$\text{unit cost} = \frac{\text{total costs}}{\text{total units}} = \frac{\text{fixed costs} + \text{stockholding costs}}{\text{total units}}$$

$$= \frac{£100}{20}$$

$$= £5 \text{ per unit}$$

If an order is placed for 2 periods, the unit cost will be £3.71:

$$\frac{\text{fixed costs} + \text{stockholding costs}}{\text{total units}} = \frac{100 + 15 \times £2 \times 1}{35}$$

$$= £3.71 \text{ per unit}$$

If the analysis is now performed over the 6 periods, the following schedule is obtained:

Number of periods for which demand is satisfied	Unit costs per item
1	£5
2	£3.71
3	£3.80
4	£4.43
5	£5.73
6	£6.87

Satisfying demand up to and including period 2 achieves the lowest unit cost and hence 35 items are reordered.

As the demand for this item of stock is not uniform throughout the 6 periods and the EOQ method assumes steady demand, then it is likely that it will give a more costly result than the least-unit-cost algorithm. Total demand over the 6 periods is 150 units and hence average demand is 25 units, the fixed costs per order, 0, total £100, the total usage of this item of stock per period, T, is 25 units and the storage costs per unit per period, S, are £2. The EOQ is thus 50 units calculated as follows:

$$EOQ = \sqrt{\frac{2 \times 25 \times 100}{2}}$$

$$= \sqrt{2500}$$

$$= 50$$

With an EOQ of 50, unit cost is £3.80:

$$100 + \frac{15 \times 2 + 15 \times 2 \times 2}{50} = £3.80$$

Therefore, by using the EOQ method the costs on just one order would be 2½ per cent more; over the full 6 periods, this differential will increase. It will also increase with greater variability of demand from month to month.

Summary

Economic order quantity and the least-unit-cost algorithm are two fairly straightforward and robust methods. More complex systems have been developed, relying, for example, on probablistic information on ordering and scheduling routines. Different algorithms are available for different demand patterns. In the simple case, where demand is stable, EOQ may be used. If demand is not stable, the least-unit-cost method gives a better result. Management must determine, on the basis of past and projected demand patterns, which approach is most suitable to its particular needs: this may involve using a more complex process than the two techniques outlined above.

Vendor stocking

The discussion so far has concentrated on the supply side of the equation. However, a firm may also be able to influence the demand side. One common method is to persuade vendors to hold specific amounts of high-turnover items for individual companies. A large customer may be able to obtain this service free of charge. The advantages include savings in working capital and storage space. It may achieve a further objective of reducing lead times so that lower levels of stocks are required.

Establishing the value of stock

Stocks often represent a significant investment of working capital. The accounting definition of the book value of stocks is the lower of cost or net realizable value. Many companies tend to assume that net realizable value is always above the original cost and enter stocks in the books at cost. However, this assumption is sometimes wrong and a company should always take care that its stock investment has not deteriorated in value. If a company believes that part of its stock should be valued at below cost a provision should be made in the balance sheet not only to ensure its accuracy but also to secure tax advantages. Such a provision is a legitimate tax deduction and will reduce the company's tax liability.

As a very general rule, the older the stock the more likely that its value will be reduced. Hence reports of the number of months' sales represented by stock and an ageing analysis can provide an alert mechanism.

When particular stocks start to increase faster than sales, their average age is also increasing and management can investigate quickly and decide if their market value is decreasing and whether remedial action or write-off are necessary. The financial analyst must always appreciate that the ratio of stock to sales, which gives the number of days' sales that can be met by current stock, is only an average and will take account both of goods just brought into stock and those that have been there for a considerably longer period than the ratio indicates.

Lines Brothers Ltd and stock control

An interesting example of the necessity and relevance of stock control is the Lines Bros toymaking company which finally went into liquidation in September 1971 although signs of serious financial weakness were evident several years earlier. The balance sheet for 31 December 1968 is shown in a simplified form in Figure 3:1.

At just under £12 million, stocks represent a very significant investment for a company with total assets of £21 million. The balance-sheet date is 31 December; a toy company has highly seasonal sales and one would expect a very low stock figure just after Christmas. If stocks were valued at cost and this was 60 per cent of their retail value, then £12 million of stocks at cost would have had a retail value of £20 million (£12 million x 5/3). The average annual sales were £38 million, so approximately six months stock was being held (12 months x £20 million/£38 million).

The 1969 interim report disclosed that sales in the first six months of that year totalled £12 million, confirming the seasonality of sales; this suggests that on 31 December 1968 there was more than six months stock in hand. (The estimate in the previous paragraph was computed on the annual sales figure of £38 million). On the basis of the previous year's figure, second-half sales would have been £26 million and they would have occurred mainly in the 2-3 months before Christmas. It is, therefore, likely that the December 1968 stock would have covered sales over the first 8-9 months of 1969. This

Figure 3:1 Lines Brothers Ltd consolidated balance sheet as at 31 December 1968

		£ million
Capital employed		
	Shareholders' funds	13.9
	Minorities and deferred tax	1.2
	Long-term debt	6.0
	Capital employed	21.1
Employment of capital		
	Fixed assets (net)	12.0
	Investments	0.5
	Intangibles (goodwill etc.)	1.9
		14.4
Current assets		
	Stocks	11.9
	Debtors	11.7
	Cash	0.3
		23.9
Less		
Current liabilities		
	Creditors	8.9
	Overdraft	7.2
	Tax	0.4
	Dividends	0.7
	17.2	6.7
	Total assets	21.1

is an enormous amount of stock for a company to hold at its seasonal low point in sales, and should raise questions among financial analysts about its value, since the toy industry is susceptible to changes in tastes and some items may not be in demand a year after manufacture. Stocks at £11.9 million constitute over one-half of the total asset figure. If their value was only, say, 50 per cent of cost, shareholders' funds would have been reduced from £13.9 million to £6.9 million. When the company did go into liquidation, stocks only realized a small fraction of their book value.

Measuring turnover of stocks and asset utilization

The turnover-of-stock ratio is an indicator of stock usage:

$$\text{turnover of stock} = \frac{\text{cost of goods sold}}{\text{average cost of stock}}$$

The cost of goods sold is computed for the period being considered; the average stock figure is usually the average of stocks held at the beginning and end of the period. However, when there is a strong seasonal element, as in the case of Lines Bros, it is necessary to compute a more sophisticated average.

Generally, the higher the turnover-of-stock ratio, the more efficient the stock management of the firm. However, a relatively high stock-turnover ratio may be the result of too low a level of stocks and frequent stockouts. This situation could be more costly for the firm than carrying a larger level of stocks and having a lower turnover ratio. When the stock-turnover ratio is relatively low, it may indicate slow-moving stock or obsolescence of some stock. Obsolescence may necessitate large write-downs, which would affect both the net assets of the company and its profitability.

Utilization of computer facilities

With the use of computers, great improvements in stock control are possible. Computer facilities can be used to:

1   Print out purchase orders automatically.
2   Compute batch sizes (using the most suitable algorithm).
3   Print out automatically the items on which stockouts have occurred.
4   Record and report the level of service being achieved by the stock-control system.

Many companies already have computer facilities and the marginal cost of using them to produce stock-control information periodically is not great. The savings can be substantial in enabling buyers to devote more time to negotiating prices with customers and reducing lead times rather than filling out order forms.

Summary

Stocks often require a significant investment of working capital and a framework must be provided in which the manager can appreciate the important variables. Stock control has become a specialist field of study and management frequently turns to professional assistance when implementing new stock-control systems. Obviously stock control is not the prime responsibility of financial management: production and marketing have their own objectives and constraints and an efficient stock policy will try to balance all these needs.

Notes

1   J. F. Magee, 'Guides to inventory policy: 1. Functions and lot sizes',
      Harvard Business Review, vol.34, no. 1 (January–February 1956),
      pp.49–60.
2   D. S. Ammer, 'Materials management as a profit centre', *Harvard
      Business Review*, vol.47, no. 1 (January–February 1969), pp. 72–82.
3   H. M. Wagner, *Principles of Operations Research–with
      Applications to Managerial Decisions* (Englewood Cliffs, NJ:
      Prentice-Hall, 1969).
4   A. Snyder, 'Principles of inventory management', in *Foundations
      for Financial Management: A Book of Readings*, edited by J. Van
      Horne (Homewood, Ill: Irwin, 1966), pp.72–4, 89–90.

Further reading

K. J. Arrow, S. Karlin and H. Scarf, *Studies in the Mathematical Theory of
Inventory and Production* (Stanford, Calif: Stanford University Press,
1958).
W. Beranek, 'Financial implications of lot-size inventory models',
Management Science, vol. 13 (1967), pp. B-401–8.
J. Buchan and E. Koenigsberg, *Scientific Inventory Management*
(Englewood Cliffs, NJ: Prentice-Hall, 1963).
G. Hadley and T. M. Whitin, *Analysis of Inventory Systems* (Englewood
Cliffs, NJ: Prentice-Hall, 1963).
F. Hanssmann, *Operations Research in Production and Inventory Control*
(New York: Wiley, 1962).
G. A. Hay, 'Production, price, and inventory theory', *American Economic
Review*, vol. 60 (September 1970), pp. 531–45.
W. A. Lampkin, 'A review of inventory control theory', *Production
Engineer* (February 1967).
E. S. Mills, *Price, Output and Inventory Policy: A Study in the Economics
of the Firm and Industry* (New York: Wiley, 1962).
E. Naddor, *Inventory Systems* (New York: Wiley, 1966).
M. K. Starr and D. W. Miller, *Inventory Control: Theory and Practice*
(Englewood Cliffs, NJ: Prentice-Hall, 1962).
A. F. Vienott, Jr, 'The status of mathematical inventory theory',
Management Science, vol. 12 (1966), pp. 745–77.
A. F. Vienott, Jr and H. M. Wagner, 'Computing optimal (s, S) inventory
policies', *Management Science*, vol. 11 (1965), pp. 525–552.
T. M. Whitin, 'Inventory control in theory and practice', *Quarterly Journal
of Economics*, vol. 66 (November 1952), pp. 502–21.

PART TWO
FIXED ASSETS

4

Methods of project appraisal

The profitability of a firm is primarily a function of its ability to generate projects or investments that provide returns greater than the cost of funds. Often management must choose between different projects, perhaps because they are mutually exclusive, or because there is a temporary shortage of funds and managerial skills. This chapter examines three appraisal methods and discusses their relative advantages and disadvantages.

We believe that the discounted cash flow method is often the most useful and that the payback period and accounting rate of return methods are of very limited value.

It is evident that whichever method is used, the accuracy of the result depends on management's forecasting ability and the information base. Discounted cash flow is only useful for measuring the profitability of a given projection of cash flows or returns; if the projection or management's forecasting ability is poor, DCF may not produce a better result than other methods. Furthermore, the forecasts of costs and revenues incorporated into the appraisal must reflect the markets for the products and their competitive structure. Profitable investment opportunities usually imply a comparative advantage in the production, marketing process etc. and it is this phenomenon that provides the justification for investment.

Payback method

The payback method is one of the most popular evaluation methods in current use. It is more a measure of the liquidity than of the profitability of a project. The payback period of a project is defined as the number of years required to return the project's initial outlay (including any working capital) and should be computed after taxes and investment incentives. If a project is expected to produce constant net revenue the payback period can be determined by a simple formula:

$$\text{payback period} = \frac{\text{capital cost--cash grant--(initial allowance} \times \text{tax rate)}}{\text{revenue (1-tax rate)}}$$

If the projected net revenues cannot be represented as constant annual amounts, the formula has to be modified. To obtain the project's payback period, it is necessary to add the after-tax revenues for each year of the project until the accumulated sum equals the net capital cost (capital cost--cash grant--tax benefits of capital allowance). An explanation of the

system of cash grants and tax allowances is given in Chapter 5.

Consider three five-year projects, all with capital outlays of £100 in year 0, as shown in figure 4:1. If taxation and investment incentives are ignored, all the projects have a payback period of four years as computed in Figure 4:2. In the first two years the projects recover entirely different percentages of their capital cost, 50, 80 and 20 per cent respectively.

Figure 4:1   Cash flows for three projects

Year	Project 1 £	Project 2 £	Project 3 £
0	−100	−100	−100
1	+25	+40	+10
2	+25	+40	+10
3	+25	+10	+40
4	+25	+10	+40
5	+25	+10	+40

Figure 4:2   Calculation of payback period
Taxation and tax allowances are ignored

Year	Project 1 £	Project 2 £	Project 3 £
1	+25	+40	+10
2	+25	+40	+10
3	+25	+10	+40
4	+25	+10	+40
Cash inflows	+100	+100	+100
Capital outlay	−100	−100	−100
Balance	0	0	0

If taxation is now taken into account, the payback period and the ranking of the projects change radically. Assume a 20 per cent cash grant (£20) and a 100 per cent first-year capital allowance (£100) with corporation tax at 50 per cent. Using the previous formula, the payback period for project 1 falls from 4 years to 2.4 years:

$$\text{payback period} = \frac{£100 - £20 - (£100 \times 0.5)}{£25 \times (1 - 0.5)}$$

$$= \frac{30}{12\frac{1}{2}}$$

$$= 2.4 \text{ years}$$

In this example, the value of the cash grant and the capital allowances is greater than the corporation tax payments on the project's net revenue stream.

For project 2 (using the modified method), the payback period is reduced when cash grants and allowances are introduced (see Figure 4:3).

Figure 4:3   Calculation of payback period for project 2

Year		Net cash in flow
0	Net capital cost	−30
	[capital cost − cash grant − (initial allowance × tax rate)]	
	− [100−20−(100 × 0.5)]	
1	40 × (1−0.5)	+20
2	40 × (1−0.5)	+20

As the gross revenues total £40 each year and tax is 50 per cent, net revenues are reduced to £20 per year. After tax and investment incentives, the project's net capital cost of £30 is recovered in 1½ years. For project 3, the payback period after tax and incentives is 3 years.

The payback method has a number of significant disadvantages. It neglects the exact timing of the cash flows and excludes all cash flows after the payback period. For example, the payback period for a mine may be seven or eight.years, but it could still be a very profitable investment if the cash flows extended significantly after the project had repaid its capital cost. In this sense payback is not a good measure of a project's viability as it understates the project's profitability and the total cash flow. Conversely, on a short-life project where cash is generated rapidly, the payback would be short – for example, 3 years – but cash flows may terminate in the third year. Although the payback period is low the project is not attractive. If the payback method is to be used as a criterion for project acceptance, several minimum payback periods should be estimated for projects with different lives and risks. Clearly payback should not be used as the main method of appraisal. Nevertheless, the payback period is a useful figure to have. For small businesses it may be of critical importance for both the lender and the borrower to know if the project can generate sufficient cash to repay borrowings in a specific period: the after-tax payback period can play a useful role here.

Accounting rate of return

The *accounting rate of return* is defined as the average annual profits after tax and depreciation as a percentage of the capital outlay:

$$\text{accounting rate of return} = \frac{(\text{net revenue} - \text{accounting depreciation}) \times (1 - \text{tax rate})}{\text{capital cost} - \text{cash grant}} \times 100\%$$

One may substitute in the formula the first year's capital outlay or take an annual average of the capital outlays if these are spread over a number of years. The averaging procedure subjects this method of appraisal to much abuse as a project, where capital outflows occur over a number of years, will seem to have a much greater return than if those outflows were incurred in the first year. We believe all major capital outlays from the inception of the project should be included in the capital cost when the accounting rate of return is computed.

Book depreciation rates are commonly used and not the rates permitted for tax purposes. The two statistics could differ substantially if high initial capital allowances are available for tax purposes but the capital outlay and the tax benefits are spread over a number of years for accounting depreciation purposes. In this respect the accounting rate of return will understate project profitability. .

Figure 4:4 gives cash inflows for three projects. The initial capital costs on each are £50, annual straight-line depreciation is 20 per cent and corporation tax is 50 per cent.

Figure 4:4   Cash inflows for three projects

Year	Project 1 £	Project 2 £	Project 3 £
1	+25	+40	+15
2	+25	+40	+20
3	+25	+15	+30
4	+25	+15	+30
5	+25	+15	+30
	125	125	125

For all projects the accounting rate of return is 15 per cent:

$$\frac{(£25-£10) \times (1-0.5)}{£50} \times 100\% = \frac{£7.5}{£50} \times 100\%$$

$$= 15\%$$

However, if a cash grant of £20 was available and credited to the profit and loss account, the rate of return would rise to 25 per cent:

$$\frac{(£25-£10) \times (1-0.5)}{£30} \times 100\% = \frac{£7.5}{£30} \times 100\%$$

$$= 25\%$$

This highlights a problem: a change in the firm's tax or profit reporting basis can change a decision to accept or reject a project. For example, if an initial, or first year, allowance of 100 per cent was available for a particular investment in machinery but was later reduced to 80 per cent, the change would not be reflected in this type of computation because depreciation rates used for reporting profits to shareholders are unrelated to the capital allowances which permit the company to write off part or all of the cost of an asset and thereby reduce the firm's tax payments. Thus the firm's cash flow would be affected by a change in tax allowances and this change should be reflected in the appraisal exercise and its result, the project's expected returns.

All three projects are ranked equally, even though the timing of cash flows is substantially different in each case. Clearly, all managers would prefer project 2 to any of the others because of the large cash flows occurring in the early years. However, some managers feel more concerned with the way projects are reported to shareholders in a particular year and consequently use the accounting rate of return. Although a change in the timing of cash flows might not affect the profit and loss account in a particular year it would affect the shareholders' wealth as they value both current and future profits. Therefore, we do not recommend the use of this appraisal method, which confuses reported profits with net cash flow. This problem will be elaborated later in the chapter.

Discounted cash flow (DCF)

The methods previously reviewed have failed to account for the timing of cash flows in a consistent manner. They have not embodied a generally accepted concept that is the basis of the DCF approach, namely, that £1 now is worth more than £1 in a year's time. Discounting cash flows is conceptually the reverse of compounding. For example, £100 invested at 10 per cent compounded annually becomes £121 after two years. Therefore £121 received in two years discounted at 10 per cent has a value of £100 today (£100 is the present value of £121 due at the end of two years).

The DCF method, unlike other methods discussed, includes all cash flows in the calculation when they actually occur. Taxes are included (capital allowances are only included in so far as they reduce the physical outflow of taxes) when they are paid, not when they fall due, and any working capital involved in the project must be incorporated. A simple example will illustrate the discounting method.

Figure 4:5   Calculation of the present value of a cash flow

			Year			
	0	1	2	3	4	
Cash flow (£)		100	150	180	150	= £580
Discount factor (at 10%)		0.9091	0.8264	0.7513	0.6830	
Present value (£)		90.91	123.96	135.23	102.45	= £452.55

Figure 4:5 shows four cash payments discounted at 10 per cent yielding a present value (in year 0) of £452.55. This means that if the individual investor's reinvestment rate is 10 per cent, he would be prepared to offer up to £452.55 for that particular stream of cash flows; these cash flows are received at the end of each year. The discount factors are to be found in Appendix 1.

The discounting process can be illustrated by analysing an investment of £452.55 compounded at 10 per cent annually. The cash flows that occur in each year in Figure 4:5 are deducted from the compounded sum, to obtain a zero cash balance at the end of year 4. Figure 4:6 shows that the present value of £452.55 compounded at 10 per cent is equivalent to the pattern of cash flows occurring in years 1 to 4 in Figure 4:5. Thus, discounting is shown to be the reverse of compounding.

Figure 4:6   The relationship between compounding and present value

	£	Paid by investor £	Paid to investor £
	452.55	452.55	
10% p.a. year 1	45.26		
	497.81		
Less cash flow year 1	100.00		100.00
	397.81		
10% p.a. year 2	39.78		
	437.59		
Less cash flow year 2	150.00		150.00
	287.59		
10% p.a. year 3	28.76		
	316.35		
Less cash flow year 3	180.00		180.00
	136.35		
10% p.a. year 4	13.65		
	150.00		
Less cash flow year 4	150.00		150.00
Balance	—		580.00

There are two different ways of using the DCF process to calculate a project's returns. They are the Net Present Value (NPV) and Internal Rate of Return (IRR) methods.

Net present value (NPV)

The net present value method discounts a project's cash flows back to the present day, usually referred to as year 0; the discount rate used represents the investor's minimum required rate of return for a project of that risk. If the discounted cash flow or net present value is positive, then the project is acceptable, as the investor will achieve more than the equivalent required rate of return available in the capital market. If the NPV is negative, then the project is unacceptable. In the example in Figure 4:7 the cash flows discounted at 12 per cent produce an NPV of £23.97. As the NPV is positive, the project is acceptable. If another project under review had a capital outlay in year 0 of £200 and an NPV of £30 then it would also be acceptable.

Figure 4:7   Calculation of net present value

	0	1	2	3	4	5
			Year			
Cash flow (£)	–100	+25	+35	+40	+40	+35
Discount factor (at 12%)	—	0.8929	0.7972	0.7118	0.6355	0.5674
Present value of cash flows (£)	–100	+22.32	+27.90	+28.47	+25.42	+19.86
Net present value	£23.97					

It is important for the analyst to understand the meaning of a positive net present value in competitive market terms. In forecasting such a profit, which is estimated after accounting for the cost of funds, the firm implies that either the product to be sold is in short supply (with consequent high prices) or the firm has some competitive advantage over other companies. Short supply may be an inadequate justification since, if there are few barriers to entry, the supply gap and consequent high price will give way to lower prices and more normal profits by the time the investment comes on stream. What we want to emphasise is that the analyst cannot separate a study of markets and competition from the forecasts of costs and revenues incorporated into the cash flow analysis. A positive net present value implies abnormally higher profits and the firm should justify how such a profit can be obtained and for how long it can be sustained.

Internal rate of return (IRR)

The internal rate of return (IRR) is the return or discount rate which equates the present value of the cash inflow stream with the present value of the cash outflow stream. For example, the following series of cash flows has an IRR of 20.7 per cent:

Year	0	1	2	3	4	5
Cash flow (£)	–100	+25	+35	+40	+40	+35

For this project, the positive cash flows discounted at 20.7 per cent produce a present value of £100, which constitutes the capital outlay in year 0. How do we arrive at a discount rate of 20.7 per cent? There is an element of trial and error in computing the IRR. If the stream of cash flows is not uniform, as in the above example, some approximation to uniformity is made. Cash inflows are divided by the number of years over which they occur (£175/5 = £35) and in this example adjusted downwards to take account of the fact that the larger cash inflows occur in later years and hence are less valuable when discounted. Assume that the cash-flow series is equal to an annuity of £33 a year for 5 years.

Appendix 2 shows the present values of £1 per year received over n years discounted at r per cent. Thus, if a cash flow of £30 per year is received over

5 years and the cost of capital for the project is 12 per cent the present value can be computed at £108.

$$\text{Present value} = £30 \times a_{5,12}$$

where $a_{5,12}$ is the annuity factor for £1 per annum over 5 years discounted at 12 per cent

$$= £30 \times 3.6048$$
$$= £108$$

So the cash-flow series has been approximated to an annuity of £33 per year for five years. To approximate the IRR it is necessary to find the discount rate which equates this annuity over 5 years with the original capital outlay of £100. Thus

$$£33 \times a_{5,r} = £100$$

$$a_{5,r} = \frac{100}{33} = 3.030$$

Appendix 2 shows that for a five-year annuity, the annuity factors are 3.0576 and 2.9906 for discount rates of 19 and 20 per cent, respectively. As it is only an approximation, 20 per cent can be used as the discount rate. At this rate the NPV is +£1.64 (Figure 4:8). As the NPV is positive, the discount rate is too low: the present value of the cash inflows is greater than that of the capital outlay. Therefore, a higher discount rate, for example 21 per cent, must be used (Figure 4:9). At 21 per cent, the NPV is negative, so 21 per cent is above the IRR for the project.

Figure 4:8 IRR estimated at 20 per cent

Year	Cash flow (£)	Discount factor (at 20%)	Present value (£)
0	−100	—	−100
1	+25	0.8333	+20.83
2	+35	0.6944	+24.30
3	+40	0.5787	+23.15
4	+40	0.4823	+19.29
5	+35	0.4019	+14.07
		NPV	+1.64

Figure 4:9   IRR estimated at 21 per cent

Year	Cash flow (£)	Discount factor (at 21%)	Present value (£)
0	-100	—	-100.00
1	+25	0.8264	+20.66
2	+35	0.6830	+23.91
3	+40	0.5645	+22.58
4	+40	0.4665	+18.66
5	+35	0.3855	+13.49
		NPV	-0.70

Therefore the IRR is between 20 and 21 per cent. Between discounting at 20 and 21 per cent there is a difference in NPV of £2.34 (1.64 + £0.70). The IRR is the discount rate that produces a zero NPV. The IRR can be obtained by assuming that the NPV equals 0 at a point represented by the fraction 1.64/2.34 between 20 and 21 per cent:

$$\text{IRR} = 20.0\% + \frac{1.64}{2.34} \times (21\% - 20\%)$$

$$= 20.0\% + 0.7\%$$

$$= 20.7\%$$

If the final discounting had been at 20 and 25 per cent then this method of interpolation would have been conducted between the limits 20 and 25 per cent. The assumption that the relationship between NPV and IRR is straight line or linear is only an approximation and interpolation should be confined to reasonable bounds.

After computing a project's IRR, the latter should be compared with the minimum required rate of return for a project of that risk in order to assess its adequacy.

It is useful at this stage to plot the relation between the NPV and IRR for this project. This is shown in Figure 4:10 which plots the results shown in Figure 4:11. When the discount rate is zero, the NPV is simply the sum of the cash inflows and outflows – that is, no account has been taken of the time value of money. As the discount rate increases, the NPV decreases. The graph cuts the discount rate axis at the project's IRR, or where the NPV equals zero.

Figure 4:10   Relationship of NPV to IRR
For the series of cash flows –100, +25, +35, +40, +40, +35

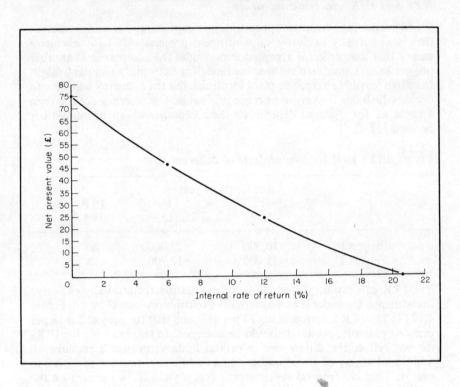

Figure 4:11   Relationship between NPV and IRR
For the series of cash flows –100, +25, +35, +40, +40, +35

Discount rate (%)	NPV (£)
0.0	+75.0
6.0	+46.2
12.0	+24.0
20.7	0.0

Comparison of DCF methods

NPV and IRR – incremental yields

When evaluating investment proposals it is important to consider whether
they are mutually exclusive or contingent projects. *Mutually exclusive*
means that if a project is accepted, it precludes the acceptance of another
project being considered at the same time. For example, a company might
have two feasible alternative plant locations, but the company will have to
decide which one is likely to be more profitable. *Contingency* occurs when
acceptance for a project depends on the acceptance of one or more other
projects.[1]

Figure 4:12   IRR for two projects of different size

| | Cash flows in year | | IRR |
	0 (£)	1 (£)	(%)
Project 1	–10,000	+12,000	20
Project 2	–15,000	+17,700	18

The IRR can produce a wrong recommendation for mutually exclusive
investments. Consider the two mutually exclusive projects shown in Figure
4:12.[2] The IRR for project 1 is 20 per cent and that for project 2 is 18 per
cent. Apparently, project 1 should be accepted. In this example the IRRs
do not reflect the differences in capital outlays; project 2 requires an
additional outlay of £5000 and produces additional revenue of £5,700 in
year 1. This incremental revenue produces a yield of 14 per cent on the
additional investment. If a company can obtain funds at less than 14 per
cent then project 2 is preferable to project 1.

Figure 4:13   IRR for two projects of the same size

| | Cash flows in year | | | IRR | NPV |
	0 (£)	1 (£)	2 (£)	(%)	(Discount rate 5%) (£)
Project 1	–10,000	+2,000	+12,000	20	2,789
Project 2	–10,000	+10,000	+3,125	25	2,358

Consider another case where two projects have the same capital outlay, but
have different IRRs and are mutually exclusive (Figure 4:13). The
IRR of project 1 is 20 per cent and that of project 2 is 25 per cent. However,
the NPV at 5 per cent is £2,789 for project 1, and £2,358 for project 2. The
discrepancy arises because the pattern of cash flows differs and the
generated funds are reinvested at different rates. In the case of the IRR

method, the reinvestment rate is the project's IRR, whereas under an NPV assessment, the reinvestment rate for both projects is the relevant cost of capital or discount rate for the project given its risk (in this example 5 per cent).

In order to compare both projects on the same basis the net present value can be used or the incremental return or yield must be computed on the incremental cash flow, as in Figure 4:14. Using the latter method, an incremental yield of 10.9 per cent is produced and thus with a cost of capital of, for example, 5 per cent, project 1 is to be preferred.[3] It should be clear that the net present value method will always provide the correct answer. If management wishes to use the IRR, an incremental analysis must be made where the projects are mutually exclusive.

Figure 4:14   Incremental yield of project 1

| | Cash flow in year | | | |
	0 (£)	1 (£)	2 (£)	IRR (%)
Project 1–project 2	0	–8,000	+8,875	10.9

NPV and IRR – multiple solutions under the IRR method

So far the projects that have been considered have involved a negative outflow followed by positive inflows. In these circumstances, the IRR method is generally satisfactory. However, in the situation where a project has negative cash flows at various stages in its life (other than its initial outflows), the IRR method should be modified because more than one solution could be obtained. To give a simple example, consider the two-year project shown in Figure 4:15. If the cash flows are discounted at both 10 and 25 per cent the NPV is zero. As apparently there are two IRRs, it is useful to plot the NPVs for a variety of discount rates as shown in Figure 4:16.

Figure 4:15   Project with two IRRs

| | Year | | | |
	0 (£)	1 (£)	2 (£)	NPV (£)
Project cash flows	–1,000	+2,350	–1,375	—
PV at 10% discount rate	–1,000	+2,136	–1,136	0
PV at 25% discount rate	–1,000	+1,880	–880	0

Figure 4:16   IRR method and multiple solutions

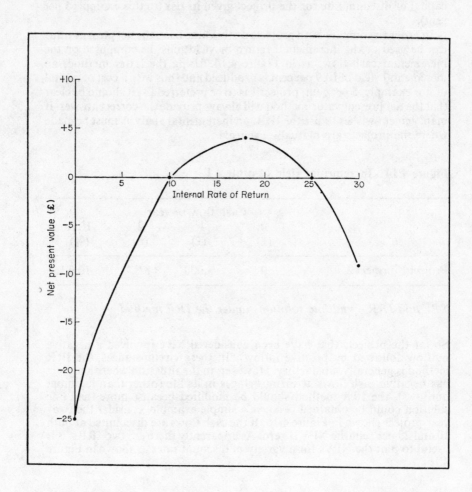

The graph no longer exhibits a uniformly negative slope in contrast to the graph in Figure 4:10. Where multiple solutions occur, the number of solutions is limited to the number of reversals in the cash flow stream (thus, if there are three reversals, the maximum number of IRRs is three). In situations where multiple solutions arise, the IRR method is confusing.

Figure 4:17 Eliminating a negative cash flow

	Year					
	0	1	2	3	4	5
Cash flows (£)	– 4,277	+1,000	+1,000	+1,000	+1,000	+1,000
Adjusted cash flows (£)	– 4,277	+1,000	+1,000	+1,000	+1,000	+1,000

	Year				
	6	7	8	9	10
Cash flows (£)	+1,000	+1,000	+1,000	+1,100	–2,000
Adjusted cash flows (£)	+1,000	+1,000	+188	0	0

This confusion with the IRR, can be avoided by using the 'extended yield' method. First note the periods in which cash flows are negative (excluding initial negative flows). Starting at the most distant negative cash flow and working backwards, discount the cash outflow to the previous period at the cost of capital for the project until the adjusted cash flow is positive. The internal rate of return is then computed on the remaining cash flows (Figure 4:17). To obtain the adjusted cash flows discount the outflow of £2,000 in year 10 at the cost of capital (say 7 per cent) to year 9:

$$£1,000 - \frac{£2,000}{1.07} = -£869$$

As this is negative, discount –£869 at the cost of capital to year 8:

$$£1,000 - \frac{£869}{1.07} = +£188$$

This is a positive cash flow and the standard IRR approach can be used from then on. The extended yield method of computation gives an IRR of 14.6 per cent. It should be noted that the net present value method does not cause such problems because the discount rate used always reflects the required rate of return for the project, that is, the opportunity cost on invested funds for a project of that risk.

Comparison of payback, accounting rate of return and internal rate of return

Rockley[4] computed IRRs for projects with various lives and payback periods. Certain of his results are shown in Figure 4:18. He assumed cash flows took the form of annuities and that the equipment or plant had no value at the end of the project's life – that is, the project's terminal value was zero.

Figure 4:18   Comparison of the payback and IRR
IRRs for projects of various lives and pay-back periods

Life of asset (years)	Payback Period (years)		
	2.0	4.0	6.0
5	41.0	7.9	N.A.
10	49.1	21.4	10.6
15	49.9	24.0	14.5

Figure 4:18 shows that the longer the life of the project, the closer the IRR approaches the reciprocal of the payback period or the payback yield (the reciprocal is 1 divided by the payback period). Thus a payback period of 4 years has a reciprocal of 25 per cent ($\frac{1}{4}$) and one of 5 years, 20 per cent ($\frac{1}{5}$). For a four-year payback project (payback reciprocal = 25 per cent) with a 15 year life the DCF yield or IRR is 24 per cent. A project that has the same payback of 4 years but a life of only 5 years provides a DCF return of only 7.9 per cent compared to the payback yield of 25 per cent. Clearly, if the life of the project shortens, the difference between payback yield and IRR increases. The conclusion is that payback can be grossly misleading as a criterion of profitability for short-life projects under these assumptions.

Rockley also compared different payback periods with the accounting rate of return on total and average investment. The results for payback periods of 2, 4 and 6 years are summarized in Figures 4:19, 4:20 and 4:21. Figure 4:19 gives results for projects with lives ranging from 5 to 15 years; all these projects have a two-year payback (payback yield of 50 per cent). Each project has a capital outlay of £200 and the average investment percentage return is based on a capital cost of £100, ($\frac{1}{2} \times £200$ = average = £100), while the total investment percentage return is based upon the total capital outlay of £200. It should be apparent that the total investment percentage return will always be half the average investment return. The following conclusions can be drawn from these tables:

1   The IRR is always lower than the payback yield. This difference is greatest for short-life projects.

Figure 4:19 Comparison of accounting rate of return (based on total investment of £200 and an annual net cash flow of £100) and IRR for projects with a payback period of two years (payback yield of 50%).

1 Life of asset (years)	2 Average investment (% return)	3 Total investment (% return)	4 IRR
5	60.00	30.00	41.04
10	80.00	40.00	49.08
15	86.67	43.33	49.88

Figure 4:20 Comparison of accounting rate of return (based on total investment of £400 and an annual cash flow of £100) and IRR for projects with a payback period of four years. (payback yield 25%)

1 Life of asset (years)	2 Average investment (% return)	3 Total investment (% return)	4 IRR
5	10.00	5.00	7.93
10	30.00	15.00	21.41
15	36.67	18.33	24.01

2 The average investment return is greater than the IRR, payback yield and total investment return.
3 The accounting rate of return on total investment (column 3) is below all other returns. This method understates a project's profitability.

All returns have been computed on an after-tax basis, assuming 100 per cent first-year allowance (that is, the project's capital cost can be written off in the first year for tax purposes) and 50 per cent corporation tax.[5]
As the payback period is increased to four and six years (Figures 4:20 and 4:21) the following additional conclusions may be drawn:

1 The longer the payback period, the greater the divergence between payback yield and the IRR.
2 The accounting rate of return on total investment remains below the IRR for all asset lives.

Figure 4:21   Comparison of accounting rate of return (based on total investment of £600 and an annual net cash flow of £100) and IRR for projects with a payback period of six years (payback yield 16.67%).

1 Life of asset (years)	2 Average investment (% return)	3 Total investment (% return)	4 IRR %
5	N.A.*	N.A.*	N.A.*
10	13.33	6.67	10.56
15	20.00	10.00	14.47

*If the life of the asset is less than the payback of the project then the total and average investment returns as well as the IRR will be negative.

It should be clear that the use of one payback criterion or one accounting rate of return provides very crude results which differ significantly from those produced by a DCF calculation. If the payback or accounting rate of return criteria are used various minimum rates should be developed for projects of different lives and risks. Many managers may feel these methods do not deserve such complexity and therefore may prefer the DCF approach.

Capital rationing

A company may not have adequate funds to finance all prospective profitable projects. A situation in which sufficient funds cannot be generated internally at a particular time and it is inopportune to resort to the capital markets is called 'capital rationing'.

Under capital rationing it is necessary to rank projects. This can be done by relating the present value of a project's cash inflows to its outflows (capital expenditure). This ratio constitutes a profitability index.

$$\text{profitability index} = \frac{\text{present value of cash inflows}}{\text{present value of cash outflows}}$$

Figure 4:22   Five alternative projects

Proposal	Profitability index	Initial outlay (£)
1	1.25	40,000
2	1.18	20,000
3	1.12	17,500
4	1.09	22,500
5	1.05	10,000

To illustrate the capital rationing problem, consider the projects listed in Figure 4:22. If the budget ceiling is £100,000 and these proposals are independent of each other, projects 1–4 inclusive would be selected. If projects are dependent in the capital rationing situation, the capital expenditure and the net revenues are added and the profitability index on the combined projects is computed.

The situation is usually more complex than in the above example, as it is seldom possible to combine the most profitable projects and exhaust the capital budget. Consider now the set of projects in Figure 4:23. If the capital budget constraint for this period is £30,000, proposals 2 and 3 would be accepted and proposal 1 rejected. The total NPV of projects 2 and 3 is higher than that of project 1 and, if the capital budget is to be fully utilized, it is best tor reject the most profitable project. (For simplicity, it has been assumed that these are the only projects and that surplus cash can only be reinvested at a zero interest rate.

Mathematical programming has been used to produce optimum decisions subject to restrictions.[6] Simple programming packages are available to accomplish this.

Figure 4:23   Four alternative projects

Proposal	Profitability index	Initial outlay (£)	Net present values (£)	
1	1.20	20,000	20,000 (1.20 − 1) = 4,000	
2	1.17	18,000	18,000 (1.17 − 1) = 3,060	} 4,740
3	1.14	12,000	12,000 (1.14 − 1) = 1,680	
4	1.09	15,000		

Effect of DCF on reported earnings

If DCF is used in investment appraisal to rank projects, the projects with the highest NPVs should be accepted. One aspect in making this decision has not been taken into account: this is the impact on reported earnings.[7] Accounting earnings or unadjusted earnings per share (EPS) as distinct from cash flows may influence shareholders and share prices; some analysts believe that if earnings fluctuate significantly, a share price will be lower than if there was a steady growth in earnings. They suggest that a constraint should be incorporated into the DCF analysis.

Suppose that a company is faced with the opportunity of investing in the projects listed in Figure 4:24. The company employs a formalized profit-planning system with a five-year time horizon and estimates the contribution to the profit and loss account from each project as in Figure

Figure 4:24   Three alternative projects

	Cash flows (£) in year						
	0	1	2	3	4	5	6
Project 1	−5,000	+500	+1,000	+1,500	+4,000	+5,000	
Project 2		−9,500	+2,000	+800	+5,000	+8,000	+2,000
Project 3		−3,000	+1,200	+1,000	+ 800	+ 500	+ 500

4:25. A project's cash flow and its contribution to the profit and loss account in a particular year can differ substantially for the following reasons:

1 The period in which cash grants and depreciation allowances are credited to the profit and loss account often differs from the period when they are received. Substantial cash grants received in year 1 will greatly improve the cash flow and DCF returns; however, many companies would not credit them to the profit and loss account in the period they are received. Usually, the benefits are spread over a period of years by reducing the cost of the asset in the balance sheet by the amount of the cash grant and depreciating the remainder (cost of asset – cash grant) over the life of the asset.
2 Capital outlays affect the cash flow in the year they occur, but in the profit and loss account they are spread over a period of years.
3 Receipt of cash may occur at a different time to that when sales are made and credited to the profit and loss account. If cash is received after sales are made, then reported earnings will be higher than cash flow at a particular point in time. Construction companies and shipbuilders often take revenue into their profit and loss account before money is received. If the time differential is more than a year, earnings per share can differ significantly.

Which of the three projects would the company adopt if it uses the DCF approach? If the firm adopts a discount rate of 20 per cent then the NPVs of the projects are as in Figure 4:26. The company would therefore accept projects 1 and 2 on a DCF basis. However, if the two projects are accepted,

Figure 4:25   Capital budget's contribution to the profit and loss account

	Contribution (£) in year				
	0	1	2	3	4
Project 1	−5,000	+300	+700	+1,200	+3,000
Project 2		−9,500	+2,000	+800	+5,000
Project 3		−2,000	+800	+1,000	+900

the earnings reported to the shareholders over the next five years would be as in Figure 4:27. If the reported earnings to shareholders have a bearing on efforts to maximize shareholder wealth and if a target of sustainable and consistent growth in earnings is one of management's aims, then the figures show that the DCF method may not produce a result that is consistent with this aim. The dramatic decline in year 1 and the rise in earnings in year 2 followed by a decline in year 3 could give rise to the impression that the company is subject to cyclical swings. Investors may respond by placing a lower value on these reported earnings than they would on a more stable earnings stream and the share price will suffer accordingly.

Figure 4:26   NPVs of the projects in Figure 4:24

Project	NPV (£) Discount rate 20%
1	+918
2	+278
3	−401

Figure 4:27   Projected earnings for next five years

Year	Projected earnings on existing project (£)	Projected earnings including projects 1 and 2 (£)
0	10,000	5,000
1	9,500	300
2	9,000	11,700
3	9,000	11,000
4	8,500	16,500

If the company wishes to report to its shareholders a growth of at least 10 per cent a year in earnings during this period, then acceptance of projects 1 and 2 clearly would not be appropriate. What would be the effect on reported earnings of accepting projects 1 and 3 (project 3 would be rejected on cost-of-capital grounds)? Reported earnings would be as in Figure 4:28. This earnings stream would achieve at least a 10 per cent growth in earnings per year and a more stable earnings stream. Clearly, however, on a cash-flow basis shareholders would be worse off. Research indicates that if shareholders are aware of cash flow and reported earnings, they base share valuation on cash flow. Thus management should provide more information on the sources and disposition of funds so that analysts can adjust reported earnings and provide an explanation for changes that occur.

Figure 4:28   Projected earnings from projects 1 and 3

Year	Earnings (£)
0	5,000
1	7,800
2	10,500
3	11,200
4	12,400

It is important to realise that if a firm chooses a portfolio of projects because this results in a smooth earnings trend, then it may fail to maximize its earnings on a discounted cash flow basis. As a result, shareholder wealth may be reduced rather than increased. Management should appreciate that it cannot reduce the degree of risk inherent in the business, and therefore in the earnings stream, by choosing projects on the basis of their impact on reported earnings. If this basis is adopted there is little point in using systematic appraisal techniques such as DCF.

Summary

The present-value approach to capital budgeting requires that projects with the highest present values should be adopted first and projects which provide a return below the company's cost of capital – that is, projects with a negative NPV – should be rejected. However, the imposition of an earnings-growth constraint changes the approach to capital budgeting in three important ways:

1 It makes reported income flows as well as cash flows relevant to the investment decision. It may therefore result in a portfolio of accepted projects that has a lower present value than that obtained by the unconstrained method and therefore in a lower growth in shareholder wealth.
2 It raises a policy question of what planning horizon a company should use in preparing its capital budget.
3 Management must remember that it is running the company for its shareholders. The shareholders have purchased shares in that company and industry knowing the business risks; thus they must have accepted any earnings fluctuations that may take place. Management should not and need not reject profitable projects in order to smooth out these fluctuations.

Notes

1   See, H. M. Weingartner, 'Capital budgeting of interrelated projects: survey and synthesis', *Management Science*, vol. 12 (1966), pp. 485–516. Reprinted in *Managerial Economics: Selected Readings,*

edited by G. P. E. Clarkson (Harmondsworth:Penguin, 1968), pp. 194–234.

2   This example is taken from H. Bierman and S. Smidt, *The Capital Budgeting Decision*, third edition (New York: The Macmillan Company/London: Collier-Macmillan, 1971). See: E. Solomon, *The Theory of Financial Management* (New York: Columbia University Press, 1963), pp. 134–5.

3   It should be noted that small differences in the project's cash flows will be exaggerated in the incremental cash flows. The result may be a high yield on the incremental cash flow, but if this is a small fraction of the project's cash flow, that high yield is relatively insignificant.

4   L. E. Rockley, *Capital Investment Decisions: A Manual for Profit Planning* (London: Business Books, 1968). See also M. Sarnat and H. Levy, 'The relationship of rules of thumb to the internal rate of return: a restatement and generalization', *Journal of Finance*, vol. 24 (June 1969), pp. 479–90.

5   As an example, consider a project in Figure 4:20 with a life of 5 years. The cash flow is

Year	0	1	2	3	4	5
	–400	+100	+100	+100	+100	+100

The accounting rate of return on total investment is

$$\frac{[(500\text{-}400)]\ 1/5}{400} = 5\%$$

6   H. M. Weingartner, *Mathematical Programming and the Analysis of Capital Budgeting Problems* (Chicago: Markham Publishing Co., 1967).

7   E. M. Lerner and A. Rappaport, 'Limit DCF in capital budgeting', *Harvard Business Review*, vol. 46, no. 5 (September–October 1968), pp. 133–9.

Further reading

R. J. Ball, 'Risk, Return and Disequilibrium: An Application to Changes in Accounting Techniques', *Journal of Finance*, 27 (May 1972), 343–54.

W. J. Baumol and R. E. Quandt, 'Investment and discount rates under capital rationing – a programming approach', *Economic Journal*, vol. 75 (June 1965), pp. 317–29.

R. H. Bernhard, 'Mathematical programming models for capital budgeting – a survey, generalization, and critique', *Journal of Financial and Quantitative Analysis*, vol. 4 (June 1969), pp. 111–58.

H. Bierman, Jr, and S. Smidt, *The Capital Budgeting Decision*, third edition (New York: The Macmillan Company/London: Collier-Macmillan, 1971).

D. Bodenhorn, 'On the problem of capital budgeting', *Journal of Finance*, vol. 14 (December 1959), pp. 473–92.

P. L. Cheng and J. P. Shelton, 'A contribution to the theory of capital budgeting – the multi-investment case', *Journal of Finance*, vol. 18 (December 1963), pp. 622–36.

J. Dean, *Capital Budgeting* (New York: Columbia University Press, 1951).

E. J. Elton, 'Capital rationing and external discount rates', *Journal of Finance*, vol. 25 (June 1970), pp. 573–84.

M. J. Gordon and E. Shapiro, 'Capital equipment analysis: the required rate of profit', *Management Science*, vol. 3 (October 1956), pp. 102–10.

J. H. Lorie and L. J. Savage, 'Three problems in rationing capital', *Journal of Business*, vol. 28 (October 1955), pp. 229–39. Reprinted in *Foundations for Financial Management: A Book of Readings*, edited by J. Van Horne (Homewood, Ill: Irwin, 1966), pp. 295–309.

J. C. T Mao 'Survey of capital budgeting: theory and practice', *Journal of Finance* (May 1970), pp. 349–60.

J. C. T. Mao, 'The internal rate of return as a ranking criterion', *Engineering Economist*, vol. 11 (Winter 1966), pp. 1–13.

P. Marsh and R. Brealey, 'The Use of Imperfect Forecasts in Capital Investment Decisions', *London Business School Working Paper*, (January 1975).

P. Massé, *Optimal Investment Decisions: Rules for Action and Criteria for Choice* (Englewood Cliffs, NJ: Prentice-Hall, 1962).

A. J. Merrett and A. Sykes, *Capital Budgeting and Company Finance* (London: Longmans, 1966).

J. M. Samuels and F. M. Wilkes, *Management of Company Finance* (London: Nelson, 1971).

E. Solomon, *The Theory of Financial Management* (New York: Columbia University Press, 1963).

D. Teichroew, A. A. Robichek and M. Montalbano, 'An analysis of criteria for investment and financing decisions under certainty', *Management Science*, vol. 12 (1965), pp. 151–79. Reprinted in *Managerial Economics: Selected Readings*, edited by G. P. E. Clarkson (Harmondsworth: Penguin, 1968), pp. 159–93.

D. Teichroew, A. A. Robichek and M. Montalbano, 'Mathematical analysis of rates of return under certainty', *Management Science*, vol. 11 (1965), pp. 395–403.

J. C. Van Horne, *Financial Management and Policy* Fourth Edition (Englewood Cliffs, NJ: Prentice-Hall, 1977).

D. Vickers, *The Theory of the Firm: Production, Capital and Finance* (New York: McGraw-Hill, 1968).

H. M. Weingartner, 'Some new views on the payback period and capital budgeting decisions', *Management Science*, vol. 15 (1969), pp. B-594–607.

5

The impact of tax allowances on project appraisal

This chapter outlines the old system of corporation tax applicable in the UK and the new 'imputation' system which has been in operation since April 1973. Some explanation is given of the investment incentives available to industry, introduced in April 1976, and of how they should be incorporated in an investment appraisal.

Company taxation before April 1973

Before April 1973, UK company profits were liable for corporation tax at 40 per cent; from the profits net of corporation tax, any distribution (that is the dividend) made was liable to income tax. For example, a company that produced a pretax profit of £100,000 would pay £40,000 in corporation tax.

If the company distributed £40,000 it would be liable to income tax totalling £15,500 at the standard rate of 38.75 per cent. Put another way, the company needed to earn £40,000 in profits after corporation tax to give shareholders £24,500 in dividends. Clearly, under this system there was discrimination against distributed profits in that they suffered both corporation tax and the individual shareholder's income tax and surtax, whereas the earnings that were retained only incurred corporation tax.

Although retained earnings did not attract income tax, if they were reinvested profitably so that the share price rose, a shareholder would be liable to capital gains tax when his shares were sold at a profit. However, capital gains tax was only paid on disposal of the shares and at a maximum rate of 30 per cent. This compares with the much higher rates of income tax and surtax that were charged on dividends.

	£'000
Profits before tax	100
Corporation tax at 40%	40
Profit net of corporation tax	60
Distribution (gross)	40
Retained earnings	20

The 'imputation' system

A new system has operated from 1 April 1973. Under this system, corporation tax includes a payment for shareholders' income tax at the appropriate standard rate.[1]

Under the imputation system, all company profits whether distributed or not, are taxed at the current rate of 52 per cent. When dividends are paid out of profits net of corporation tax, they are treated in the hands of shareholders as if they had incurred income tax at the rate of 35 per cent. Thus, a company earning pre-tax profits of £100,000 will pay £52,000 in corporation taxes. Let us assume it declares a dividend of £22,750 and retains £25,250.

	£'000
Profits before tax	100
Corporation tax at 52%	52
Profits net of corporation tax	48
Net dividend	22.75
Retained earnings	25.25

The £22,750 net dividend will count as a gross dividend of £35,000 ($\frac{22{,}750 \times 100\%}{65\%} = £35{,}000$) in the hands of shareholders on which income tax at the basic rate of 35% (£35,000 × 35% = £12,250), will be deemed to have been borne by ('imputed to') the shareholder. This £12,250 will be available for repayment to the shareholder if he is entitled to pay a lower rate of income tax than the basic rate of 35 per cent. Similarly, if a shareholder's marginal rate (highest rate) is higher than 35 per cent, he will have to pay the difference.

Timing of corporation tax payments

Corporation tax is due nine months after the end of a company's financial year (except for companies that were liable to income tax before 1 April 1965). However, when a UK company pays a dividend it has to pay 'advance corporation tax' (ACT) to the Inland Revenue. ACT is 35/65 of the net dividend (that is, 35 per cent of the gross dividend) and must be paid within 14 days of the end of the quarter in which the dividend payment occurs. Nine months after the end of its financial year the company will have to pay the balance of its corporation tax ('mainstream' tax liability).

If, in the previous example, the company's financial year ended on 31 October 1976, then corporation tax due for the year would be £52,000 (52 per cent of £100,000). If the £22,750 net dividend was paid on 1 February 1977, ACT of £12,250 would have fallen due on 14 April 1977 – that is, within 14 days of the end of the quarter in which the dividend was paid. The balance of the corporation tax, £39,750 ('mainstream' tax liability) would be due on 31 July 1977.

ACT cannot be used to reduce the mainstream corporation tax liability below 20 per cent of the taxable income. This restriction operates when a company's dividends are greater than after-tax earnings. If a company's taxable income is £50,000, then its corporation tax liability is £26,000. If the company pays a dividend of £32,500 (part being paid from previously retained earnings) then its ACT will be £17,500 (£32,500 × $^{35}/_{65}$). The mainstream corporation tax liability will be £10,000 not £8,500, as the maximum that can be set off against mainstream tax liability is £16,000. The balance of £1,500 may be carried forward to set against future mainstream corporation tax liabilities or carried back to the two previous financial years.

Companies' capital gains

Under the old taxation system, companies' chargeable gains were subject to corporation tax of 40 per cent. Under the new system only $^{30}/_{52}$ of companies' chargeable gains are subject to corporation tax. Thus the effective rate of tax is only $^{30}/_{52}$ of 52 per cent or 30 per cent. This is the same as the maximum rate of tax on personal capital gains.

Accounting for tax

In principle the accounting position has not changed under the imputation system except that dividends are shown net of corporation tax and basic-rate income tax. Investors must note that under the new system, distributions have already incurred basic-rate income tax. Under the old system, gross dividend yields were quoted before deduction of standard-rate income tax.

Investment incentives

There are two basic forms of investment incentive: investment grants and capital allowances. (To simplify examples in this section a corporation tax rate of 50% has been assumed.)

Investment grants

Investment grants are cash sums paid by the government to a company for making an eligible investment. For example, a 20 per cent cash grant would entitle a company to receive £20 on a £100 investment. Such grants are treated as non-taxable capital receipts. When cash grants have been assigned, there has been a delay in receipt of between 9 and 18 months.

Capital allowances

Capital allowances are concessions whereby the value of an asset can be written off for tax purposes. The type of allowance which has been used in recent years has been the *initial allowance* or *first-year allowance*. A company may write off for tax purposes a large amount of the capital cost of an asset in the first year of ownership. If a company was granted an 80 per cent first-year allowance on a £100 investment, it would be able to write off part or all of the remaining £20 in the second or subsequent years.

	£
Capital cost	100
Initial allowance 80%	80
To be written off in subsequent years	20

The £80 initial allowance is written off against profits. At a corporation tax rate of 50 per cent the tax saving would be £40 (£80 × 50% = £40).

A company must have profits available against which to write off allowances. If the company has inadequate profits to utilize all the available allowances, the balance can be carried forward and utilized in later years. With a cash grant, payment is made irrespective of the company's profit position.

Annual allowances

Annual allowances are proportions of an asset's capital cost that may be written off in each year for tax purposes. Under the present system of investment incentives, annual allowances are based on the capital cost after deduction of the initial allowance. The main method of writing down the asset is on a reducing balance basis whereby a fixed percentage is allowed each year on the preceding year's written-down value. The major exception to this is industrial buildings, where annual allowances are on a straight-line basis.

Balancing allowances and charges

When an asset is disposed of and the selling price is above the written-down value of the asset for tax purposes the company is liable to pay corporation tax on the difference. If the selling price is below the written-down value, then a tax allowance against profits is given on the book loss. If an 80 per cent initial allowance and a 25 per cent annual allowance are available, the write-off against profits would be as in Figure 5:1. Up to the end of year 3, the company would have reduced its tax payments by £44.37, or, put another way, the asset would have cost £55.63 against its original cost of £100. If the asset is sold at the end of year 3 for £10, then a balancing allowance of £1.25 (i.e. £11.25–£10) would be permitted. If there is a balancing charge against the company it may be able to avoid the tax by purchasing another piece of similar equipment (rollover provisions).

It should be noted that the writing-down rates used for tax purposes will generally be different from the provisions for depreciation used in the preparation of a profit and loss account and balance sheet.

Figure 5:1 Tax savings from the initial and annual allowances

	£	Tax saving (50% corporation tax) £
Capital cost	100	
Initial allowance 80%	80	40
	20	
Annual allowance (year 2) 25%	5	2.5
	15	
Annual allowance (year 3) 25%	3.75	1.87
	11.25	44.37

Present system of investment incentives

Since the war regional investment incentives have been given by the government. During the period since 1966, the main differential has been between the development areas (DAs) and the non-development areas (NDAs). Figure 5:2 shows the investment incentives introduced in April 1976. A combination of cash grants and tax allowances are available.

Figure 5:2   Investment allowances and grants introduced in April 1976

	New plant and machinery		New industrial buildings	
	Development areas	Non-development areas	Development areas	Non-development areas
Cash grant	20%	—	20%	—
Initial allowance	100%*	100%*	40%§	40%§

* If 100% is written off in the first year, there are no annual allowances
  thereafter.
§ In addition, annual allowances of 4% straight line apply.

For simplicity only development and non-development areas are referred
to although there are also special development and intermediate areas. The
cash grant for plant and machinery in development areas is given over and
above the initial allowance. Thus on a plant project with a capital cost of
£100 attracting a 20 per cent cash grant, the initial allowance would still be
£100.

Methods of assessing tax and investment incentives

For a correct assessment of taxation and investment incentives, the
discounted cash flow technique must be used. Consider the case of an
investment in plant and machinery totalling £100, earning a before-tax
internal rate of return of 20 per cent in a 5-year period. How should the
after-tax return be computed? Assume that the investment is in a
development area so that there is a 20 per cent cash grant and a 100 per cent
initial allowance. The rate of corporation tax is taken at 50 per cent and is
paid one year after the end of the financial year. The cash grant is paid after
a delay of twelve months. The cash flow is shown in Figure 5:3. It produces
an internal rate of return of 33.6 per cent after tax.

The importance of accounting for tax and investment incentives is
brought out by this example, where the return is 20 per cent before tax and
grant but as much as 33 per cent after tax and grant.

It should be clear that investment calculations should be based always on
after-tax profits as different projects attract varying levels of tax benefits.
In addition, evaluation of past investment performance should be
considered on an after-tax basis in order to be consistent and take account
of all cash flows that affect the original decision to invest.

This method of assessment can be used to compute the returns after tax
and incentive for plant and machinery with particular before-tax returns.
The results of a set of projects are summarized in Figure 5:4.

Figure 5:3 **Analysis of after-tax cash flows**

	0	1	2	Year 3	4	5	6
Net revenue cash flows		33.4	33.4	33.4	33.4	33.4	
Taxation			−0.5 ×33.4	−0.5 ×33.4	−0.5 ×33.4	−0.5 ×33.4	−0.5 ×33.4
Capital cost	−100						
Cash grant		+20					
Initial allowance		+0.5×100					
Net cash flow	−100	+103.4	+16.7	+16.7	+16.7	+16.7	−16.7

Figure 5:4 **comparison of pre-tax and after-tax IRRs for investments in plant and machinery in development and non-development areas as at April 1976.**

Tax allowances and grant rates are given in Figure 5:2. Corporation tax is 50 per cent

	Non-development areas			Development areas		
Before-tax returns	10%	20%	30%	10%	20%	30%
After-tax returns						
Five-year life	10.0%	20.0%	30.0%	23.7%	33.6%	43.7%
Twenty-year life	10.0%	20.0%	30.0%	16.1%	27.5%	38.9%

The reintroduction of a cash grant for development areas in the Industry Act 1972, with the existing 100 per cent initial allowance in the first year and the introduction of 100 per cent initial allowances for NDAs, has produced the greatest incentives in absolute terms as well as the largest regional differential since 1966.[2] It is apparent from Figure 5:4 that there is a great advantage on an after-tax DCF basis of investing in plant and machinery in a development area as opposed to a non-development area, and this should be considered in factory location.

Effectiveness of investment incentives

It is exceedingly difficult to analyse the effectiveness of investment incentive schemes, mainly because they have been changed repeatedly and therefore the time period for analysis of a particular scheme is too short. These frequent changes have meant that, from a company's point of view, the advantages cannot be relied on to stay in force for a substantial period. This point, however, can be overemphasized, as the types of investment incentives to be received by the company are those operable at the time the order for equipment is placed. Thus the investment incentive received is dependent on when the decision to invest is made and not when the investment takes place. It is only when the expansion scheme is planned well into the future that such uncertainty arises.

There is considerable evidence that many firms fail to take account of investment incentives and taxation and fail to use the DCF method of appraisal in assessing their investments. Clearly this can lead to a poor utilization of companies' funds, especially when there are large incentives to invest in development areas. There is, however, an important qualification. Such incentives are provided presumably because the level of investment in such areas is low. This may be due, for example, to higher costs of transport to the main markets, or a shortage of skilled labour. It is important not to assume that the government is giving such 'free meal tickets' without good reason.

Notes

1   The revision and the decision to employ the 'imputation' system are discussed in the green paper, *Reform of Corporation Tax* (Cmnd. 4630) (London: HMSO, March 1971), *Report from the Select Committee on Corporation Tax* (House of Commons Papers, Session 1970–71, number 622) (London: HMSO, 1971), and the white paper, *Reform of Corporation Tax* (Cmnd. 4955) (London: HMSO, 11 April 1972).
2   See Harry Scholefield, 'Taxation commentary: what has happened to investment incentives', *Journal of Business Finance*, vol. 3 no. 4 (Winter 1971), pp. 54–62; and H. H. Scholefield and J. R. Franks, 'Investment incentives and regional policy', *National Westminster Bank Quarterly Review*, February 1972, pp. 34–40.

Further reading

H. H. Scholefield and J. R. Franks, 'The new policy for the regions', *Journal of Accountancy* (July 1972).
R. Thomas, 'The new investment incentives', *Bulletin of the Oxford University Institute of Economics and Statistics*, vol. 33 (May 1971), pp. 93–105.
R. Thomas, 'The new fiscal incentives to invest: liquidity and profitability aspects', *Scottish Journal of Political Economy*, vol. 19 (1972), pp. 273–86.
R. Thomas, 'Taxation commentary: the new fiscal incentives to invest – manufacturing and service industries compared', *Journal of Business Finance*, vol. 3 no. 4 (Winter 1971), pp. 63–6.

6

Inflation and the investment decision

In this chapter we shall discuss some of the implications of changes in the rate of inflation on the profitability of a capital investment. We shall show how progressive income taxes, corporation taxes levied on a nominal trading profit and stock gains can affect the profitability of capital investment in real terms during periods of inflation. Using an example, we measure the impact of changes in the rate of inflation on the present value of a project.

Interest rates and inflation

The risk-free rate of interest can be said to reflect the expected rate of inflation together with the real rate of return in one period and any changes in that rate of inflation are assumed to be reflected fully and speedily in interest rates. Clearly, if interest rates do not reflect expected rates of inflation, markets may be uncompetitive and there may be an opportunity to make money as the market adjusts. For example, suppose the anticipated price increase for wheat for a particular period is 15 per cent, the nominal interest rate is 10 per cent and the real rate of interest is zero. How will consumers or wholesalers behave? Presumably some will borrow and buy wheat until either the price rises to a level where the expected price increase equals 10 per cent or until the rate of interest increases to 15 per cent. The proposition that interest rates fully reflect anticipated rates of inflation or price changes was made by Irving Fisher and is known as the 'Fisher Effect'.[1] Of course this hypothesised relationship between interest rates and inflation cannot be perfect as there are storage costs and other expenses to consider and for some assets the market may not be very efficient.

The Fisher Effect is often used as a basis for the assertion that a change in the anticipated rate of inflation should have no effect on the profitability of capital investment. For example, a 10 per cent a year discounted-cash–flow (DCF) rate of return on a project would increase to 16 per cent if the rate of inflation were to increase from zero to 6 per cent a year. However, the increase in the rate of return on the project would be offset entirely by a corresponding increase in its required rate of return or cost of capital.

It is of great importance for the analyst to understand the relationship between forecast price changes and current interest rates. To assume blithely that prices of some goods or services will increase at a greater rate than the expected rate of inflation implies that the particular market in the item is inefficient. It also implies that by holding that item or commodity, a profit will be made. Will most markets make available such free meal tickets?

If Fisher's proposition were not an accurate reflection of the effect of expected rates of inflation on required rates of return, then there would be no obvious reason to suppose that the profitability of capital investments could remain unchanged by changes in the anticipated rates of inflation. In a recent paper, Fama[2] tests whether the market for one to six-month US Treasury Bills, during the period 1953–71 was efficient and correctly used all information about future rates of inflation. He concludes that 'there are definite relationships between nominal interest rates and the rates of inflation subsequently observed. Moreover, during this period, the bill market seems to be efficient in the sense that nominal interest rates summarise all the information about future inflation rates that is in a time series of past inflation rates.' He also suggests that evidence implying contrary conclusions is based on earlier periods, when the market may have been less efficient and when only poor data was available.

In order to isolate the effect of other changes, we shall assume that the Fisher Effect is the best available approximation to the relationship between inflation and interest rates.

Income effects

A change in the general level of prices due to inflation should not of itself alter the allocation of consumer expenditure between different goods and services. However, in a progressive income tax system inflation will change the marginal rates of tax paid by individuals if income for tax purposes is not adjusted for the rate of inflation. Even if inflation were to affect pre-tax incomes and prices uniformly, some consumers would still be worse off as they moved into higher tax brackets. As a consequence, they would alter their consumption patterns. The resulting shifts in demand for different goods and services will have varying effects on project revenues depending on the responsiveness of prices and costs to these shifts in demand.

An income effect may also be present if some consumer groups such as pensioners live on fixed incomes that are unrelated or react slowly to changes in the rate of inflation. Such forms of income redistribution which take place as a consequence of a change in the rate of inflation will alter the demand pattern for goods and services and also have different effects on the revenues of specific capital investments in real terms.

Inflation and capital allowances

Where capital allowances extend beyond the first year of a project's life, unanticipated changes in the rate of inflation will affect their real value. Let us compare a project's profitability under two sets of assumptions about the rate of inflation.

In Figure 6:1 we have computed the net present value of a risk-free project assuming a zero expected rate of inflation. In Figure 6:2 we have incorporated a forecast rate of inflation of 10 per cent a year. The net present value of the project declines as the anticipated rate of inflation increases, simply because the capital allowances do not change with the inflation rate, whereas costs, revenues and interest rates do. We have assumed that the required rate of return for the project reflects fully the change in the rate of inflation.

Figure 6:1   Risk-free project with zero inflation

	0	1	2	3	4
Capital cost	−100				
*CT savings on capital allowance at 50%		12.5	12.5	12.5	12.5
Net revenues		75	75	75	75
*CT on net revenues		−37.5	−37.5	−37.5	−37.5
Net cash flows after tax	−100	50	50	50	50
NPV at discount rate of 1%	= +95				
*CT = Corporation tax					

Figure 6:2   Risk-free project with 10% inflation

	0	1	2	3	4
Capital cost	−100				
CT savings on cap. allowance at 50%		12.5	12.5	12.5	12.5
Net revenues		82.5	90.75	99.82	109.80
CT on net revenues		−41.25	−45.38	−49.91	−54.90
Net cash flows after tax	−100	53.75	57.88	62.4	67.40

NPV at discount rate of 11% = + 85.43

Clearly, where capital allowances are spread over a number of periods, inflation reduces their value in real terms. Although a capital allowance of 100 per cent in the first year is provided for plant and equipment, many companies which are not currently in a tax-paying position must delay taking capital allowances until sufficient taxable income becomes available in the future. Also investment in industrial buildings involves the spreading of capital allowances over twelve years. In these circumstances increases in the rate of inflation will have an adverse effect on the profitability of capital projects because capital allowances are not indexed.

Corporation tax, stockholding and project profitability

The taxation of company profits is based upon monetary gains rather than real gains. Also, in the past stock has been valued on a first-in-first-out (FIFO) basis in the UK. This method of taxing stock gains has given rise to controversy, as some commentators have suggested that stock gains are not real gains and should not therefore be taxed. A simple example illustrates the controversy.

		Period 1	Period 2
Purchases	100 units	£100	£120
Sales	100 units		£120

Profit & loss A/C for period 2

	£
Sales	120
Purchases	100
Profit	20
Tax (50%)	10
Profit after tax	10

In the above example the reported profit for tax purposes is £20 and the tax payable is £10. However, if the firm has t replace the stock, which now costs £120 for 100 units, the firm has a cash-flow loss represented by the 'tax leakage' on the stock gain. Alternatively, if the tax system were based on the last-in-first-out system (LIFO), the profit for tax purposes during the period would be zero.

	£
Purchases	120
Sales	120
Profit	0

Under LIFO a tax on the stock gain is paid only when the stock ceases to be replaced. In this section we shall try to clarify the issues and demonstrate their importance in the investment decision.

In the above example, under FIFO, the firm has made a 10 per cent return on its investment after tax. The firm can either sell the stock for £100 in period 1 or wait and sell it at the end of period 2 at an expected nominal profit of 10 per cent. If the after-tax cost of finance is less than the nominal gain less the tax, the firm would find it attractive to hold the stock until the end of period 2. Clearly the stock gains are a part of expected trading profit and cannot be described as 'unreal'. By definition an investment's profitability cannot be affected by a rate of inflation that has been expected and incorporated into the original investment decision.

The above analysis assumes that the volume of stock can be changed at the end of each period. Although a dealer in, say, copper, can realize his stock profits at any time, one should recognise that a minimum stock of raw materials and of work-in-progress is required to keep most manufacturing processes going. For much of manufacturing industry, the level of stock becomes relatively insensitive to changes in the rate of inflation and interest rates for the life of the particular project or process. Consequently, the tax leakage resulting from the FIFO method of assessment may continue each year for the life of the project. Although the adverse effect of taxation on stock gains may not be sufficient to justify abandonment of an existing project, project profitability will be affected adversely by these taxes when the rate of inflation exceeds the rate which

Figure 6:3   Project with zero inflation

	End of year						
	0	1	2	3	4	5	6
Plant and machinery	-1000					100[1]	
CT savings on cap. allow. (at 50% tax)		500					-50[2]
Building*	-1000					800[1]	
CT savings on cap. allow.		270	20	20	20	20	-250[2]
Cash grants[3]		400					
Stock**	-1000					1000	
Net revenues		600	600	600	600	600	
CT on net revenues			-300	-300	-300	-300	-300
	-3000	1770	320	320	320	2220	-600

Net present value at 7% = 622

*Usually land should be included.
** Other working capital assumed to be negligible

1   Estimated residual value

2   -250 = 20-270
    Balancing charges
    | Cost of building | £1000 |
    | Capital allowances absorbed | 740 |
    | Written down value (Yr5) | 260 |
    | Sale proceeds | 800 |
    | Gain for tax purposes | 540 |
    | Tax payable (50%) | 270 |

3   Cash grants of 20% for building and plant and machinery

Figure 6:4 Inflation at 20% with tax on stock gains under FIFO and no relief

	End of year						
	0	1	2	3	4	5	6
Plant and machinery	-1000					249	
CT savings on cap. allow. (at 50%)		500					-125
Building*	-1000					1991	
CT savings on cap. allow. on building		270	20	20	20	20	-350[1]
Capital gains tax on building (at 30%)							-297[1]
Grants		400					
Stock**	-1000					+2488	
Net revenues		720	864	1037	1244	1493	
CT on net revenues			-360	-432	-518	-622	-746
CT on stock gain			-100	-120	-144	-173	-207
	-3000	1890	424	505	602	5446	-1725

Net present value at 28.4% = 365

* Land should usually be included.
** Other working capital assumed to be negligible

Key

1 -350 = 20 - 370

Cost of building	£1000
Capital allowances	740
Written down cost	260
Sale proceeds	1991
Gain for tax purposes	1731
Tax payable 740 × 50% = 370	
991 × 30% = 297	647

had been expected. When a higher rate of inflation is anticipated, investment in stock intensive projects must be lower as a result. Later in the chapter we shall incorporate such tax effects into an example.

Project profitability under inflation – an example

In this section we quantify the effect of different assumptions about the anticipated rate of inflation on the profitability of a particular capital investment. The project investment consists of plant and machinery, buildings and stock. Therefore we can consider the result of a change from FIFO to the LIFO system of stock valuation and compare this with the current government measures for tax relief on stock.

The net cash flows of the project assuming zero inflation are outlined in Figure 6:3. Assuming a real rate of interest of 1 per cent and a 6 per cent risk premium in an all-equity financed firm, the net present value of the project is £622. Next, if we assume an anticipated rate of inflation of 20% per annum through to the sixth year and that this is reflected in interest rates, costs and revenues, and that FIFO is used for valuing and taxing stock, the net present value of the project is only £365. What causes the decline in the value of the project? There are two main causes; the tax on stock gains and the loss in real terms of the value of the capital allowances.

In Figure 6:5 we have computed the effect on profitability of a change (for tax purposes) from the FIFO to the LIFO system of taxing stock gains. If we assume that the tax on stock gains is paid at the end of year six, the net present value of the project increases from £365 to approximately £465. Alternatively, if we incorporate the stock relief measures introduced by the government in April 1976 (Appendix 6:1), the net present value becomes £638. Thus, in our example at high rates of inflation with equivalent high discount rates, the government has provided relief exceeding that which would be available under the LIFO valuation formula. To the extent that interest rates did not fully reflect higher rates of inflation, stock relief would be found to be even more generous in net present value terms.

Figure 6:5   Net present value of the project example using different stock valuation methods

Stock valuation Method	Expected rate of Inflation	Discount rate	NPV
FIFO	0%	7%	£622
FIFO	20	28.4	365
LIFO	20	28.4	465
FIFO with stock relief	20	28.4	638

Money terms or real terms

It is often assumed that calculations performed in real terms avoid the necessity to project forward costs and revenues and therefore avoid forecasts of the rate of inflation. This view is mistaken as the real rate of return must be used in the discount rate and to estimate the rate requires a forecast of the expected rate of inflation. Thus, it is not possible to avoid the problem of forecasting general and specific price changes.

Inflation often provides capital gains on fixed and current assets and in order to estimate the taxes payable, the computations must be made in the money of the day. In addition, particular components of the cash flow calculations for example, capital allowances, may be fixed in nominal terms, and therefore should be treated separately. The forecasts of specific revenues and costs should be related to market expectations about changes in the general price level and the consequent changes in the specific components of the project's costs and revenues. For example, the expected effects of price control and incomes policy on the project must be included in the analysis. If one wishes to estimate the effect of a deviation in expected price changes, it should be clear whether such a change is based upon a general price level change which is different from that estimated by the market. If so, the interest rate or discount rate should be altered correspondingly to reflect the anticipated rate of inflation assumed in the altered forecasts of costs and revenues.

Conclusions

Even when perfectly competitive markets are assumed, we have shown that a change in the anticipated rate of inflation can affect corporate profitability in real terms as a result of personal and corporate taxation levied on a nominal basis. Managements who ignore income effects of inflation under progressive tax systems on consumer spending will make incorrect forecasts of product revenues for capital projects. Corporation tax based on the FIFO stock valuation method will reduce profitability in real terms under inflation as a result of a tax leakage on stock gains unless offsetting stock relief provisions are granted. Without stock relief management's ability to restore profitability through price increases would depend upon the competitive structure of the market for its products. However, as prices on products requiring investment in stock have to increase at a greater rate than the prices of other goods or services requiring less stock, it would be surprising if real profitability were unaffected.

It should be clear that project cash flows must be estimated in nominal terms because the Corporation tax system is not indexed. Also, estimates of the effects of differential rates of inflation and price controls on product inputs and outputs require nominal forecasts. Even should it be thought desirable to deflate these forecasts, the problem of assessing the expected rates of inflation reflected by the market in interest rates for this purpose cannot be avoided.

Notes

This chapter is based on a teaching note by J. R. Franks and J. E. Broyles, 'Inflation and the Investment Decision', London Graduate School of Business Studies, 1976.

1 Irving Fisher, *The Theory of Interest*, Macmillan, New York, 1930.
2 Eugene F. Fama, 'Short Term Interest Rates as Predictions of Inflation', Unpublished Working Paper, September 1974.

Further reading

J. E. Broyles and J. R. Franks, 'Some Implications of Change in the Rate of Inflation for Capital Investment', Unpublished paper, London Graduate School of Business Studies.

J. R Hicks, 'Inflation and Interest Rates', *Banca Nazionale de Lavoro*, 1974.

M. A. King, 'The United Kingdom Profits Crisis: Myth or Reality?' *The Economic Journal*, March 1975.

Robert Mundell, 'Inflation and Real Interest', *Journal of Political Economy*, June 1963.

Charles R. Nelson, 'Inflation and Capital Budgeting', *Journal of Finance*, June 1976, No. 3, Vol. XXXI.

R. Roll, 'Interest Rates on Monetary Assets and Commodity Price Index Changes', *Journal of Finance*, May 1972, pp. 251-78.

Peter Swoboda, 'The Value of Shares and Project Appraisal under Inflation', Unpublished Manuscript, University of Graz, Austria.

Appendix 6:1   Inflation at 20% p.a. with stock relief

	End of year						
	0	1	2	3	4	5	6
Plant and machinery	-1000					249	
CT savings on cap. allow. (at 50%)		500					-125
Building*	-1000					1991	
CT savings on cap. allow. on building		270	20	20	20	20	20
							-350
Capital gains tax on building (at 30%)							-297
Grants		400					
Stock**	-1000					+2488	
Net revenues		720	864	1037	1244	1493	
CT on net revenues			-360	-432	-518	-622	-746
CT on stock gain			-100	-120	-144	-173	-207
CT: stock relief***		616	34	40	49	54	-1251
	-3000	2506	458	545	651	5500	-2976

Net present value at 28.4% = 638

*   Land should usually be included
**   Other working capital assumed to be negligible
***   See next fig. for calculations

Appendix 6:2   Computation of stock relief as at April 1976

| | End of year | | | | | |
	0	1	2	3	4	5
Net revenues	0	720	864	1037	1244	1493
Stock gain on goods sold	0	200	240	288	346	414
Trading income before capital allowance	0	920	1104	1325	1590	1907
Capital allowance	1540	40	40	40	40	−949
Trading income less capital allowances	−1540	880	1064	1285	1550	2816
Closing stock less opening stock (includes changes in physical volume)	1000	200	240	290	340	−2074
Less 15% trading income (less allowances)	−231	132	160	193	233	422
Stock relief (received with one year's delay)	1231	68	80	97	107	−2502
Tax savings at 50% (received with one year's delay)	616	34	40	49	54	−1251

An all-equity financed company is assumed and therefore interest changes have not been subtracted from trading income.

For definitions and assumptions see next page.

Definitions

Net revenue	=	Current sales – current expenses – costs of stock replaced.
Stock gain on goods sold	=	Difference between stock costs on FIFO basis and replacement basis.
Trading income	=	Current sales – current expenses (excluding stock replacement)
		– FIFO cost of stock used.

Therefore:

Trading income	=	Net revenue + stock gain

Assumptions

This analysis looks at the incremental effect of the project assuming:

(1) The company is in a tax paying position and can utilise all of its capital allowances and tax savings

(2) The company is in a net stock profit relief position in all years of the project.

(3) The project is an incremental activity in an ongoing business. If this were not the case and, for example, a new subsidiary were set up to operate the project, the initial purchase of stock would be treated differently by the Inland Revenue.

(4) There are no interest charges to be set against trading income.

7

Project appraisal under conditions of uncertainty

Our analysis of the capital-budgeting decision has so far been based upon a state of certainty regarding the future. For example, when cash flows have been forecast for a particular project, the DCF return has been computed on the assumption that only those cash flows would occur. In reality, the outcome will usually be different from that predicted. For a number of reasons, cost and revenue factors may not move in line with original expectations. Management must be able to incorporate uncertainties into any project appraisal and the various techniques used for this purpose come under the general heading of risk analysis. This chapter reviews the main methods of risk analysis, but it is only an introduction to the subject. Any discussion of risk analysis must involve probabilities and probability distributions. Readers who are not conversant with these terms should read the explanatory section at the end of the chapter.

Risk analysis

Project appraisal involves future cash flows which must to some extent be thought of as uncertain or risky. They are uncertain in so far as the investment may result in returns ranging, for example, from 5 to 25 per cent. Unless stated otherwise, the terms risk and uncertainty will here be used synonymously.

When dealing with uncertain proposals, two questions arise: is the uncertainty of the cash flows significant and, if so, what can be done to take this into account? There seems little doubt that uncertainty is important if actual project returns are compared to those predicted. For a variety of reasons, the two are rarely the same. Although little post-audit analysis has been done in the UK, every company can point to capital projects that have exceeded or failed to come up to expectations. There are two ways in which risk analysis can help managers:

1   Risk analysis can provide a more explicit view of the underlying economics of a project. The probability of the major variables changing and the conditions underlying such a change can be translated into a range of returns to provide an improved framework for the decision-maker.
2   The analytical methods to be discussed not only provide a framework to examine the project's risk characteristics, but also suggest ways of limiting or shifting the risks facing a firm if a particular project is to be accepted.

Methods of adjusting for risk

The list of methods discussed below whereby management can make allowance for risk is not exhaustive, but is designed to cover methods at present in general use and others which have potential.

Payback

When the payback method was examined in Chapter 4, we noted that one advantage of the method was an implicit risk-averseness in its use, if we assume that one of the major determinants of risk is time. This appears intuitively reasonable to many managers as it is usually easier for them to predict events occurring in the short term than in the long term. For example, it may be possible to estimate the rate of inflation over the next six months, but very few would be willing to predict inflation rates for the next ten years.

If cash flows are riskier the further ahead they occur, payback may be thought of as discriminating against risky projects, as it ignores all cash flows beyond the payback period. However, there are good reasons why payback is not a suitable risk discriminator. Projection of revenues may be easier to predict in the long term than in the short term. Furthermore, payback does not measure profitability adequately and hence does not allow the decision-maker to compare a project's profit and risk. Some such balance or trade-off must be made, for it is surely worth while accepting a risky project if the potential return is sufficient. How much is sufficient is the sort of question more sophisticated methods attempt to answer, but this tradeoff cannot be made with the payback method.

Despite its drawbacks, many companies still use payback because they believe it discriminates adequately against risky projects. This is not so, for, as described in Chapter 4, a project may repay its capital cost rapidly but remain unprofitable because cash flows or net income dry up soon after the capital cost has been recovered. Similarly, a project with a long life, such as a mine, will rarely repay its capital costs in less than four years yet it may be very profitable because of a long life.

As an example consider two projects with the after-tax costs and revenues shown in Figure 7:1. Project 1 produced a rapid return with a payback of 4 years, whereas project 2 takes $5\frac{1}{3}$ years to return its capital. However, because project 2 has more substantial cash flows after the payback period, it has the higher IRR, and therefore is more profitable. Managements would accept project 1 if they assumed payback to be the only measure of return.

Figure 7:1   After-tax costs and revenues from two projects

		Project 1	Project 2
Cash flow year	0	–£100	–£100
	1	+£25	+£10
	2	+£25	+£10
	3	+£25	+£20
	4	+£25	+£20
	5	+£25	+£30
	6	0	+£30
	7	0	+£40
	8	0	+£40
Payback period		4 years	$5\frac{1}{3}$ years
IRR		7.9%	14.2%

Figure 7:2   Return from projects in Figure 7:1 if revenues are reduced by £5 a year

		Project 1	Project 2
Cash flow year	0	–£100	–£100
	1	£20	£5
	2	£20	£5
	3	£20	£15
	4	£20	£15
	5	£20	£25
	6	0	£25
	7	0	£35
	8	0	£35
Payback period		5 years	$6\frac{2}{3}$ years
IRR		0%	8.8%

Suppose that cash flows do not arise as expected, but fall short of estimates by £5 every year. The new cash-flow position and rates of return would be as in Figure 7:2. The payback on projects 1 and 2 increases and the DCF returns diminish, but clearly project 2 is more profitable than project 1 and is less sensitive to identical reductions in revenue. The payback criterion does not help in examining project risk in any consistent way. If annual cash flows were £10 less than predicted, project 1 would make a substantial loss, whereas project 2 would still show a 3 per cent return. Obviously, payback is not a suitable risk criterion in this case as project 1 appears more likely to make a loss than does project 2. Even if it is believed that later cash flows are riskier, a tradeoff must still be made between risk and return, and the payback method, unlike DCF, cannot make such an adjustment. It should be possible to construct a set of minimum payback rules for projects of different risks and different lives but then, this dispenses with the prime virtue of payback, its simplicity of calculation. The conclusion is that payback is not a good measure of risk. Its prevalence as an appraisal device is probably due to force of habit, simplicity and because it produces a workable result. We believe that this result is not good enough and that in certain cases, where the payback has obscured other risk considerations, it can be seriously wrong.

Decision trees [1]

Investment decisions sometimes involve a complex interlocking of decisions and outcomes in which later decisions depend upon the outcomes of earlier decisions. A useful way of dealing with such problems is to use a decision tree, which is simply a sequential statement of all possible actions and outcomes. Probabilities are assigned to the outcomes of particular actions and it is possible to compute the best decisions, given these probabilities and their associated returns.

To illustrate this approach, consider the following example: a company is expecting a substantial increase in demand for one of its products in the near future. The firm has three possible courses of action which will enable it to meet this demand: increase shiftwork in its existing plant, extend the existing plant or build a new plant. The amount of additional output increases with each choice, but so does the cost. The company is not sure of the actual increase in demand and thus cannot with certainty relate the correct capacity decision to the expected rise in demand. The increases in capacity which can be achieved by the different actions are given in Figure 7:3. The marketing department has supplied the data given in Figure 7:4 on demand increases and their associated probabilities.

Figure 7:3   Potential increases in capacity

Action	Capacity increase (units per year)
Shiftwork	100,000
Extension	150,000
New building	300,000

Figure 7:4   Potential increases in demand

Increase in demand		Probability of occurrence
Low	100,000	0.3
Medium	250,000	0.6
High	400,000	0.1

The proportion of fixed costs is known to be different for each expansion scheme, so that, for example, building a new plant will incur losses if demand turns out to be low, but it may produce very large profits if demand turns out to be high. This information can be presented in the form of a decision tree as in Figure 7:5. The revenues projected for each course of action in the decision tree are after the deduction of all costs. Then, over the life of the project, the discounted sum of future revenues for each combination of outcomes can be calculated and these can be balanced against the initial capital cost. This will provide an NPV for each course of action.

Suppose the decision is to extend the plant. This choice is represented by the middle line, or path, leading from the decision box on the extreme left of the tree. If the plant is extended there are three possible demand outcomes. Each outcome has a *payoff* which consists of the revenue from expected sales to meet the particular level of demand less expected costs. Multiplying each payoff by the probability of each outcome yields the *expected monetary value* (EMV), or mean, of the decision to extend the plant. The EMV is the sum of the payoffs multiplied by their respective probabilities for all possible outcomes from a particular actioin:

$$\text{EMV} = 0.3 \times £50,000 + 0.6 \times £150,000 + 0.1 \times £150,000$$
$$= £120,000$$

The EMV is calculated for each choice and the choice with maximum payoff is the choice which is statistically most favourable. In the present case, building the new plant is the best choice. Although it is the most risky course of action, incurring heavy losses if demand is low, it yields high profits if demand is high and on balance has the greatest EMV.

A relatively simple example has been used to illustrate the application of decision trees in risk analysis. In most cases the tree would not be used for just one set of decisions and outcomes, but for a whole series. Instead of having a payoff as a result of each outcome, there might be a further decision and trees can be developed for a whole series of decisions and outcomes.

The method of dealing with one-stage decision/outcome problems reduces a number of possible outcomes to the most favourable one based on estimates. This process may be used to 'roll back' a more extended tree. Starting from the right with the final payoffs, the correct decision is evaluated at each final decision box. Then the EMV of the most favourable action at each final decision box can be regarded as the payoff for the

Figure 7:5   Decision tree

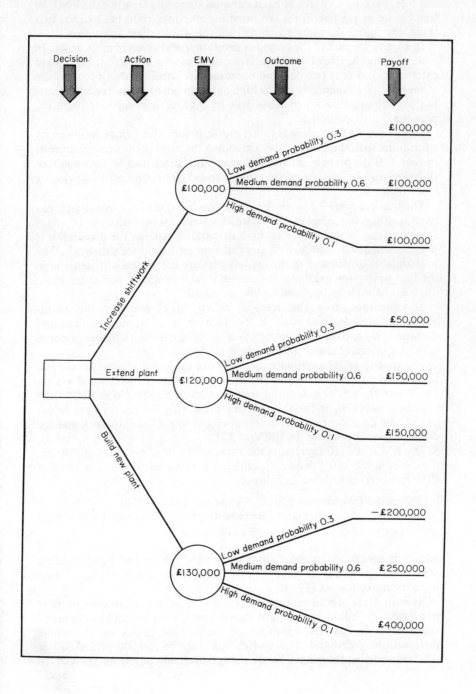

outcome that leads to that decision box. Thus one can move back through the tree, making a choice at each decision stage and treating the EMV of that choice as the payoff for the previous outcome, right back to the first stage, the initial decision which will set the whole chain in motion.

In Figure 7:6 part of the previous decision tree is given in more detail. In order to limit the size of the overall tree, only two choices, overtime or plant extension, and only two demand outcomes are considered in a two-period model. Demand increases can be high or low in both first and second years; the probability that an increase will be high or low depends upon the previous year's outcome.

If the first-year outcome is to extend shiftwork this can be followed by continuing with the shiftwork or extending the plant in the same manner as in year 1. If the plant is extended in year 1 this can either be done again or shiftwork can be introduced into the extended plant to increase its capacity still further.

The tree in Figure 7:6 is similar to the one in Figure 7:5 except that it has two decision/outcome stages instead of one. The outcome of plant extension can be either low or high demand. Whatever the demand, it is possible either to continue on normal time or introduce shiftwork. The probabilities of demand in the second year are correlated with demand in the first year – for example, if demand is high in year 1, it is much more likely to be high as opposed to low in year 2.

To illustrate how the tree is 'rolled back' consider the plant-extension/high-demand path. If the decision is to extend the plant and demand is high, then a further decision has to be made on whether or not to continue normal time or to introduce shiftwork.

The first stage is to estimate the EMVs of the last decisions in the tree; these EMVs are shown within circles at the final branch-points of Figure 7:6. These show that extending shiftwork has a higher EMV (£210) than normal time (£176) and so the branch representing normal time can be cut off; at this decision box, the better choice is to extend shiftwork and the decision would produce an EMV of £210.

The EMV of £210 represents the expected value of extended shiftwork; the decision is taken if demand is high in the previous period. The EMV of £210 has been calculated as follows:

high demand (probability of 0.8) × expected value (£250)
+ low demand (probability of 0.2) × expected value (£50)
= £210.

Working backwards sequentially through the tree shows that extending plant size produces a much more favourable EMV (£172.4) than introducing shiftwork (£118).

Decision trees do have certain drawbacks as far as risk analysis is concerned. It should be apparent that the high, medium and low demand occurrences in the first example are really only points on the whole distribution of demand. Demand cannot only be 100,000 or 250,000 or 400,000 units but these have been used as convenient points for analysis. In

Figure 7:6 Extended decision tree

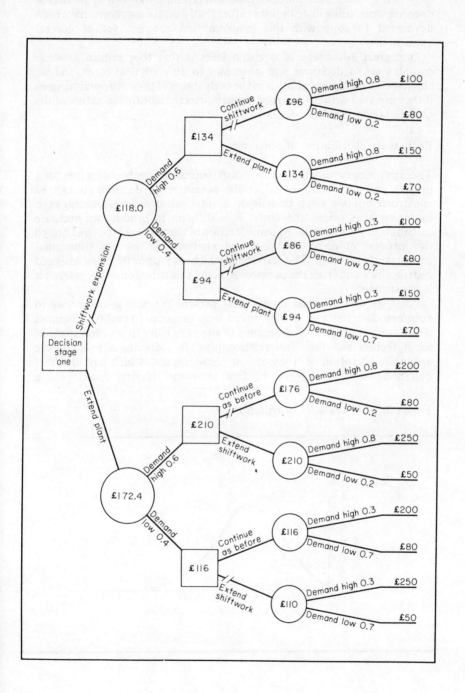

practice, errors may be introduced if the whole distribution is reduced to only two or three such point estimates. Techniques known as stochastic decision trees, using distributions rather than discrete outcomes, have been developed to cope with this problem, but are not yet of general applicability.

One great advantage of decision trees is that they reduce a whole complex set of decisions and outcomes to an analytical form, and we suggest that their great utility is in the early stages of project appraisal, even if they are used without assigned probabilities to indicate the nature of the choices facing the decision team.

Probability distribution of outcomes

This approach considers the entire distribution of possible outcomes for a project and how this can affect the accept/reject decision. It can be constructed in two ways: by estimating total values or by estimating each input, such as prices and costs. It is difficult to produce an accurate distribution without detailed consideration of the relevant inputs, although this process of data collection and analysis can involve substantial manpower and cost. The variables which are uncertain are assigned distributions and from the composite model a distribution of the outcomes is constructed.

Analysis of individual inputs is at present the best possible way to accommodate risk in a one-off investment decision. In reality, outcomes differ from those expected because of the variability in a wide variety of input factors and their interrelationships. By adopting a probabilistic approach attention is focused on these inputs, which are the real determinants of change in the final outcome. Having constructed a

Figure 7:7   Probability distribution

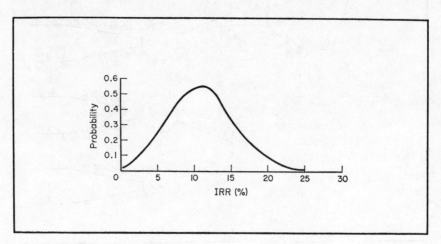

distribution of outcomes, known as a *risk profile*, the problems of risk criteria still remain – given a particular risk profile, how can one decide whether or not it is acceptable? Individuals' attitudes towards risk differ; acceptability may be a function of shareholders' risk preferences (or rather of managements' perception of those preferences); different managers have different attitudes towards risk and hence make different decisions. No hard and fast rules can be given, but a framework can be provided within which a decision can be made.

Figure 7:7 shows a risk profile that has been developed for a project. It is easier to deal with the distribution if it is converted into a cumulative profile by consecutively adding portions of the curve. To show how cumulative profiles are developed and what such a profile means, consider another project with the discrete outcomes shown in Figure 7:8.

Figure 7:8   Discrete probability distribution

DCF rate of return	Probability of outcome
5%	0.05
10%	0.05
12%	0.2
14%	0.2
16%	0.2
18%	0.2
20%	0.1
	1.0

The cumulative probability is obtained by adding in each new probability as a new DCF figure is reached (Figure 7:9).

For each DCF rate, the cumulative figures express the probability of obtaining less than, or equal to, that particular rate.

This example has used a discrete series of events, but the method can also be applied to a continuous distribution. Any point on the curve represents the probability of getting less than or equal to the associated DCF value. If the process is inverted, subtracting successive probabilities from 1, a curve is obtained which represents the probability of achieving *more* than any particular value on the curve. Figure 7:10 shows such a cumulative probability distribution curve. Either can be used depending on how one likes to receive information.

Figure 7:9   Cumulative probability from Figure 7:8

DCF rate of return	Cumulative probability	
10% or less	0.1	
12% or less	0.3	(0.1 + 0.2)
14% or less	0.5	(0.3 + 0.2)
16% or less	0.7	(0.5 + 0.2)
18% or less	0.9	(0.7 + 0.2)
20% or less	1.0	(0.9 + 0.1)

This cumulative curve gives the probability of making more than a given rate of return, which is more useful than simply knowing the probability of each particular return. The curve starts at a probability of 1 of achieving more than the minimum value of the risk profile and ends up with a zero probability of achieving more than the maximum possible return. As an example, consider a DCF rate of return of 20 per cent. From the cumulative graph, there is a 0.05 chance (that is 5 per cent) of making 20 per cent or more on the project.

Precise criteria for the decision have yet to be defined. One criterion should be based on the relationship of the expected value of all possible outcomes to the minimum acceptable return. Usually, a project would not be accepted if it had an expected value less than the hurdle rate (some risk takers might gamble with such a project if there is the possibility of a very high return, even though the most likely return is poor). Assuming that the most likely point is above the hurdle rate, the first point to consider is the probability of exceeding this rate. In Figure 7:10, if the hurdle rate is 10 per cent, there is a 0.625 (62.5 per cent) chance of exceeding this value. This must now be weighed up against the chance of failing to meet the hurdle rate and the chance of actually making a loss (in this example 5 per cent).

Armed with this information about a particular risk profile, management can decide on its acceptability, taking account of their own risk preferences. Some managers may take on a project with heavy downside risk because it also has considerable upside potential, whereas others will be more cautious and favour those projects limited in their downside risk. It is important to realize at this point that we have only mentioned the cost of money and the capital market in an indirect way. We have suggested that the expected value and probability distribution of returns should be used to assess risk. The trade-off between risk and expected value has only been mentioned in a casual way. In the next chapter we suggest that the capital market provides us with the trade-off and permits management to assess the profitability of a project from the point of view of shareholders' and market values. This does not diminish the value of previous analysis, rather it changes the purpose. Management must compare the expected returns of an investment with the risk. Such a trade-off should be examined from the standpoint of the shareholders. In addition, management must then decide whether such risks are acceptable to them in the context of ensuring company survival. Risk analysis serves both these purposes and we shall return to this question in the next chapter.

Sensitivity analysis

This technique is used by many companies to determine a project's risk characteristics. Selected input factors, such as prices, are varied and the consequent change in the DCF return is computed. This process highlights the most sensitive factors and a range of returns can be related to the risks attached by management to the most sensitive factors.

Figure 7:10   Cumulative probability distribution

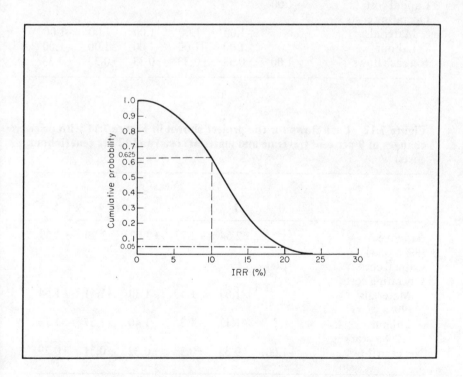

Figure 7:11 shows cash flows in current prices which produce a 20 per cent DCF return on a five-year project. If management's best estimates are that over the project life, prices for sales and materials will rise 9 per cent a year and wages will increase at 12 per cent a year then the adjusted cash flows will be those shown in Figure 7:12. These adjusted cash flows produce a DCF return of 17.9 per cent. If the project's cost of capital is 13 per cent then this project is acceptable. But how sensitive is the DCF return to relative changes in the price of labour as compared to material and product prices: if, instead of the 12 per cent forecast, wage rates were expected to rise by 13 per cent, how would the project's returns be affected? The adjusted cash flows are shown in Figure 7:13.

Figure 7:11   Project cash flows in current prices producing a DCF return of 20 per cent

	Year					
	0	1	2	3	4	5
Revenue		+2.33	+2.33	+2.33	+2.33	+2.33
Capital cost	−1.00					
Operating costs						
Materials		−1.00	−1.00	−1.00	−1.00	−1.00
Labour		−1.00	−1.00	−1.00	−1.00	−1.00
Net cash flows	−1.00	+0.33	+0.33	+0.33	+0.33	+0.33

Figure 7:12   Cash flows for the project shown in Figure 7:11 with price changes of 9 per cent (revenue and material costs) and 12 per cent (labour costs)

	Year					
	0	1	2	3	4	5
Revenue (9% a year)		+2.54	+2.77	+3.02	+3.29	+3.59
Capital costs	−1.00					
Operating costs						
Materials (9% a year)		−1.09	−1.19	−1.30	−1.41	−1.54
Labour (12% a year)		−1.12	−1.25	−1.40	−1.57	−1.76
Net cash flows	−1.00	+0.33	+0.33	+0.32	+0.31	+0.29

Figure 7:13   Effect on the cash flows in Figure 7:12 of an increase of 1 per cent in the forecasting price change for labour costs

	Year					
	0	1	2	3	4	5
Revenue		+2.54	+2.77	+3.02	+3.29	+3.59
(9% a year)						
Capital costs	-1.00					
Operating costs						
Materials		-1.09	-1.19	-1.30	-1.41	-1.54
(9% a year)						
Labour		-1.13	-1.28	-1.44	-1.63	-1.84
(13% a year)						
Net cash flows	-1.00	+0.32	+0.30	+0.28	+0.25	+0.21

A forecast of 13 per cent for wages reduces the project DCF return to around 12 per cent and if the cost of capital is 13 per cent the project becomes unacceptable. In this case the DCF return on the project is very sensitive to small increases in wage rates.

The main problem with sensitivity analysis is deciding the amount by which each factor should be altered. The analyst cannot change numbers at random or simply assume that wage costs will move up without considering the causes of the expected wage increase and the implications for the other inputs and outputs. Thus the wages increase may reflect a general change in price levels with corresponding changes in prices of all other components of the cost and revenue streams of the project. Alternatively, he may forecast a relative change in the price of labour and materials but there must be some underlying economic rationale for those assumptions.

Sensitivity analysis can be used in conjunction with risk profiles. If changes in input variables are analysed, the analytical team can concentrate on those variables most likely to affect the outcome and most worthy of detailed study; it is a waste of time to spend effort synthesizing the likely shape of an input probability distribution if, in fact, the final profile is hardly affected by that distribution. When the report is written, management attention should be focused on the most sensitive variables and how changes in particular variables alter the final profile or distribution of outcomes.

Not only does sensitivity analysis indicate which variables require further study, it shows where resources can be most effectively utilized. In conjunction with probability distributions, it provides a powerful management tool. Attention can be concentrated on the sensitive variables in order to reduce the overall risk of the project. If, for example, price is a far more sensitive variable than product costs, resources should be concentrated on the marketing side to reduce risk by negotiating fixed price contracts or index-linked terms.

We suggest that sensitivity analysis is a useful tool for gauging risk and focusing attention and resources on sensitive variables. We recommend that sensitivity analysis should be used in conjunction with probability analysis in large projects, or on its own for smaller projects. However, the numbers used in such analysis must reflect the underlying economic relationships between the variables.

Correlation and multi-project choice

The preceding discussion has involved the assumption that there is no interrelationship between the outcomes of different projects.

Consider two projects, A and B. Suppose that the risks inherent in each have been analysed and two distributions have been derived of expected returns in terms of present values. One distribution for project A has a mean of μ_A, and a standard deviation of σ_A, and one for B with a corresponding mean and standard deviation of μ_B and σ_B respectively. (The concepts of mean and standard deviation are described in the final section of this chapter.) If only one project is accepted then the risk to be taken is σ_A for project A, or σ_B for project B. But what are the implications of accepting both projects? The expected value from accepting both projects is simply the sum of the expected values of the individual projects – that is, $\mu_A + \mu_B$. The risk involved in accepting both projects depends on the extent to which the projects are interrelated. It can be shown that the standard deviation of expected returns from accepting both projects, μ_{A+B}, is given by the formula:

$$\sigma_{A+B} = \sqrt{(\sigma_A^2 + 2\rho_{AB}\sigma_A\sigma_B + \sigma_B^2)}$$

Where ρ_{AB} is the *correlation coefficient* between the expected returns from projects A and B and is a mathematical expression of the interrelationship between them. The value of ρ lies in the range -1 to $+1$. A value of $+1$ means complete correlation; whatever the actual outcome of project A in terms of μ_A and σ_A, the outcome of project B will move in the same direction and at the same rate. A value of 0 means that there is no correlation or interrelationship between the two projects. A correlation coefficient of -1 suggests an inverse correlation; for example, if in the actual outcome project A's returns were near the upper end of the distribution, then B's returns would be at a similar point near the lower end of the distribution.

Only two projects were considered in the example, but the analysis can be extended to cover a number of projects, treating each different combination or portfolio of projects as a new subject with its own mean and standard deviation. Furthermore, each project should also be considered in relation to the characteristics of the whole firm. Suppose the expected returns for the firm can be represented by a distribution with mean μ_F and standard deviation σ_F, then if project A is accepted the new profile for the firm will have a mean μ_N,

$$\mu_N = \mu_F + \mu_A$$

and a standard deviation of expected returns given by

$$\sigma_N = \sqrt{(\sigma_F^2 + 2\rho \ \gamma \ \sigma_F\sigma_A + \sigma_A^2)}$$

If project A is relatively small compared to the firm as a whole, then σ_A will be much smaller than σ_F, and σ_A^2 will be even smaller compared to σ_F^2. In the short term, σ_F is constant, and thus the first term does not change and the last term is very small. Hence the main explanation for the *difference*, if any, between σ_N and σ_F will be the expression,

$$2\rho_{FA}\sigma_F\sigma_A$$

A similar expression can be derived for any other project or set of projects facing the company. If the standard deviations of these projects are reasonably similar – that is, all σs are of the same order of magnitude as σ_A, then the main determinant of the changes in risk from accepting any particular set of projects will be the correlation coefficient ρ_{FA}.

Obviously data requirements increase substantially if correlation is to be taken into account and the implications of this increase will be discussed following the development of a framework for the multiproject investment decision. However, management should appreciate, without the use of complex analysis, that the risk attached to a particular project should be considered in the light of the total capital budget. Projects that are not confined to existing activities may not constitute diversification if their correlation coefficients are positive. Moving into a different product line or geographical area may not amount to diversification if the outcomes, or returns, move in the same direction, simultaneously.

Efficiency frontiers

The means and standard deviations of the outcomes of a number of projects have been plotted in Figure 7:14. The mean μ, is a measure of the likely return or present value of a project and σ is a measure of the associated risk. It is apparent that many of the projects in Figure 7:14 are inferior to others because of their lower return and/or higher risk. For example, project P is inferior to project A because it carries more risk (has a greater σ) for the same return; P is inferior to project B because it has a lower return (smaller μ) for the same risk, and finally, P is inferior to project C because it has both lower return and higher risk.

In fact most of the projects in the graph are inferior to other projects and so will be discarded before a final accept/reject decision is made. Having rejected these because of their inferiority, the only projects which require a choice are those which are not inferior in both μ and σ to other projects; these projects lie on the curve drawn on the graph.

Figure 7:14   Efficiency frontier

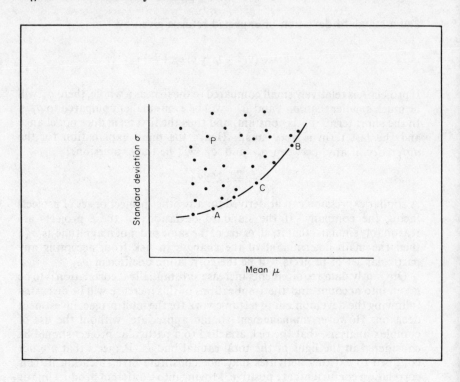

Figure 7:15   Efficiency frontier

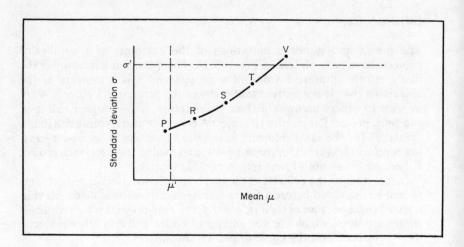

This line is known as the efficiency frontier. Moving along the efficiency frontier from left to right increases return as measured by μ but also increases risk σ. Management must choose which combination of μ and σ best meets its risk/return preferences. This may be accomplished by formal rules or by consideration of the actual profiles of those projects most likely to be chosen.

For example, consider the efficiency frontier in Figure 7:15. Management has decided that it wants to see a return of at least μ', and is unwilling to accept any greater risk than σ'. Hence the final choice is between the three projects R, S, and T. Of course such an analysis is really of interest only to management. Shareholders usually spread their risks widely by investing in the shares of a variety of companies. The diversification of risk within a company is important to management as a safeguard against the potential loss of their jobs or those of other employees in the company. However, shareholder wealth is not altered by the simple act of diversification.

Summary

In this chapter we have given some details of current methods of risk analysis. These methods have two important purposes. Firstly, they help to isolate the areas where project profitability is most sensitive, thereby enabling management to monitor more carefully particular costs and revenues, and make decisions to reduce or shift risk. Thus it is part of the financial planning process to know how possible changes in a project's returns will affect the solvency and profitability of the company. Secondly, management may wish to reject projects or manage them in a different way as a result of analysing how economic changes may affect the project and the firm.

What these methods do not do, is to provide us with a criterion that will measure the impact of the project on the share price of the firm and consequently on shareholders' wealth. To accomplish this, we need to know whether the expected return from the project is greater than its required return, given the risk characteristics. This specifically concentrates attention on the opportunity cost of funds, that is what return the shareholder would obtain if he invested his funds in a security of similar risk to that project. If the project is expected to provide a greater return the shareholder is better off, and the share price will increase. The next chapter tells us how to relate the expected returns of a project to the required return given the opportunities available in the money markets and stock market.

Explanatory section: probabilities and probability distributions

Any discussion of risk analysis must involve probabilities and probability distributions; these topics are briefly covered in this section.

Probabilities

Probabilities are numbers between 0 and 1 expressing the likelihood of a particular occurrence. A probability of 0 means that the outcome will certainly not occur, whereas a probability of 1 suggests that the outcome will definitely occur. Values between 0 and 1 express a varying probability of occurrence, and the nearer the probability is to 1, the more likely is that outcome. If a situation exists where more than one outcome is feasible, then the probability of occurrence of all possible outcomes must sum to 1 – after all, something must happen!

As an example, consider an ordinary 1p piece spun in the air. Each face will have an equal chance of landing uppermost and as the sum of probabilities must equal 1, each has a 0.5 chance of showing. Similarly, if an unbiased six-sided dice is tossed, each face has a $\frac{1}{6}$ chance of landing uppermost.

Probabilities simply express the likelihood that a particular event (in the examples, that one face of a coin or side of a dice lands uppermost) takes place. One cannot say with absolute certainty what will happen: quite simply, we do not know. We *can* express relative chances of outcomes by stating their respective probabilities.

Some prefer probabilities to be expressed as percentages, and this can be done by multiplying the 0 to 1 numbers by 100. The example of tossing a coin would then be rephrased to say that each face has a 50 per cent chance of showing.

Expected monetary value

Associated with probabilities is the concept of expected monetary value (EMV). Suppose, in the coin-tossing example, a bet had been made on the result. If the coin shows heads, the gambler receives £1, if it shows tails he has to pay £1. The EMV is obtained by multiplying the value of each possible outcome by its related probability. In the present case, the possibility of heads or tails is 0.5 in each case; the EMV is given by

$$\text{EMV} = 1 \times 0.5 + (-1) \times 0.5$$
$$= 0$$

This may at first seem a paradoxical result; in any one throw a pound is either given or received, but some transaction must always result; money must change hands. This is perfectly true, but the EMV does not attempt to measure the actual outcome of just one event. It can be thought of as the average return which could be obtained from repeating the same event a large number of times – in the present case, with an even chance of winning or losing, the average result over a large number of throws will be close to zero.

The EMV is a statistical measure of the relative advantages of different courses of action; by comparing the EMVs of different actions a choice can be made between them on the grounds that the action with the highest

EMV will probably produce a greater return than will any other action. In this way, the EMV is a useful method for selecting between alternatives, especially when dealing with decision trees.

Probability distributions

Probabilities describe the chance of a particular discrete outcome occurring where the number of possible outcomes is known and finite – in other words, when only a certain limited number of outcomes can occur from a particular action such as throwing a dice. However there are many circumstances in which there are an unlimited number of outcomes. For example, consider the weight of selected children of a particular age. It is obvious that out of a sample of, say, 100 there will be very few children of the same weight. Furthermore, given that there will be some natural limits to the weight ranging from that of the smallest to the largest, the weight of any one child can fall anywhere within these limits. The act of weighing a particular child does not have a limited number of outcomes, as do coins showing either heads or tails; instead literally any weight within certain limits may show up.

Figure 7:16   Histogram

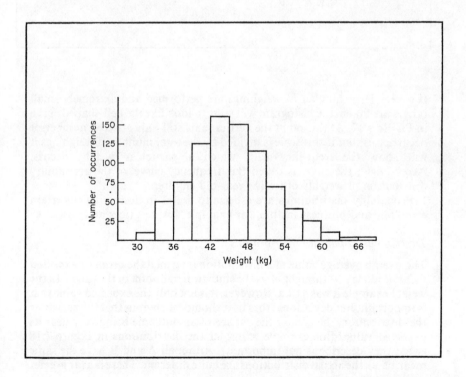

Suppose that a large number of twelve-year-old children are weighed and their weights are classified into ranges of 3 kg. Figure 7:16 shows a graph known as a histogram, on which numbers of occurrences are plotted against range of weights. The height of each rectangular box indicates the number of weights found within the limits of the box. For example, 125 children had weights of between 39 and 42 kg.

Figure 7:17   Number of occurrences

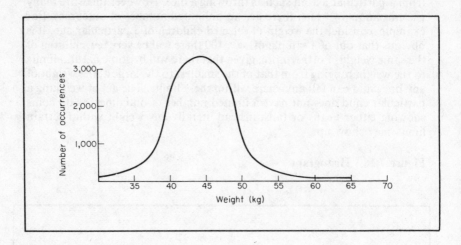

If a very large number of weighings are performed and extremely small ranges are taken, the histogram will start to look like the bell-shaped curve in Figure 7:17. At this point the vertical axis still indicates the number of occurrences, but if this scale is divided by the total number of weighings it will show the frequency with which a particular weight occurs. Accordingly, the curve is called the 'frequency curve' of the probability distribution of weights of twelve-year-old children.

Probability distributions are especially useful in describing uncertain economic and business factors, for example, future prices and costs.

Describing probability distributions

The overall average value of a distribution is termed the *mean* or *expected value*, and may be thought of as the statistical midpoint of the range. In the weight example it was 44 kg. However, it is not only the expected value that is important, but deviations from it. It should be obvious that the narrower the distribution, the greater the chance of an outcome being very near its expected value. For example, consider the distributions in Figure 7:18 (what they describe is not important). Although A and B have the same mean of 30, the actual distributions are quite different. There is a far greater chance of an outcome for distribution A being near the mean than for distribution B. To describe this difference, it is usual to state not only the mean but also the standard deviation (s.d.) for any distribution. The standard deviation is a statistical measure of the spread of the distribution: the larger the s.d. the wider the distribution. In Figure 7:18 the s.d. of B would be much larger than that of A.

Figure 7:18   Two distributions with the same mean but different standard deviations

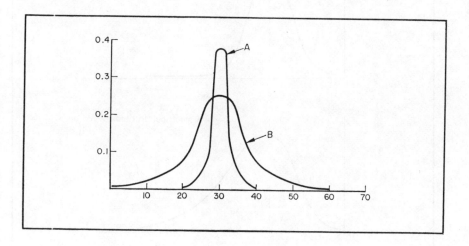

Common symbols for the mean and standard deviation are μ and σ respectively.

The standard deviation may be thought of as a simple measure of risk. B is a riskier distribution than A as there is more chance of getting a value widely removed from the mean. In fact, the larger the σ the greater is this chance, and in situations where the variability of occurrences implies risk, is a good measure of such risk. Similarly, μ is an approximate measure of the return offered by any distribution.

The mean and standard deviations cannot fully describe distributions which are not symmetrical about the mean unless these happen to conform to well-known asymmetrical distributions. Asymmetrical distributions in general are known as skew distributions (Figure 7:19).

To describe skew distributions, they can either be approximated to one of the known skew distributions, such as the Poisson or binomial, or a third term can be given with mean and standard deviation to take account of the skew.

Figure 7:19   Symmetrical and asymmetrical distributions

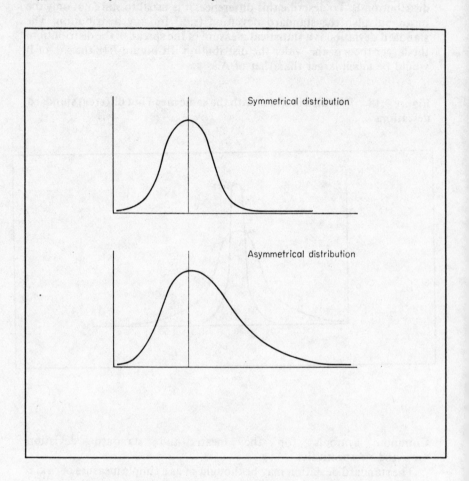

In most circumstances the mean and standard deviation are sufficient to describe a distribution with reasonable accuracy. The mean indicates where the average lies, and the standard deviation indicates the spread of the distribution around the mean. (For a more detailed discussion of methods of computing μ and σ, see the first two items under 'further reading'.)

Notes

1 For an introduction to decision analysis see: P. G. Moore and H. Thomas, 'How to measure your risk – Pethow Company' and 'A tree to tease your mind – Pethow Company', *Financial Times*, 18 and 19 January 1972, and H. Thomas, *Decision Theory and The Manager*, Pitman: London, 1972.

Further reading

Statistics
T. Cass, *Statistical Methods in Management* Cassell: London, 1969.
J. C. Van Horne, *Financial Management and Policy*, second edition, Englewood Cliffs, NJ: Prentice-Hall, 1971, especially ch. 2 and 5.

Certainty equivalents
A. A. Robichek and S. C. Myers, *Optimal Financing Decisions*, Englewood Cliffs, NJ: Prentice-Hall, 1965, pp. 79–93.

Decision trees
J. R. Franks, J. E. Broyles, C. J. Bunton, 'A Decision Analysis Approach to Cash Flow Management', *Operations Research Quarterly*, 1974, Dec. 25 (4).
R. F. Hespos and P. A. Strassman, 'Stochastic decision trees for the analysis of investment decisions', *Management Science*, vol. 11 1965, pp. B-244–59.
H. Raiffa, *Decision Analysis*, Addison-Wesley: Reading, Mass, 1968.

Risk profiles
D. B. Hertz, 'Risk analysis in capital investment', *Harvard Business Review*, vol. 42, no. 1, January–February 1964, pp. 95–110.
D. B. Hertz, 'Investment policies that pay off', *Harvard Business Review*, vol. 46, no. 1, January–February 1968, pp. 96–108.

Portfolio selection techniques
H. A. Latané and W. E. Young, 'Test of portfolio building rules', *Journal of Finance*, September 1969.
J. C. T. Mao, *Quantitative Analysis of Financial Decisions*, Macmillan: New York, Collier-Macmillan: London, 1969.
J. C. T. Mao, 'Essentials of portfolio diversification strategy', *Journal of Finance*, vol. 25 December 1970, pp. 1109–21.
H. M. Markowitz, *Portfolio Selection: Efficient Diversification of Investments*, Wiley: New York, 1959.
G. A. Pogue, 'An Extension of the Markowitz portfolio selection model to include variable transaction costs, short sales, leverage policies and taxes', *Journal of Finance*, September 1967.

8

The stock market and capital project appraisal

The principal objectives of management when undertaking capital investment are to increase the value of the firm. The simplest measure we have of value is based on the price of the firm's securities traded in the capital market. In order to predict the likely effect of a proposed capital project on the value of the firm, management must discount expected cash flows at the market's required rate of return for the risk class of the project. In this chapter we explain how we can obtain an estimate of the market's discount rate for projects within the firm.

Efficient capital markets

The concept of an efficient capital market is important as such markets are the prime source of profitability criteria for decisions relating to investment in fixed assets by firms. An efficient capital market is defined as a market in which prices reflect all relevant information. Therefore, if the stock market is efficient, equity prices will reflect the favourable or unfavourable effects of capital investments in fixed assets with complete accuracy. For example, a project which has just been accepted by management and has a net present value of £100, will add the same amount to the market value of the firm's equity, assuming the market accepts management's forecasts of cash flows and the discount rate.

Empirical studies[1] to date have resulted in no convincing evidence contrary to market efficiency. For example, work conducted both in the US[2] and the UK[3] on the reaction of the share price to news of forthcoming takeovers suggests that there is a rapid response by the respective stock markets to changes in expectations about company developments affecting the welfare of shareholders. How can the market be efficient when the market index fluctuates far more than expected earnings? It has to be remembered that market swings reflect changes in risk as well as changes in expected earnings. Therefore, we turn to the way the market relates rates of return to risk for capital investments.

Risk and required rates of return

Every investor knows that dividend expectations and capital gains are not the only factors to be considered in evaluating a security: something called risk lurks in the background of every investment decision, whether the investment is being made by a private investor or by management on his behalf.

No discussion of risk in the field of finance is complete without consideration of possible risk reduction. Given that risk can be reduced substantially by means of diversification, should one be concerned if the firm itself is not well diversified? From the shareholder's point of view the diversification of the firm is of little or no consequence because he can diversify his holdings at least as easily and as cheaply as can the firm. In fact, most shareholders own diversified portfolios, so management need not diversify for the sake of shareholders or imagine that such diversification will, of itself, improve the share price. The motive for diversifying the firm concerns risk to management and employees – not to shareholders.

If portfolios can reduce risk, cannot all risk be diversified away and so become irrelevant to the investment decision? Unfortunately, this happy state cannot be achieved even by means of the widest possible diversification. A holding in each of the investments quoted on the London Stock Exchange would still leave one with a very considerable degree of risk – as typified by the fluctuations in the Financial Times–Actuaries Index! The risk that cannot be diversified away is that in the economy at large. This remaining risk is usually termed 'non-diversifiable' or 'systematic' risk.

Why can't risk be completely eliminated by means of diversification? One could then ignore risk in decision making with a clear conscience. If each investment were undertaken in a different national economy and each national economy were wholly independent of the others, then after, say, twenty such investments very little risk would be left. However, the economies of most countries have become interrelated through trade. World-wide economic changes affect to greater or lesser degrees the returns for most investment projects. Of course, this point holds even more strongly for investments within the same national economy.

The phenomenon of the co-relationship between the returns of an investment and the economy can be observed in the stock market. It is well known that share prices tend to 'move with the market'. The stock market index may be regarded as an indicator for the economy as a whole and the price of a share may be regarded as the corresponding indicator for the economic activities of the firm. It would not be surprising to find that share price changes for the firm are correlated with changes in the stock market index for the country to which the firm's activities are principally related.

This rather plausible hypothesis is born out by numerous tests in university research and in more recent years by stockbrokers in New York, London, Paris and elsewhere. Simply stated, the hypothesis suggests that the price (adjusted for dividends) of an individual security is expected to move with the market. Should, for example, the Financial Times Index rise or fall 10 per cent, we would expect the security's price to change in the same direction on average. The sensitivity of the security's price to changes in the index depends upon the security's risk relative to the market index. If the security is riskier than the index we would expect its rises and falls in price to exceed those of the market index. The ratio that expresses the volatility of the security compared with the market is a risk index and is referred to as the 'Beta' co-efficient. The so-called 'Beta Co-efficient' measures the sensitivity of the security's returns to market returns. A Beta value of zero means that the investment is riskless. A Beta value of one means that the investment is equally as risky as the market index, while a value of two indicates that the price of the security is twice as volatile as the market index.

Figure 8:1   The trade-off between risk and return in the capital market

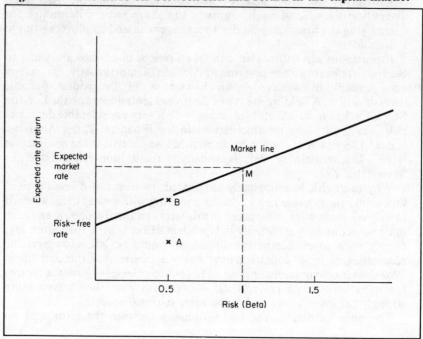

The Beta measure has its counterpart in capital investments undertaken by companies and relates to the same common economic factors that explain Beta values for different equities. We shall need to know the way the capital market relates required rates of return to systematic risk or Beta in order to establish profitability criteria for capital projects.

The fact that investors hold portfolios is as good evidence as any that investors are 'risk averse'. To be risk averse means that one requires returns which are higher than average to justify taking above-average risks. Also, as the capital markets reflect the behaviour of diversified investors, it is systematic or non-diversifiable risk for which the market in aggregate will require a premium. Thus, we have an hypothesis that the capital markets require higher returns for increasing levels of risk from investments.

The Capital Asset Pricing Model[4] proposes a linear relationship between returns and risks and empirical studies[5] provide some support for this hypothesis. This relationship is shown in Figure 8:1.

The horizontal axis measures the degree of systematic risk represented by the Beta co-efficient and the vertical axis measures the expected rate of return. The minimum required rate of return when Beta is zero is the risk free rate of interest. The slope of the line is seen to be determined by a second point M representing the expected return on the Market portfolio i.e. where Beta equals 1.

What reason is there to believe that individual investments within the Market Portfolio might also be found on this line at locations depending on their Beta values? Suppose an individual security having a Beta value of 0.5 was so over-priced that its rate of return fell below the Market line (Point A in Fig. 8:1). How many would buy it? Any investor could create for himself a better investment by putting half his money into a risk-free asset and the other half into the Market Portfolio. He would then have an investment on the Market line at Beta equals 0.5 (Point B) which is superior to our hypothetical investment below the line. Clearly, the investment below the line is over-priced and would not be expected to attract much demand until the price fell sufficiently to put the security back on the line. Anyone investing in securities which are on the line would not buy the security until it found its way back onto the line.

Why required rates of return must be related to risk

Figure 8:1 represents the way in which capital markets are understood to relate increasing expected rates of return to increasing risk. If management is representing the interests of shareholders when appraising capital projects, it must employ these rates of return (adjusted for tax) which shareholders expect.

However, few companies in the UK systematically adjust project required rates of return for risk. There is a widespread belief that a single cut-off rate for all projects reflecting average risk for the company will result in correct capital investment decisions on average. We will show that this notion is false.

Figure 8:2   Capital market opportunities and the test discount rate

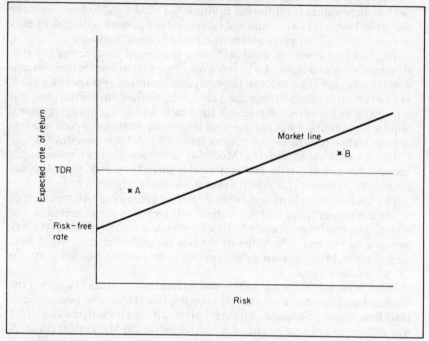

In Figure 8:2 we have plotted the market line of Figure 8:1 and superimposed on this the horizontal line representing a single test discount rate (TDR), or single cut-off rate, for capital projects regardless of differing levels of systematic risk for projects. The point at which the two lines cross represents average risk and average return for the company.

The risk-return characteristics of two capital projects A and B are also plotted in Figure 8:2. Project A is a profitable low-risk project which offers a rate of return exceeding the capital-market opportunity cost. However, this project would be rejected on the basis of the test discount rate, which cannot take account of the project's attractive low risk in relation to its return. On the other hand Project B, which offers a higher return and is unacceptable because it cannot cover capital market opportunity costs, would be accepted on the basis of the single test discount rate.

Thus we find that the single average rate of return criterion does not produce correct decisions on average. It may be seen from the above example that the use of a single test discount rate as an investment criterion will bias investment towards high-risk, unprofitable projects.

Capital project risk

We have examined the way in which rates of return in the capital market are related to the risk which cannot be eliminated by diversification and we have shown that required rates of return or discount rates for capital projects are based upon investment opportunities available in the capital market. It follows that we must know the risk class of a proposed capital project in order to set a discount rate for it. Thus the two principal questions which we now wish to answer are: how can discount rates for projects be made to reflect capital market required rates of return? How can risk classification of capital projects be implemented by companies?

What are some of the specific components of systematic risk? We regard 'cyclicality' of project revenues and cost as the most important source of systematic risk. Cyclicality refers to the sensitivity of the project's cash flows to unanticipated changes in the business cycle and related macroeconomic phenomena including inflation. The risk of the project's net cash flows is the net result of the cyclicality of the project's revenues on the one hand and its costs on the other. If the project's revenues are highly cyclical but the costs are mostly variable costs(that is, low fixed costs) or can easily be reduced or shifted to other activities, then costs are also cyclical and the project is not very risky. However, if the revenues are cyclical and the costs are not (or if they should be counter-cyclical) then the project is more risky. The relationship between revenue and cost cyclicality and risk classification is illustrated by the table in Figure 8:3.

Figure 8:3   Project risk classification grid

		Revenue sensitivity to unanticipated changes in the economy		
		LOW	MEDIUM	HIGH
	LOW	A	B	C
Cost sensitivity to unanticipated changes in the economy	MEDIUM	B	A	B
	HIGH	C	B	A,B

The columns in the table represent respectively low, medium and high revenue cyclicality or sensitivity to unanticipated changes in the economy. The rows represent low, medium and high cost cyclicality, respectively. Thus there are nine boxes in the table, each representing a different combination of revenue and cost cyclicality. Low-risk combinations are indicated by the letter 'A'. Medium risk combinations are indicated by the letter 'B' and high systematic risk by 'C'. By means of such an analysis, capital projects can be screened into one of three risk classes A, B or C each with its own risk premium appropriate to the risk class. Figure 8:4 illustrates the way in which required rates of return can be related to risk classes.

Figure 8:4   Historical required rates of return for three risk classes

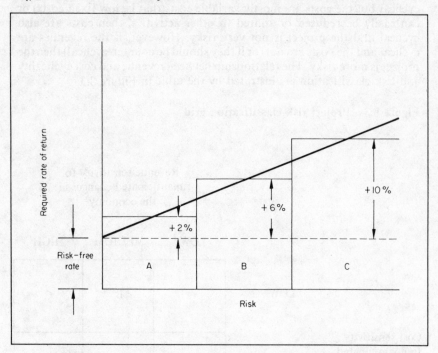

Projects which are typical of a company or an industry may be pre-classified by such a scheme into three categories A, B or C. Projects which are usually risk-free fall into the A category and high-risk projects should be put into the C category. Each risk class has its own risk premium as indicated in Figure 8:4. The risk premium is the additional return over and above the risk-free rate of interest necessary to justify investment in projects in each risk class. Setting values for these risk premiums requires an understanding of capital market required rates of return adjusted for tax.

Minimum required rates of retun for each risk class

We shall now discuss the way in which expected rates of return in the capital market can be estimated for each risk class. This task has three parts: (a) Selecting the appropriate risk-free rate; (b) Estimating the risk premium; (c) Adjusting for tax. A degree of judgement is necessary at each stage, but extreme accuracy is usually unnecessary.

Risk-free rates are to be found in prevailing interest rates on Government securities. In principle, cash flows in different future periods should be discounted at different rates depending on the term structure of interest rates. However, such refinements appear to be needlessly complicated as term structure differences are normally small in comparison to differences in risk premium. For most projects the redemption yield on the Government bond maturing at the end of the project's life will suffice as an estimate of the risk-free rate for the project. To this risk-free rate should be added the risk premium for the project's risk class. In the case of Class B projects this is identical to the risk premium of the firm, which is the risk premium for the market portfolio multiplied by the firm's Beta value. Consequently, firms with greater or less than average systematic risk will have correspondingly larger or smaller risk premiums for Class B projects.

We now require an estimate of the risk premium for the market portfolio. This has been estimated at 8.8 per cent per annum[6] in the US for the period 1926–72 and 9.1 per cent per annum[7] in the UK for the period 1919–72. The UK estimate is after the deduction of Corporation tax, which now includes payment of standard rate income tax on behalf of all shareholders. Consequently, if we assume the marginal tax rate of all shareholders is 35 per cent a risk premium of 6 per cent after personal taxes is obtained. Thus, the cash flows of a project, which has a Beta equal to 1, would be estimated after Corporation taxes and discounted at a rate that reflects the risk-free rate of interest after personal taxes of 35 per cent plus the risk premium of 6 per cent. The company must be able to earn after Corporation tax what the investor expects after personal taxes for an investment in each risk class.

For Class B projects in the average firm the required rate of return is approximately equal to the risk-free rate after personal taxes, plus the historical 6 per cent (after personal tax) risk premium. For Class A projects the risk premium would be 2 per cent: the risk premium for Class C projects would be 10 per cent (higher for extremely risky project) as may be seen in Figure 8:4. For firms with Betas different from 1, Class B projects will be based upon the risk premium of the market multiplied by the Beta co-efficient. For example, the brewery industry has a Beta of 0.8. Within that industry, Betas for individual firms range from 0.4 to 1.2 Such differences may occur because of the competitive position of one brewery compared with another in a particular region. If the Beta of a company is 0.5 then Class B projects will be based on a risk premium of 3% (0.5 × 6%). Risk premiums for Class A and C projects would be set some percentage points below and above the 3 per cent average. It is important to realise that the Beta for a firm is a dynamic factor and is dependent on the Betas of all the firm's projects weighted by their present value.

Procedure for establishing project discount rates

On the basis of the foregoing we recommend that project discount rates should be established according to a procedure which would include the following steps:

1   A common set of criteria should be developed for risk classification of capital projects. These criteria should relate to systematic risk, that portion of risk related to macroeconomic uncertainties which cannot be diversified by shareholders.
2   In each line of business a staff study should undertake to identify typical projects by risk classes according to the degree of perceived non-diversifiable risk of each category of project. As far as possible the common set of criteria for risk classification should be used in all such studies.
3   A central authority should establish the risk premium which is to be associated with each risk class for the purposes of computing a discount rate. These risk premiums may be revised from time to time due to changes perceived in the total risk for the economy as reflected in the capital markets. For example, a precipitous drop in the market index frequently results from an increase in the market's risk premium.
4   The current discount rates for projects should usually be determined by adding the risk premium for the project's risk class to the risk-free rate corresponding to the life of the project. Risk-free rates should be based on the prevailing term structure of interest rates.
5   The term structure of interest rates reflects the market's expectation of inflation. Therefore all computations should be based on projected cash flows stated in money (rather than 'real') terms reflecting forecast prices for all costs and revenues.

Summary

Risks related to unanticipated macroeconomic changes cannot be eliminated through diversification even by government. Thus, although private and institutional investors tend to hold diversified portfolios they are subject to risk. Because investors are risk averse, rates of return in the capital market have been found to reflect risk premiums. Investors can choose from a variety of investments from Government bonds paying risk-free rates of interest to equities promising higher expected rates of return but subject to non-diversifiable risk. The opportunity cost to the shareholder of investment in real assets is the rate of return obtainable from the same funds invested in the capital market in securities of equivalent risk. Managers entrusted with shareholders' funds should not invest in capital projects unless the expected returns exceed those available to shareholders in the capital markets.

Capital market opportunity costs include risk premiums. Capital projects with high risk require high rates of return to be profitable in relation to capital market opportunities. It is not valid to assume that a single discount rate representing average opportunity costs will lead to the right decisions on average. The use of a single test discount rate regardless of risk will bias capital investment towards high-risk projects which are unprofitable. Thus typical capital projects should be grouped into risk classes according to the exposure to broad economic risks that each represents. The discount rate for each risk class should reflect the appropriate capital market risk premium. The discount rate should equal the risk-free rate of interest plus the risk premium for the project's risk class.

Practical criteria for the risk classification of capital projects can be used. Non-diversifiable risk is associated with the relative cyclicality of revenues and costs and an outline of a risk classification scheme has been suggested.

If the world economy should become significantly more or less risky, occasional adjustments to the risk premium for each risk class may be required. Usually such changes should follow large and abrupt changes in capital market prices.

Thus, as we have shown, the modern theory of finance provides a coherent framework for profitability assessment of capital projects. When applied within the context of soundly based corporate planning and strategy this approach can be expected to maximise the value of the firm.

Notes

Part of this chapter has been taken from: J. E. Broyles, J. R. Franks, 'Capital Project Appraisal: a modern approach'. *Management Finance*, vol 2, No. 2, 1976.

1   Reference to tests conducted mainly on Chicago University data base containing monthly share prices for all companies listed on the NY Exchange for over 40 years.

2   P. J. Halpern, 'Empirical Estimates of the Amount and Distribution of Gains to Companies in Mergers', *Journal of Business*, October 1973, pp. 554–75.
    G. Mandelker, 'Risk and Return: the Case of Merging Firms', *Journal of Financial Economics*, Vol. 1, December 1974, pp. 303–335.

3   J. R. Franks, J. E. Broyles and M. Hecht, 'An Industry Study of Mergers in the United Kingdom', *Journal of Finance*, Forthcoming March 1978.

4   W. F. Sharpe, 'Capital Asset Prices: A Theory of Market Equilibrium Under Conditions of Risk', *Journal of Finance*, Vol. 19, September 1964, pp. 425–442.
    J. Lintner, 'Security Prices, Risk and Maximal Gains from Diversification', *Journal of Finance*, Vol. 20, December 1965, pp. 587–615.

5   F. Black, M. C. Jensen and M. Scholes, *'The Capital Asset Pricing Model: Some Empirical Tests'*, M. C. Jensen (ed.), Studies in the Theories of Capital Markets, Praeger, 1972.
6   R. G. Ibbotson and R. A. Singuefield, 'Stocks, Bonds, Bills, and Inflation: Year-by-Year Historical Returns (1926–1974)', *Journal of Business*, Vol. 94, January 1976, pp. 11–47.
7   R. A. Brealey and E. Dimson, 'The Excess Return on UK Equities: 1919–1975', Unpublished Manuscript, London Graduate School of Business Studies, 1976.

Further reading

R. A. Brealey, *An Introduction to Risk and Return from Common Stocks*, Cambridge, Mass. MIT Press, 1969.
J. Lorie (ed.) and R. Brealey (ed.), *Modern Developments in Investment Management*; A Book of Readings, Praeger Publishers, 1972.
J. Lorie and Mary T. Hamilton, *The Stock Market: Theories and Evidence*, R. D. Irwin, 1973.

9
Leasing

Leases are contracts where one party, the *lessee*, hires equipment or services from another party, the *lessor*. All such leases can be categorized as either financial or operating leases.

Financial leases. Under a financial lease the lessee agrees to make a series of payments to the lessor for the use of equipment. The contract cannot be cancelled by either side during the operating life of the equipment.

Operating leases. Operating leases are contracted for periods shorter than the operating life of the asset, allowing either side to cancel the contract upon suitable notice. In effect this cancellation clause reduces the risk of obsolescence to the lessee and possible non-utilization of the asset.

Advantages and disadvantages of leasing

Numerous claims have been made about lease financing and before we discuss an analytical approach, we should examine conceptually some of the more obvious issues.

Initially, let us confine our comments to financial leases, where the lessee agrees to make a series of payments to the lessor for the use of the asset throughout its operating life.

One of the most important advantages attributed to leasing is that the firm is permitted to acquire the use of the asset without recourse to its own funds. This claim is imprecise and even misleading as lease payments to the lessor take in the price of the equipment plus interest on capital. The lessee is in an analogous position to an individual who purchases a house with a mortgage provided by a building society or an insurance company, and repays the lender by regular instalments. Each instalment consists of part repayment of the loan and interest on the balance outstanding. In addition, since a lease, like a mortgage, requires a deposit or some form of advance payment, the lessee often contributes to the initial cost of the equipment.

It is unlikely that the lessor would advance a loan for the whole cost of the asset unless the borrower possessed other assets or equity to support the loan. Even if the lessor finances 100 per cent of the cost of the asset, all-debt financing is not necessarily implied because equity in the firm may be required to support the loan. The covenants in the lease agreement will often require a minimum level of equity and liquid assets to be maintained in the business. The lease contract is therefore similar to any other secured loan or debenture agreement.

It should be clear that leasing is a form of debt financing which provides for the effective acquisition of the asset. However, some managers believe that because future lease payments are not included as a liability in the balance sheet, investors and lenders do not include the liability as part of the debt burden of the company. Of course, intelligent bankers require information on any contractual commitments entered into by the company. Likewise, the investor is interested in both the risk and expected returns of the company. Even if the lease does not appear in the balance sheet, the financial analyst will estimate all the fixed costs of the business which contribute to the volatility or risk of the company's earnings. Lease payments clearly increase the company's fixed costs and the sensitivity of the company's earnings to changes in such costs. Recent legislation and policy papers by the Institute of Chartered Accountants now require disclosure of important financial leases in the notes to the company accounts.

Another advantage perceived by lessees is that clauses in lease agreements are thought to be less restrictive than corresponding covenants for debenture agreements. This assertion may have been a reasonable one during the early years of leasing, but it is not so today. What then are the advantages of financial leases? As our subsequent analysis will show such advantages, where they exist, derive mainly from the special tax position of the lessor or lessee.

The credit function.

For operating leases, where the lessee has no significant long-term contractual commitment, the credit-granting function is probably not very important. In a financial lease, the ability of the lessee to obtain the use of the asset for its operating life without the initial outlay of capital is usually the primary reason for seeking the lease. Because of the cost of the money that the lessor has invested in the purchase of the equipment, the aggregate total of a series of lease payments should be greater than the purchase price of the equipment to recover the cost of financing the purchase and to provide the lessor with a premium for the risk that the value of future rentals will be lower when the asset is re-leased.

Analysis of the leasing decision

The advantage of operating leases from the lessee's point of view is that cancellation can be made at short notice. The lessee is therefore not involved in any significant commitment to continue to lease the equipment and is thus making an investment decision rather than a financial decision. Because of this cancellation option, an operating lease invariably costs more than any other form of financing and the main decision for the lessee will depend upon whether the additional cost of the operating lease compensates for the reduced risk of obsolescence, or the need to satisfy a short-term demand for the equipment. Generally, the lessor performs more functions under an operating lease than a financial lease. Normally, operating leases are 'maintenance leases' where the lessor maintains the asset and pays insurance, whereas financial leases are 'net leases' where the lessee pays maintenance and repairs, insurance and other expenses.

Figure 9:1   Total cost of ownership of a petrol truck
Four-year life. Figures in parentheses represent cash inflows

	Year				
	0 (£)	1 (£)	2 (£)	3 (£)	4 (£)
Operating costs		590	850	710	770
Less 50% corporation tax		295	425	355	385
Net cost after taxes		295	425	355	385
Tax recovery from investment incentives*					
100% first-year allowance (equals the cost of the asset)	3,650				
Cash inflow based on a 50% tax rate (value of the initial allowance)	(1,825)				
Cost of truck	3,650				
Net cash outflows after tax	1,825	295	425	355	385

*For simplicity it is assumed that there is no delay in tax payments.

Operating leases – the lease-or-buy decision

A company considering the acquisition of a new piece of equipment by
means of an operating lease has three possible courses of action.

1 Decide against the acquisition.
2 Purchase the equipment.
3 Enter into an operating lease.

Consider the example of a truck that is four years old with maintenance
costs that have been rising steadily. The possibilities facing its owner are to
purchase or lease either a petrol- or battery-driven truck. The terms of the
operating lease are £207 per month and £267 per month for the petrol- and
battery-driven trucks respectively; the payments would be for a minimum
of 4 months with a 30-day cancellation clause thereafter.
   Assuming that savings would occur regardless of whether a petrol- or a
battery-powered truck is used, the first pertinent question to ask is: Which
type of truck is cheaper to use? Figure 9:1 shows the total cost of purchasing
a petrol truck and Figure 9:2 shows the costs of a battery-powered truck.

Figure 9:2   Total cost of ownership of battery-powered truck
Five-year life. Figures in parentheses represent cash inflows

		Year				
	0 (£)	1 (£)	2 (£)	3 (£)	4 (£)	5 (£)
Operating costs		300	300	300	300	300
Less 50% corporation tax		150	150	150	150	150
Net cost after taxes		150	150	150	150	150
Tax recovery from investment incentives*						
100% first-year allowance	6,250					
Cash inflow based on 50% tax rate	(3,125)					
Cost of truck	6,250					
Net cash outflows after tax	3,125	150	150	150	150	150

*For simplicity it is assumed that there is no delay in tax payments.

If a 10 per cent return after tax and investment incentives is required, then the cash flows for the two trucks must be discounted at this rate to take into account the time value of money. However, each calculation computes the cost of owning the truck for a different life. At the end of year 4 the petrol truck must be replaced, but the battery-powered truck would be retained for a further year; therefore it is necessary to take into account the replacement cycles for both types of truck. To do this the cash flows are converted into equivalent annual costs. This procedure takes advantage of the assumption that the same set of cash flows will occur for each replacement cycle and computes the present value cost for only one cycle. The results of applying this technique to the after-tax net cash flows of the petrol and battery-powered trucks are shown in Figure 9:3.

Figure 9:3 shows that the present value costs of purchasing a petrol truck and a battery-powered truck are £2,974 and £3,693 respectively, the petrol truck having an estimated life of 4 years and the battery-powered truck one of 5 years. The following formulation may be used to find the equivalent annual cost of the lease:

present value cost = equivalent annual cost
$\times$ annuity factor for *n* years discounting at *r*%

Petrol truck
The annuity factor from Appendix 2 for discounting £1 per year for 4 years at 10 per cent is 3.17.

$$£2,974 = X \times 3.17$$

where X = equivalent annual cost. Therefore

$$X = \frac{£2,974}{3.17}$$

$$X = £938$$

Battery-powered truck
The annuity factor for discounting £1 per annum over 5 years at 10 per cent as shown in Appendix 2 is 3.79.

$$£3,693 = X \times 3.79$$

where X = equivalent annual cost. Therefore

$$X = \frac{£3,693}{3.79}$$

$$X = £974$$

Figure 9:3   Present value costs of the petrol- and battery-powered trucks
Discounted at 10 per cent

Year	Petrol truck After-tax costs		Battery-powered truck After-tax costs	
	Cash flow (£)	Present value (£)	Cash flow (£)	Present value (£)
0	1,825	1,825	3,125	3,125
1	295	268	150	136
2	425	351	150	124
3	355	267	150	113
4	385	263	150	102
5			150	93
		2,974		3,693

Therefore, ownership of a petrol truck for four years (£938 per year) is cheaper than ownership of a battery-powered truck (£974 per year). After-tax savings of £36 per year are expected, but the differential is so small in this case that the decision is marginal.

 With the analysis completed for the investment decision, the next stage is to examine the leasing plans offered so that the financing decision can be made. In each of the operating leasing plans, the lessor maintains the equipment, pays insurance, etc., leaving the lessee to pay fuel costs, which amount to £300 and £60 per year for the petrol truck and battery truck respectively (Figure 9:4). For the purposes of exposition, calculations are shown for both trucks.

Figure 9:4   Cost of leases on trucks

	Petrol truck (£)	Battery-powered truck (£)
Fuel costs	300	60
Lease payments for 12 months	2,484	3,204
Total annual costs	2,784	3,264
Less 50% corporation tax	1,392	1,632
Annual costs after tax	1,392	1,632

For either type of equipment the operating lease costs are significantly more than the costs of ownership. Why do the operating leases appear so expensive? As the lease is shorter than the asset's operating life, the value at the end of the period of the lease is important in assessing the value of all future rental payments. The shorter the lease, the more uncertain are future rental payments. Thus the cost differential between an operating lease and purchase is accounted for by the time value of money and a risk premium. The risk premium reflects uncertainty about the future value of the leased asset when the particular agreement comes to an end. The lessee must pay a premium for the option to discontinue rental payments before the end of the asset's operating life.

In this case the lessee must decide whether the difference of £454 between the annual costs of leasing the petrol truck (£1,392) and the equivalent annual costs of ownership of £938 is worth the reduced risk of obsolescence and the ability to cancel the lease at short notice.

Financial leases – the lease-or-borrow decision

In a financial lease the analysis from the lessor's viewpoint must be more rigorous since the investment usually has a longer term and is of substantially greater value. Financial leases are, in effect, only another way of raising capital; they represent a long-term contractual commitment to make periodic payments that are equivalent to the cost of the equipment plus financing charges. The lessee's obligations are therefore similar to those incurred if he raised further debt capital.

Importance of the discount rate

Many managers who lease equipment have wondered how leasing could be quite so advantageous as it appears. They adopted a sensible discounted cash flow approach to the lease versus buy decision. However, leasing was analysed like any other capital budgeting decision and the rate used to discount the cash flows was the one required for the investment decision. In fact the decision to lease is both a financing and investment decision. The interest rate the lessor is charging should be compared with the lessee's marginal borrowing rate. The lessee frequently ignores the importance of an accurate discount rate and thereby inadvertently increases the apparent attraction of the leasing alternative. Let us illustrate this point with a simple example.

A company has the opportunity to purchase an asset for £1,000. If the company buys the asset, it obtains a 100 per cent initial tax allowance. The alternative is to lease the equipment for its operating life. Let us assume that the lease consists of five payments of £230 a year the first of which is required in advance and all payments are tax deductible. The company's tax rate is 50 per cent, the lessee's marginal borrowing rate is 10 per cent before tax and an after tax discount rate of 15 per cent is used for all risky investment projects. Figure 9:5 shows how the use of a high discount rate reduces the cost of the lease and makes purchase appear relatively less attractive. The net present value at 15 per cent is £442 and would imply that the leasing alternative is more attractive when compared with the £500 cost of the asset net of the tax benefits accruing from the capital allowances. Since the correct discount rate is nearer 5 per cent with a corresponding net present value of £522, an incorrect decision would be made.

Figure 9:5   The discount rate and value of the lease

Year	Lease payments (£)	Tax relief* (£)	Net cost (£)
0	230	115	115
1	230	115	115
2	230	115	115
3	230	115	115
4	230	115	115

Net present value discounted at 15%	£442
Net present value discounted at 5%	£522

*Effect of lag in payment of Corporation tax has been ignored

The choice of discount rate is clearly very important. Since the alternative to leasing is purchase and debt financing, the appropriate rate of discount is usually close to the company's marginal borrowing rate after taxes. Let us now look at the analysis of the lease more closely.

Borrowing opportunity rate

Initially we shall examine the borrowing opportunity rate method originally proposed by Vancil.[1] We have incorporated a number of changes in that method reflecting current thinking on risk and we have provided further exposition on the measurement of the debt equivalent, being subsumed in the lease. The basic assumption in this approach is that leasing is equivalent to purchase with 100 per cent debt financing, that is, leasing displaces debt on a pound-for-pound basis. We shall relax this assumption later. Vancil[2] suggests that the lease payments should be discounted by the pre-tax borrowing rate and the tax benefits by an after-tax rate to obtain the net present value of the lease. The net present value of the lease can then be compared with the after-tax cost of purchase. However, two problems arise. The lease payments consist of the repayment of the loan and interest on the outstanding balance. In addition the lessee obtains tax benefits on the total lease payments (interest plus principal). As we have not included interest charges in the evaluation of the purchase cost of the asset we must exclude the interest charges from the lease payments.

Similarly, we must establish the value of the lease in order to measure the debt capacity and the consequent tax advantage. Thus a two-stage analysis is required in the Vancil method.

Initially we discount the lease payments by the pre-tax interest rate, in effect subtracting the interest charge. Now all that remains is to compute the tax benefits so that they may be deducted from the present value cost of the lease. However, we must estimate the tax benefit not on the total lease payments, but only on the repayment portion, that is the tax benefit on the lease repayment minus the imputed interest charges. This raises the problem of how to estimate the debt repayment schedule which is subsumed in the lease in order to derive the imputed interest payments.

Let us use our previous example to demonstrate the method. The gross cost of purchase is £1,000 and the initial allowance of 100 per cent is worth £500 assuming a tax rate of 50 per cent. If the tax advantage is received over more than one period, we discount it at a relatively low rate, reflecting the low risk of the tax allowances. For simplicity, assume it is the company's borrowing rate (10 per cent pre-tax or 5 per cent after taxes). What is the cost of the lease? Let us compute the net present value of the gross lease payments. To do this we discount the lease payments at the marginal borrowing rate, which is the rate we would have to pay if we were buying the asset and borrowing the funds for the equivalent period of the lease, that is 10 per cent (Figure 9:6).

Figure 9:6   The present value of the lease discounted at the pre-tax borrowing rate

Year	Lease payment (£)	Present value discounted at 10% (£)
0	230	230
1	230	209
2	230	190
3	230	173
4	230	157
Total present value		959

We must now subtract the present value of the tax benefits from the lease payments, but only after excluding the estimated interest charges. In order to estimate the interest charges we must assume a debt repayment schedule. This schedule is analogous to the one adopted by the building society lending money for the purchase of a house. The repayments consist of principal plus interest charges. As each repayment is made the outstanding balance of the loan is reduced. Vancil does not state how the precise loan schedule is to be estimated but we shall assume the repayments are constant from year to year and therefore the repayment of principal increases with time and the interest portion declines with time.

We shall assume that the lessee borrows an amount equivalent to the value of the lease which is approximately £959 and repays the loan in five equal annual instalments (the first is made in advance) with an interest rate of 10 per cent. What equal annual instalments would repay the interest and the loan over four years? We can solve for the annual instalment using the following expression where X is equal to the annual payments.

$$X = \frac{\text{Loan}}{\text{Annuity factor for four years at } 10\%}$$

In our example the loan is only £729 because £230 is paid immediately.

Therefore,

$$X = \frac{729}{3.17}$$

$$= £230 \text{ (after rounding to nearest whole number)}$$

The interest payments are computed for each period on the outstanding balance of the loan (Fig. 9:7).

Figure 9:7   The estimation of interest charges subsumed in the lease payments.

Year	Outstanding loan* (£)	Interest portion (£)	Annual payments (£)	Repayment portion (£)
0	729			
1	571.9	72.9	230	157.1
2	399.09	57.19	230	172.81
3	208.999	39.909	230	190.091
4		20.8999	230	209.1

*Rounding error

We can now compute the tax benefits on the loan repayment portion of the lease payments. We discount the tax benefits at a rate that reflects the risk of such inflows, approximated by the after-tax borrowing rate.

Figure 9:8   The present value of the tax benefits excluding the imputed interest charges

Year	Lease payments (£)	Imputed interest charge (£)	Lease payment imputed interest charge (£)	Tax benefits at 50% (£)	Present value discounted at 5% (£)
0	230	0	230	115	115
1	230	72.9	157.1	78.5	74.8
2	230	57.1	172.9	86.45	78.4
3	230	39.9	190.1	95.1	82.1
4	230	20.9	209.1	104.5	86.0
			959.2		436.3

Since the present value of the lease payments is £959.2 the net cost of the lease is £522.9 after the deduction of the tax benefits (959.2-436.3 = 522.9). The result is larger than the cost of purchase, totalling £500, so that, the company should buy rather than lease.

We must make two qualifications to the previous analysis. We have assumed an interest rate schedule based on an estimate of the present value of the lease and equal annual repayments. However, we are trying to estimate the value of the lease, which is in part dependent on the loan repayment schedule and imputed interest charges. Also we have assumed that the lease displaces debt on a pound-for-pound basis. How critical are these assumptions to the lease decision? Finally, although, Vancil did not identify or stress the importance of the discount rate used to obtain the present value of the tax benefits, such a rate should reflect the risk characteristics of the particular earnings stream. This may be different from the after-tax borrowing rate or the rate that is used to discount the net cash flow stream of the project.

Incremental leasing analysis

So far, leasing and purchasing have been compared on the basis of the net present value of cost after excluding interest charges. The comparison could be conducted on an incremental yield basis, computing the internal rate of return on the extra amount the lessor is charging. Consider the previous example of purchasing a machine for £1,000 or the alternative of leasing it with five annual payments of £230. Figure 9:9 shows the annual cash flows under both plans incorporating the tax relief that accrues from the investment allowances associated with purchasing and leasing.

Figure 9:9 Incremental analysis comparing purchasing and leasing

	Year				
	0 (£)	1 (£)	2 (£)	3 (£)	4 (£)
Purchase					
Capital cost	1000				
100% depreciation with 50% corporation tax	−500				
Total cash flow	500				
Leasing					
Lease payments	230	230	230	230	230
Tax relief at 50% corporation tax	−115	−115	−115	−115	−115
Total cash flow	115	115	115	115	115
Leasing − purchasing					
Net cash flows	−385	+115	+115	+115	+115

The next step is to compute the DCF rate of return (IRR) that will equate the lease payments to the purchase cost, net of taxes, using the annuity tables in Appendix 2.

$$115a_{4,r} = 385$$

$$a_{4,r} = \frac{385}{115}$$

$$= 3.3478$$

An annuity factor of 3.3478 corresponds to an IRR of between 7.5 and 8 per cent.

$$a_{4,7.5} = 3.3493$$

$$a_{4,8} = 3.3121$$

$$a_{4,7.5} - a_{4,8} = 0.0372$$

By interpolation, the internal rate of return can be computed.

$$\text{IRR} = 7.5\% + \frac{0.0015}{0.0372} \times 0.5\%$$

$$\text{IRR} = 7.52\%$$

In other words, the lessor is charging an interest rate of 7.5 per cent after tax, whereas the company is able to borrow at a pre-tax rate of 6 per cent (3 per cent after tax, assuming a 50 per cent corporation tax rate). This lease evaluation method is simpler than the adjusted Vancil approach. However, there are the usual problems associated with the internal rate of return computations.

S. Myers[3] has recently shown that if the appropriate discount rates are used, the incremental cash flow approach is not only simple but can be rigorously derived. Providing the Vancil method is properly adjusted, the results from the two methods will be equivalent. In the next section we use the incremental approach to evaluate a lease when one party does not pay tax.

Situations where leasing can be advantageous

In our discussion of the supposed advantages of leasing we tended to dismiss such advantages as generally illusory. Then why has leasing grown so popular? One could simply answer that it is a useful financing arrangement just like the overdraft system or a debenture agreement. However, we believe that tax frequently provides a source of benefit to those parties who engage in leasing. That is, when a company is in a non-tax paying position, permanently or temporarily, it is advantageous to lease. The lessor is able to acquire ownership of the asset, obtain the tax benefits from the capital allowances when they arise and pass part of them back to the lessee, in the form of lower rental payments. The fact that the initial capital allowances on plant and machinery, ships and aircraft are so high, provides an important attraction to leasing.

The tax advantage of leasing can be estimated using the incremental cash flow approach. Taking the previous example, let us assume the lessee is in a permanent non-tax paying position. The purchase cost of the asset is £1000 and no tax benefits accrue because of the lessee's tax position. The present value of the tax payments can be computed by merely discounting the lease payments at the pre-tax interest rate.

$$£230 + £\frac{230}{(1+.10)} + £\frac{230}{(1+.10)^2} + £\frac{230}{(1+.10)^3} + £\frac{230}{(1+.10)^4}$$

$$= £985.13$$

The pre-tax interest rate is used because the firm will be unable to deduct interest charges for tax purposes and we are assuming that leasing displaces debt finance on a pound-for-pound basis. The value of the lease is £958.13 which is less than the purchase cost of the asset.

Many UK companies are in a temporary non-tax paying position. The timing of the capital allowances and the adjustment to a pre-tax interest rate should be incorporated into the lease-versus-buy decision.[4] Clearly, the lessee's non-tax paying position could make leasing profitable. Any net present value arising from the leasing decision should be added to the value of the project which has been estimated assuming a non-tax paying period.

Capitalization of lease payments

It has already been stated that financial leases are equivalent to the purchase of the equipment through 100 per cent debt financing. In assessing the firm's ability to borrow, both the borrower and lender must include in the debt ratio the long-term debt recorded in the balance sheet and the debt equivalent inherent in long-term leases.

Using the previous example again, column 4 of Figure 9:8 gives the lease payments less the imputed interest charges; they total £959. Thus the lessor has effectively borrowed £959 repayable over four years. It is this amount that should be added to the long-term debt in the balance sheet when the firm's total debt liabilities are computed.

Summary

We have outlined the advantages and disadvantages of leasing and explained the functions performed by leasing companies. We have shown how both operating and financial leases should be analysed.

Although leasing is invariably more expensive than debt, there are reasons why leasing may be preferable. A company that is unable to absorb capital allowances or other tax benefits for a limited period should consider leasing in order to accelerate the take-up of the tax advantages. In addition, leasing provides a useful financial instrument for the long-term financing of fixed assets.

Notes

1   R. F. Vancil, *Leasing of Industrial Equipment* (New York: McGraw-Hill, 1963).
2   R. F. Vancil and R. N. Anthony, 'The financial community looks at leasing', *Harvard Business Review*, vol. 37, no. 6. November–December 1959, pp. 113-30.
3   S. C. Myers, David A. Dill and Alberto J. Batisto, 'Valuation of financial leases', *Journal of Finance*, June 1976, vol. XXXI, no. 3.
4   J. R. Franks and S. D. Hodges, 'Valuation of Financial Leases: A Note', Unpublished Note, London Graduate School of Business Studies, March 1977. (Forthcoming, *Journal of Finance*).

Further reading

R. S. Bower, 'Issues in Lease Financing', *Financial Management*, 2 (Winter 1973), 25-33.

D. R. Gant, 'A critical look at lease financing', *Controller*, vol. 29 (June 1961), pp. 274-7.

D. R. Gant, 'Illusion in lease financing', *Harvard Business Review*, vol. 37 no. 2 (March-April 1959), pp. 121-42.

F. K. Griesinger, 'Pros and cons of leasing equipment', *Harvard Business Review*, vol. 33, no. 2 (March-April 1955), pp. 75-89.

Leasing of Industrial Equipment (Washington, DC: Machinery and Allied Products Institute, 1965).

W. G. Lewellen, M. S. Long and J. J. McConnell, 'Asset Leasing in Competitive Markets', *Journal of Finance*, June 1976, Vol. XXXI, no. 3.

M. H. Miller and C. W. Upton, 'Leasing, Buying and the Cost of Capital Services', *Journal of Finance* June 1976, Vol. XXXI no. 3.

A. T. Nelson, 'Capitalizing leases – the effect on financial ratios', *Journal of Accountancy*, vol. 116 (July 1963), pp. 49-58.

R. F. Vancil, 'Lease or borrow – new method of analysis', *Harvard Business Review*, vol 39, no. 5 (September-October 1961), pp. 122-36.

R. F. Vancil, 'Lease or borrow – steps in negotiation', *Harvard Business Review*, vol. 39, no. 6 (November-December 1961), pp. 138-59.

10

Replacement decisions

A decision to replace equipment usually involves questions of both replacement and expansion. This makes it difficult to assess accurately the importance of expansion in replacement as compared with other types of investment. The conclusions from surveys[1] to date have varied considerably, but it seems reasonable to assume that in the UK 50 to 60 per cent of total investment in plant and machinery incorporates replacement.

Because of the number and magnitude of the decisions, replacement assessments require considerable care. What happens in practice? Surveys[2] show that modern techniques for appraising replacement investment are not used. The most recent survey offered the following conclusions:

1   In the majority of cases replacement is viewed like any other capital-budgeting decision. Whatever criterion of assessment is used the result is then compared with a hurdle rate and accepted or rejected on that basis.
2   Payback and accounting rate of return are used, except on large projects where DCF is employed. In the case of the first two, the method of calculation is very often erroneous.
3   Taxation and investment incentives are seldom considered except on large projects.

4   Little use is made of the more up-to-date replacement-assessment techniques.
5   Consideration of the alternatives of leasing or purchasing second-hand equipment are seldom taken into account.
6   Cost savings in over 50 per cent of the interviewed firms were treated as constant over the life of the equipment.
7   No account was taken of inflation.

These comments suggest that replacement analysis as presently practised in the UK is analytically deficient.

Objectives of replacement strategy

There are three basic questions to be examined when considering replacement:

1   When should existing equipment be replaced?
2   What policy should be pursued after the initial decision to replace or retain?
3   What is the profitability of replacing?

The first two questions involve a comparison of costs and revenues which usually change as time goes on. The effect of deterioration of existing equipment on operating costs and revenues must be compared with the capital cost of purchasing new equipment and the lower operating costs and higher revenues associated with possible technical improvement.

Deterioration means that as a machine becomes older, it cannot operate with its original accuracy and speed; it causes more wastage, requires more maintenance and generally becomes more costly to operate.

Technical improvement in new machines implies an opportunity cost in the continued operation of existing machinery. By postponing the replacement decision, a company may be foregoing the higher earning power of a new machine as well as incurring greater operating costs in order to avoid immediate capital outlay. However, this delay in purchase is justified if, later on, it enables the purchase of a more up-to-date model with even greater earning power than the machine presently available.

Variables in replacement analysis

In considering when to replace, account must be taken of the following variables and how they change over time:

1   Capital cost of new equipment.
2   Operating costs both for new and existing equipment.
3   Taxation and investment incentives.

Capital Cost of New Equipment. It may be advantageous to delay purchasing new equipment if management believes there will be significant technical improvements in the future. However, future technical improvement might have to be paid for in the form of higher equipment costs (without even considering inflation). Any anticipated increase in equipment costs must be incorporated into the replacement analysis and compared with the savings expected from technical improvements.

Operating Costs. Operating costs of an existing machine can be affected by deterioration. If output is maintained, operating costs can increase with age. This can come about because of:

1   An increase in repair and maintenance costs.
2   Greater loss of production resulting from increased downtime due to breakdowns and maintenance.
3   Lower quality production and higher material wastage.

The alternative situation of constant operating costs with declining output obviously implies increasing user costs for existing equipment. A new machine may be expected to deteriorate more slowly than existing equipment and this should be recognized in the replacement analysis.

Resale Values. If existing equipment can be sold, then replacement may be more frequent, increasing in frequency with the resale value of the equipment.

Taxation and Investment Incentives. As in any type of investment appraisal, the assessment must take account of taxation and investment incentives. This may significantly affect the decision to replace.

Methods of appraisal

It is important that the timing of these variables is taken into account and only the DCF approach can do this properly. If a straightforward investment proposal for an expansion of production is being contemplated, one would estimate the cash inflows and outflows and compare them with the alternative of doing nothing. In replacement analyses it is necessary, in addition, to consider the timing of purchasing the new equipment and replacing the old machine.

The previous section outlined the variables to be considered. Clearly, revenue and operating costs can vary in a number of ways. However, when a model is constructed restrictive assumptions invariably have to be made. In the model of equipment replacement, the element of 'pure' replacement has to be separated from expansion. 'Pure' replacement means that all or part of an investment produces the same level of output as before, but a lower operating cost, or with a lower capital cost. If an investment produces a significant increase in output, this expansion element must be dealt with separately. For replacement investment, a profit-maximization or cost-minimization approach can be employed. Both produce the same result for 'pure' replacement. The cost-minimization approach will be considered first.

Minimum equivalent annual cost

In the cost-minimization approach, the equivalent annual cost of the new machine is compared with the current annual operating costs of the old machine for the same output. The old machine is not replaced unless the equivalent annual cost of the new machine is lower.

For example, if a new machine costs £100, with a life of 3 years and estimated operating costs of £1,000 in year 1, £1,020 in year 2 and £1,040 in year 3 and the existing machine's operating costs are £1,065 for the next three years with no resale value, should the existing machine be replaced now? The operating-cost cash flows associated with the new machine are shown in Figure 10:1.

Figure 10:1 Operating-cost cash flows of new machine

Year	Operating costs (£)	Present value factor (discounting at 10%)	Present value (column 1 × column 3) (£)
1	1,000	0.9091	909
2	1,020	0.8264	843
3	1,040	0.7513	781
			£2,533

The total present value of the three years' operating costs is £2,533. The next step is to compute the equivalent annual cost for the three years which produces the same present value. The equivalent of annual cost, X, is computed as follows:

$$X \times a_{n,r} = \text{present value}$$

where $a_{n,r}$ is the factor for an annuity for n years discounted at r per cent a year (see Appendix 2).

$$X \times a_{3,10} = £2,533$$

Therefore

$$X = \frac{1}{a_{3,10}} \times £2,533$$

$$= \frac{1}{2.48685} \times £2,533$$

equivalent annual operating cost $(X) = £1,019$

The factor $1/a_{nr}$ ($1/$annuity factor) is known as the *capital recovery factor*. This term will be used in the analysis later in the chapter.

A similar computation is carried out for the *capital* cost of the new machine and results in an equivalent annual cost of £40 (£100 $\times 1/2.48685$ = £40). Therefore the total equivalent annual cost for the new machine is £1,059 or £1,019 plus £40. This compares with an operating cost per year of £1,065 for the existing machine.

On this basis the machine should be replaced immediately, because the equivalent annual cost of £1,059 is less than the cost of £1,065 of operating the existing machine for a further year. However, if the existing machine costs less than £1,059 to operate next year, it should be retained for a further year.

This method provides a useful approximation for the smaller replacement decisions; larger investments require the more sophisticated analysis discussed later in the chapter.

In the previous example an absolute comparison has been used; if relative costs had been used, as shown in Supplement 10:1 at the end of this chapter, the analysis would still have indicated that the machine should be replaced. In the remainder of this section relative costs will be used.

Although it might appear from the discussion so far that replacement analysis considers the future only to the extent of the new machine's service life, this view would be mistaken. The firm will probably also want to replace the new machine eventually and therefore replacement analysis should take into account a purchase not only of the new machine itself, but its successors. If the machine has an economic life of 10 years, this defines the date for the next replacement and thus affects the future choice of machine. A decision to buy is therefore a decision that affects the entire succession of future replacements.

It is necessary to compute whether a lower equivalent annual cost is produced by a replacement chain commencing with the purchase of a new machine or by the retention of the existing machine. The problem is that many of the machines in both chains are not yet in existence, so their capital costs and operating costs are difficult to predict.

A reasonable course, in the light of these uncertainties, is to assume that all future machines have the same minimum equivalent annual cost; consequently, attention can be confined to the machine that is presently being operated and the need for an alternative machine.

By making this simplifying assumption, attention can be concentrated on the remaining factor of uncertainty: machine life. In the previous example a life of three years was assumed without justification. In practice the life of a machine is not known with certainty and must be estimated. Two approaches are possible:

1   Alter the possible life of the existing machine so as to identify the life at which replacement and retention have the same effect.
2   Pursue a more explicit analysis defining current obsolescence and deterioration patterns.

The first approach gives information in the following form: if replacement occurs now, the new machine must have a life of at least *n* years to make replacement profitable. The decision then rests on whether the decision-maker feels that the necessary life is attainable. Although the method is not as complex as the analysis presented below, some readers may prefer its simplicity. We would only advise use of the first approach in relatively small replacement decisions.

Incorporation of obsolescence and deterioration patterns

Almost any machine is subject, as time goes on, to deterioration and obsolescence. Because of this a gap opens up between the operating performance of a machine already in service and that of new machines on the market. This gap will be called *operating inferiority*. The operating inferiority of an existing machine tends to increase with age compared with the best new machine available. The equivalent annual cost of operating inferiority will also increase as the service life of a machine is lengthened. On the other hand, the longer the period of service, the lower is the equivalent annual *capital* cost, as the original capital cost is spread over a greater number of years.

Since equivalent annual operating inferiority increases with the existing machine's service life while the equivalent annual capital cost is decreasing, it is necessary to identify the service life which produces the minimum equivalent annual total cost of operating inferiority and capital cost combined.

To simplify the analysis, it is assumed that the new machine accumulates operating inferiority at a constant rate over its service life.

The example in Figure 10:2 is a simple one in which the capital cost of the equipment totals £5,000 and the machine has no salvage value after installation and incurs no further capital cost after the original investment is made. Its operating inferiority gradient is £500 a year – that is, every year the difference in operating costs between the existing machine and the best new machine becoming available increases by £500. The discount factor for the calculation is 10 per cent.

The analysis takes the form of a relative rather than an absolute comparison. In the first year of service the present new machine is compared with the latest model on the market (a replica of itself) and consequently it has no operating inferiority. In the second year the machine, which is now one year old, is compared with the latest machine becoming available.

Column 1 gives the annual increase in the new machine's operating inferiority assuming a gradient of £500 per year. Column 2 gives the factors for computing the present value of the operating inferiorities in column 1. The present values of the operating inferiorities for each year, individually and cumulatively, are shown in columns 3 and 4 respectively. Multiplying the present values of operating inferiority in column 4 by their respective capital recovery factors in column 5, gives the equivalent annual costs in column 6. The capital recovery factors are also applied to the present value of the capital cost, £5,000, to yield the uniform annual equivalent capital costs in column 7. Finally, column 8 displays the combined sum of the equivalent annual costs of operating inferiority and capital costs.

The figures from columns 6, 7 and 8 are presented in graphical form in Figure 10:3. The graph shows that the equivalent annual capital cost declines as the service life of the machine increases, while the equivalent annual cost of operating inferiority increases simultaneously. When the two cost functions are combined the minimum equivalent total cost occurs if the machine is kept for five years. The minimum cost is £2,225. Having calculated the minimum average annual cost and optimum service life for the new machine, it remains to compute the minimum equivalent annual cost of the existing machine in service. This can be done by setting up a table similar to the one shown in Figure 10:2. At the end of the first year the operating inferiority of the existing machine relative to the latest machine is £2,000 and thereafter its operating inferiority increases by £500 per year. The present salvage value is £2,100 with values for future years as indicated in Figure 10:4.

On this basis the existing machine's minimum average annual cost is £2,970 (column 11) for two years of further service. As the minimum annual cost for the new machine is below £2,970 at £2,225, for a five-year life (Figure 10:2) a new machine should be purchased immediately.

Although taxation, investment incentives and inflation have not been included, they can be dealt with relatively easily in the computation.

Dynamic programming approach

Dynamic programming allows the maximum flexibility in the solution of replacement problems. All the variables outlined earlier in this chapter can be employed but without restrictive assumptions about how they might change. The first step is to determine a future time period on which to base the analysis. Decisions to retain or replace an existing machine will be made at various points within this period. Using dynamic programming at each decision point, purchasing a new machine can be compared with keeping a machine that is one, two, three, etc., years old. In the example below, only revenue, capital cost and operating costs will be considered and for simplicity it will be assumed that all costs and revenues occur at the beginning of the year indicated.

In the following example the analysis is based on a three-year period. Revenue, capital and operating costs for machines manufactured in each of the three years are shown in Figure 10:5. The existing machine is three years old at the beginning of year 1; its expected cost/revenue projections are

Figure 10:2 Computation of minimum equivalent annual total cost for a new machine

Capital cost of the machine is £5,000 and it has an operating inferiority gradient of £500 per year. Discount factor is 10 per cent

Year of service	1 Operating inferiority for year indicated* (£)	2 Present value factor for year indicated†	3 Present value of operating inferiority for year indicated (column 1 × column 2) (£)	4 Cumulative present value of operating inferiority (column 3 accumulated) (£)	5 Capital recovery factor for period ending with year indicated‡	Equivalent annual cost for life ending with year indicated		
						6 Operating inferiority (column 4 × column 5) (£)	7 Capital cost (£5,000 × column 5) (£)	8 Operating inferiority and capital cost combined (£)
1	0	0.909	0	0	1.100	0	5,500	5,500
2	500	0.826	413	413	0.576	238	2,881	3,119
3	1,000	0.751	751	1,164	0.402	468	2,011	2,479
4	1,500	0.683	1,025	2,189	0.315	690	1,577	2,267
5	2,000	0.621	1,242	3,431	0.264	906	1,319	2,225 §
6	2,500	0.565	1,413	4,844	0.230	1,114	1,148	2,261
7	3,000	0.513	1,539	6,383	0.205	1,309	1,027	2,335

*Operating inferiorities are treated as year-end magnitudes.
†This factor gives the present value of £1 payable at the end of the year indicated.
‡Capital recovery factor is used to convert the present value of operating inferiority and capital cost into equivalent annual costs (it is equal to $1/a_{n,r}$).
§Minimum equivalent annual cost.

Figure 10:3   Equivalent annual cost for operating inferiority, capital cost and both combined

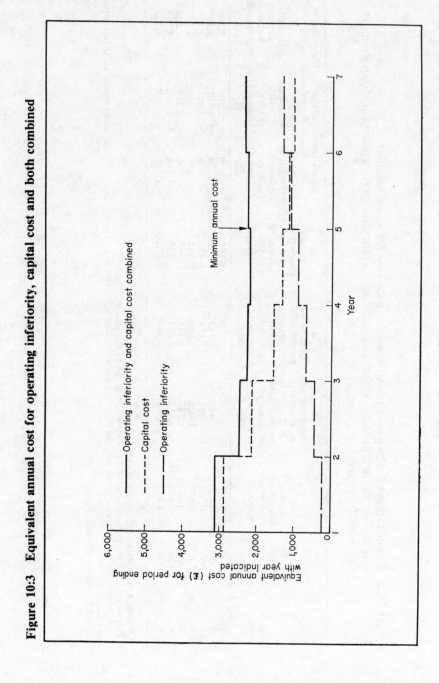

Figure 10:4 Computation of minimum equivalent annual cost for an existing machine

The machine has an operating inferiority next year of £2,000 and thereafter a gradient of £500 per year with salvage values as indicated. Discount rate is 10 per cent

	1	2	3	4	5	6	7	8	9	10	11
Year of further service	Salvage value end of year (£)	Loss of salvage value during year indicated (£)	Interest on opening salvage value of year indicated (£)	Capital cost for year indicated (col. 2 + col. 3) (£)	Operating inferiority for year indicated (£)	Capital cost and inferiority for year indicated (col. 4 + col. 5) (£)	Present value factor for year indicated (£)	Present value of capital cost and inferiority for year indicated (col. 6 x col. 7) (£)	Cumulative present value of capital cost and inferiority (£)	Capital recovery factor	Equivalent annual total cost period ending with year indicated (col. 9 x col. 10) (£)
0	2100										
1	1300	800	210	1010	2000	3010	0.909	2736	2736	1.100	3010
2	1000	300	130	430	2500	2930	0.826	2420	5156	0.576	2970*
3	800	200	100	300	3000	3300	0.751	2478	7634	0.402	3069

*Minimum equivalent annual cost.

Figure 10:5 Revenue, capital cost and operating costs of machines of different lives over a three-year period

Age at beginning of year	Year 1				Year 2				Year 3			
	Operating revenue (£)	Capital cost (£)	Operating cost (£)	Profit (loss) (£)	Operating revenue (£)	Capital cost (£)	Operating cost (£)	Profit (loss) (£)	Operating revenue (£)	Capital cost (£)	Operating cost (£)	Profit (loss) (£)
New machine	250	200	100	(50)	250	205	90	(45)	250	210	80	(40)
1 year					250	–	110	140	250	–	95	155
2 years									250	–	130	120
3 years (existing machine)	250	–	160	90								
4 years					250	–	180	70				
5 years									250	–	245	5

also incorporated in Figure 10:5. The analysis, for the dynamic programming method, starts in the final year of the period being reviewed, in this case the third year. The objective is to establish the best policy for machine replacement in year 3 and, using that knowledge, to determine the best policy in year 2, and then year 1.

The first step is to compute the profit/loss associated with machines of varying ages in year 3 to provide the basis of a decision whether to keep an existing machine or to purchase new equipment. Purchasing a new machine in year 3 produces a loss of £40. If a one-year-old machine is kept in year 3 (new machine in year 2), a profit of £155 will accrue.

The decision in this situation would be to keep a one-year-old machine, as the profit of £155 for the year exceeds the loss of £40 for purchasing a new machine. The profits associated with keeping machines aged 5 years are also shown in Figure 10:5.

The process is then repeated for year 2, except that account must be taken of what would accrue to the machine in year 3 (appropriately discounted) 'reflecting' the decision made in year 2. For this purpose let us assume a discount rate of 20 per cent (that is, a discount factor of 1/1.2).

The profit (loss) associated with purchasing a new machine in year 2 is (£45) as shown in Figure 10:5. To this must be added the profit that would accrue to the machine in year 3 discounted at 20 per cent. If a new machine was purchased in year 2 it would be one year old at the beginning of year 3. Figure 10:5 shows that a one-year-old machine would be kept in year 3 and the profit that would accrue would be £155. Thus, the discounted profit in purchasing a new machine in year 2 is

$$-£45 + \frac{£155}{1.2} = £84$$

If a one-year-old machine is kept in year 2, Figure 10:5 shows that profit would be £140. This machine would be two years old in year 3 and the associated profit is £120. Therefore, the discounted profit in year 2 of a one-year-old machine is

$$£140 + \frac{£120}{1.2} = £240$$

The profits and decisions associated with purchasing and keeping a one-year-old machine and the existing machine which would be 4 years old are summarized in Figure 10:6. The decision in year 2 would be (a) to keep a one-year-old machine rather than purchase a new machine and (b) to replace the existing machine.

Figure 10:6 Present value profits and the decisions in year 2 for machines of various ages

Option	Annual Revenue (£)	Capital Cost (£)	Operating costs (£)	Profit or loss in current year (£)	Discounted profit in future years (£)	Total profit or loss (£)	Decision to purchase a new machine or keep an old machine of the specified age
Purchase a new machine	250	−205	−90	−45	$\frac{+155}{1.2}$	+84	
Keep a one-year-old machine	250	–	−110	+140	$\frac{+120}{1.2}$	+240	Keep
Keep a four-year-old machine	250	–	−180	+70	$\frac{+5}{1.2}$	+74	Purchase

Figure 10:7 Present value of profits and decisions for the 3 year period for machines of various ages

Age at beginning of year	Profit (loss) (£)	Total Discounted Profit (£)	Decision	Value of Decision (£)	Profit (loss) (£)	Total Discounted Profit (£)	Decision	Value of Decision (£)	Profit (loss) (£)	Decision	Value of Decision (£)
New machine	(50)	150			(45)	84			(40)		
One year					140	240	Keep	240	155	Keep	155
Two years									120	Keep	120
Three years (existing machine)	90	160	Keep	160							
Four years					70	74	Purchase	84			
Five years									5	Keep	5

The decisions and associated values for the three-year period are shown in Figure 10:7. In year 1 if the existing machine is replaced at a capital cost of £200 (Figure 10:5), the new machine will produce a net revenue of £150 for its first year (£250–£100 = £150) plus the future profits of £240 discounted at 20 per cent, derived from a one-year-old machine in year 2 (Figure 10:7). The present value profit of this decision is

$$£250 - £200 - £100 + \frac{£240}{1.2} = -£50 + £200 = £150$$

Alternatively, if the existing machine is kept in year 1, the accumulated net revenue is £90 for that year (Figure 10:5, £250–£160 = £90) and the purchase of a new machine in year 2 will earn £70 (£84 discounted at 20 per cent) in all future years to produce a total present value profit of £160. Thus the incumbent machine should be kept for a further year for a net present value gain of £10 (£160–£150).

In year 2, Figure 10:7 shows that the optimum decision is to discard the existing machine (total discounted profit of £74) and purchase a new machine (total discounted profit £84).

Year 3 starts with a one-year-old machine and the conclusion from Figure 10:7 is to keep it another year to produce a present value profit of £155.

If a long enough time horizon is taken, not only is it possible to make the decision when to replace, but also to have an idea of the optimum life of the replacement machine. A calculation of this sort, performed quite easily by hand in a short period of time implicitly tests all the possible replacement schedules and chooses the best. In the above example, the immediate decision is in favour of keeping the existing machine for one more year before replacement. At the end of one year, when replacement is planned, a further assessment can be carried out based on new information available at that time.

The worked example was simplified in that the effects of taxation, investment incentives, scrap values and inflation should have been included.

Summary

We have outlined the variables to be considered in equipment replacement and followed this by an explanation of two methods of analysing the replacement problem. The first, using minimum average annual cost, has restrictive assumptions, but is applicable for replacement decisions of small magnitudes and limited information. The second, that of dynamic programming, is a more rigorous technique, but is dependent on the availability of considerably more information.

Supplement 10:1 Using relative costs

If, in the example on pages 143–4, a relative comparison had been made – that is, if all operating costs were compared with the operating costs of the new machine in year 1 – then the operating cost cash flows for the new machine would have been £0 in year 1, £20 in year 2 and £40 in year 3. The relative cost of the existing machine for a further year would have been £65.

Then the equivalent annual cost of operating the new machine is £19. (Present value of £20 and £40 in years 2 and 3 discounted at 10 per cent is £46.58. Annual cost of this over three years is £46.58/$a_{3, 10}$= £46.58/2.4869 = £19).

Similarly the equivalent annual cost of the capital outlay is £40.

So the equivalent total annual cost is £59 which is less than £65, so the machine would be replaced. (In the absolute calculation, the figures to be compared were £1,059 and £1,065.)

Notes

1 T. Barna, 'On measuring capital', in *The Theory of Capital*, edited by F. A. Lutz and D. C. Hague (London: Macmillan, 1961). P. Redfern, 'Net investment in fixed assets in the UK 1938–53', *Journal of the Royal Statistical Society*, vol. 118 (1955).
2 R. R. Neild, 'Replacement policy', *National Institute Economic Review*, number 30 (1965). H. H. Scholefield, 'Replacement of equipment', *Accounting and Business Research*, number 8 (Autumn 1972), pp. 316–24.
3 R. E. Bellman and S. E. Dreyfus, *Applied Dynamic Programming* (Princeton, NJ: Princeton University Press, 1962).

Further reading

C. W. Churchman, R. L. Ackoff and E. L. Arnoff, *Introduction to Operations Research* (New York: Wiley, 1957).

S. E. Dreyfus, 'A generalised equipment replacement study', *Journal of the Society for Industrial and Applied Mathematics*, 1960, no. 8.

R. B. Fetter and T. P. Goodman, 'An equipment-investment analog', *Operations Research*, vol. 5 (October 1957), pp. 657–69.

A. J. Merrett, 'Investment in replacement: the optimal replacement method', *Journal of Management Studies*, vol. 2 (1965), pp. 153–66.

V. L. Smith, *Investment and Production: A Study in the Theory of the Capital-using Enterprise* (Cambridge, Mass.: Harvard University Press, 1961).

R. C. Stapleton, D. B. Hemmings and H. H. Scholefield, 'Technical change and the optimal life of assets', *Operational Research Quarterly*, vol. 23 (1972), pp. 45–59.

G. A. Taylor, *Managerial and Engineering Economy: Economic Decision-making* (Princeton, NJ: Van Nostrand, 1964).

G. Terborgh, *Dynamic Equipment Policy: A MAPI Study* (New York: McGraw-Hill, 1949).

G. Terborgh, *Business Investment Policy: A MAPI Study and Manual* (Washington DC: Machinery and Allied Products Institute, 1958).

D. Teichroew, *An Introduction to Management Science: Deterministic Models* (New York: Wiley, 1964).

11

Capital budgeting and the financial process

As companies have expanded and their organizations grown more complex it has become necessary for a central corporate authority to take more responsibility for the allocation of funds between different products, departments and divisions.

The decision to accept or reject a major project can no longer be taken on a rule-of-thumb basis, or by simply making a DCF appraisal. A major project requires a substantial investigation, usually in the form of a study undertaken by a project team, that may involve several man-years of fact-finding and analysis embracing operational, strategic and financial considerations. Examination of these factors requires individuals from a variety of backgrounds and corporate sectors if the best interests of the company are to be served. Consequently, a capital-budgeting system must evolve that retains the initiative of the department or division, but which ensures that the proposition is financially viable and is in accord with the company's overall objectives.

The degree of central intervention deemed necessary to ensure that the objectives are met reflects the prevailing management philosophy. At one end of the spectrum, many of the major oil companies employ rigorous and sophisticated appraisal tools with continual evaluation procedures operating at the corporate level for major capital-budgeting projects conceived at divisional level. At the other end of the spectrum, companies in the textile industry allow divisions virtual autonomy in the investment area unless reported results suggest that funds are not being employed profitably. The latter concept may work only if top management successfully sells its own criteria for evaluation.

Divisional responsibility for costs and profits has raised potential conflicts with corporate objectives. A department is concerned primarily with its own profits, costs and expansion, whereas the company has wider responsibilities. The board is concerned not only with the search for profitable investment opportunities but with the overall allocation of funds between products and markets. Such an allocation cannot be made merely on the basis of the number and value of the projects proposed by the divisions. The board cannot resign itself to merely checking that the DCF return is adequate and therefore the projects should be financed. It has the responsibility of appraising the markets for the company's products and deciding how far its own perception of market conditions and the company's competitive advantage should influence resource allocation compared with that which would prevail if the demands of the divisional managers were satisfied. In fact, the final decision on capital allocation is derived by an iterative process between head office and division.

With these problems in mind, a formal capital-budgeting process is a prerequisite to a consistent and rational distribution of corporate funds. Within this framework there are a number of steps:

1 Establishment of long term objectives that encompass the short term and long term capital budgets.
2 Delegation of authority for the authorization and examination of proposals.
3 Establishment of criteria for evaluating investment projects.
4 Control and post-audit of project expenditure.
5 Performance appraisal and allocation of resources.

This chapter outlines a formal system that incorporates these steps.

Short and long term capital budgets

A company should define its growth objectives and decide how they might be achieved, either through expansion within its particular industry or through diversification. Both methods of growth can be implemented through internally generated projects, or through acquisition of other companies. The capital budget should summarize these aspirations for growth, but will be limited by the funds the company is able to generate from its own operations and raise in the capital markets. The budget should be split into two parts; the budget for the next financial year and summary for the next three to five years. It will include:

1 Estimated expenditures to be authorized and/or spent on projects which have been, or are expected to be, started in the current year.

2   New projects to be submitted for authorization in the next year, or subsequent two to four years.
3   Acquisitions.

The budget should outline the future direction of the company, its growth potential and the funds that will be allocated to each area of the company.

Delegation of authority for the examination and authorization of expenditure proposals

There are a number of steps in the capital-budgeting system leading to the authorization of project expenditures:

1   All capital projects within a department are reviewed by the department head.
2   They are reviewed by the divisional manager.
3   There is a final presentation to a capital appropriations committee headed by the chairman or managing director of the company.

A company must ensure that each level of management has the authority to invest appropriate amounts of capital in minor projects. These expenditure limits must be reviewed regularly, since they are too often outdated because of inflation and increased job responsibility. They can stifle or frustrate initiative and prevent senior management from concentrating on the largest and most important projects. A practical solution is to apply an inflation-related index to authority levels on a regular basis with a total update of authority schedules every 5 years.

A major project (it will usually be conceived within a department) will require an in-depth study to review its operational and financial viability. A special team from within the department may have to be set up for this examination and it is at this point that two dangers can arise.

1   A team might be expected to come up with a justification for the project after an expensive and time-consuming study. A conclusion that the project is not feasible may be unwelcome to management.
2   The operating department may not have the financial expertise necessary to produce an adequate evaluation. This will often be the case if such projects arise at infrequent intervals.

To overcome both dangers, a financial analyst or economist should be brought in from the treasurer's or comptroller's department to assist in the project evaluation; clearly this should only be done for a relatively large project.

Specialized advice from an individual outside the department will improve both the quality of the analysis and the objectivity of the study. The financial adviser's role will vary in depth and time depending on the project and the company.

Because of the shortage of such skills within a company, it may be impossible to provide operating management with such assistance. An alternative would be to use a corporate department periodically to evaluate such projects in cooperation with operating management.

In most companies, if a project's expenditure is above a specified level, it must be submitted to the board for approval. However, all too often, the board or capital appropriations committee relies on a final presentation by a department manager or study team. Some major companies invite their treasurer's or comptroller's department to make comments on the project before the board presentation. Unfortunately, this review is too often hurried and superficial, confining itself to ensuring that the DCF calculation is accurate and, possibly, that a risk analysis has been completed. This is inadequate because it does not look into the basis of the calculations; also such a review usually takes place when the project study is near or at completion, thus any opposition to it is politically difficult to mount.

We believe it is feasible and necessary for a corporate department – comptroller's or treasurer's – to review important projects at various stages in the evaluation. Their participation would lead to a more realistic appraisal and would:

1   Ensure that a comparison with existing systems takes account of any improvements that can be made before savings are computed from the new investments. The department should use the company's internal audit group to examine the efficiency of the existing system. It would be wrong to compare savings from a new investment with the existing facilities if the latter could be made more effective and costs reduced or revenues increased.
2   Ensure an examination and appraisal of alternative methods that would achieve the project's objectives.
3   Establish the appropriate life of the project. Divisional management may unjustifiably extend the project's life to increase the savings and the rate of return.
4   Verify the basis and reasonableness of savings and cost estimates.
5   Establish an appropriate minimum rate of return that takes account of the project's risk and justifies the outlay of funds.
6   Provide qualitative considerations and assess their importance in the project proposal.

These proposals should not imply that operating management cannot be trusted to examine its own investment opportunities. Most operating divisions do not have the experience or the necessary skills for the evaluation of major projects and the above framework provides a system of improving their examination and effectiveness. Figure 11:1 summarizes the relationships of each party.

Figure 11:1   Organization for capital budgeting

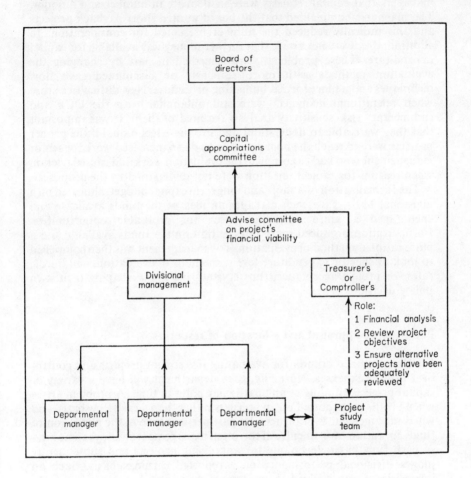

Criteria for evaluating investment decisions

A company must be aware that the kinds of capital projects generated by departments are determined in part by the particular criterion (or criteria) used for evaluating the capital projects. Thus a company that uses payback as its criterion will find that line management proposes mainly short-life projects with a short payback, and this will severely restrict their total number and profitability.

In one large company, a board member disclosed to his operating managers that capital requests were inadequate in number and amount. The managers complained that the board wanted short-payback projects and this radically reduced the number presented for consideration. In addition, they were not aware that further money was available for capital expenditure. These problems were remedied in part by changing the evaluation methods with more emphasis on discounted cash flow techniques and a more formal budgeting procedure. New difficulties arose when operational managers were still unfamiliar with the DCF and rudimentary risk/sensitivity analysis required of them. It was important that they were able to understand and use these techniques if the proper projects were to reach the board; failure to do so increased work for senior management who had to complete the evaluation work and caused friction when reasons for project rejection were not understood by the proposers.

The formalization of a short and long term capital budget, allocated on a divisional basis, gave each manager an idea of the funds available and encouraged a more energetic search for profitable opportunities. Formalization produced more information on the funds available and a more rational method of evaluation. Top management was then compelled to look at specific expenditure levels, methods of evaluation, and hurdle rates for project acceptance, thus crystallizing and reshaping their own policy decisions.

Performance appraisal and allocation of resources

We have outlined criteria for evaluating investment projects and control over project expenses. Normally, each department will have a variety of capital projects running at any particular point in time. A problem arises when profits are reported on an accruals rather than a cash flow basis, and when management is influenced by past performance in the allocation of funds for future investment. All too often management employs some kind of cash flow based technique for appraising projects and subsequently judges divisional performance on a reported earnings basis. Such an inconsistency can mislead management when capital is apportioned. As pointed out in Chapter 4 a project's cash flow and its contribution to the profit and loss account in a particular year may differ substantially. We shall show that to use reported earnings as opposed to cash flow ignores the full impact of tax and investment incentives and therefore biases the system against capital intensive projects.

In Figure 11:2 we have outlined a five-year project with associated cash flows, investment incentives and tax. In Figure 11:3 these cash flows have been converted into reported earnings before and after tax. As can be seen the reported earnings do not reflect the large cash flow generated in year 1 as a result of the investment grant and initial capital allowance.

If management was to look back at the reported earnings of the project they might wonder why the investment proposal was originally accepted.

Figure 11:2 After-tax cash flows

				Year			
	0	1	2	3	4	5	6
Net cash flows		+33.4	33.4	33.4	33.4	33.4	
Corporation tax (50%)			−16.7	−16.7	−16.7	−16.7	−16.7
Capital cost	−100						
Cash grant		+20					
Initial allowance (100%)		+50					
Net cash flow	−100	+103.4	+16.7	+16.7	+16.7	+16.7	−16.7

Figure 11:3 Reported earnings before and after tax for the project

				Year			
	0	1	2	3	4	5	6
Gross profit	—	34	34	34	34	34	
Depreciation	—	16	16	16	16	16	
Profits before tax		18	18	18	18	18	
Tax		—	—	1	17	17	
Profits after tax	0	18	18	17	1	1	

1   Assuming credit terms of 30 days (12/11 × 33.4 = 34)
2   Accounting depreciation

Cost of asset	100
Cash grant	20
Net cost	80
Annual depreciation charge	16

3   Cash grant credited directly to the balance sheet.

The transformation to reported earnings from a cash flow basis biases the system in favour of labour intensive projects. For example, if a project produces a 20 per cent IRR before tax and receives no investment incentives (labour intensive) it will produce a 10 per cent IRR after tax, with a 50 per cent tax rate. However, a project producing a 20 per cent IRR before tax and receiving a 20 per cent cash grant and 100 per cent initial allowance would provide a 33 per cent IRR after tax. The attraction of the capital intensive project would be diminished under reported earnings by the spreading of the investment incentives over the life of the project.

It is important to realize that if a firm uses reported earnings in performance appraisal and the allocation of future funds is influenced by this criterion then it is failing to maximize earnings on a discounted cash flow basis. A number of studies, by Ball and Brown[1] and Kaplan and Roll[2], have indicated that share prices respond to changes in cash flows and not to mere changes in accounting numbers. In both studies, the authors analysed the share price reaction of firms who changed their method of reporting profits by, for example, moving from accelerated to straight line depreciation in order to improve reported earnings. Their results indicate that the market is able to differentiate between accounting numbers and cash flow and that the market is impressed only by cash flows.

Control and post-audit of project expenses

Once the project has been approved and the budget appropriation has been made, some control is necessary for the ongoing project. The objectives must include:

1 Comparison of costs against budget at regular intervals.
2 Early warnings on any factors that will significantly increase costs or decrease revenues.
3 Audit of projects at various stages before completion.

Both the early-warning system and the audit are aimed at costs and methods within the project, not only to improve efficiency, but to ensure that unforeseen costs and/or delays are detected and, where possible, controlled.

In plant construction, escalation in labour costs or sudden rises in the price of an important material can substantially increase the costs of a project. Early warnings could lead to the use of other materials or to abandonment.

The sharp increase in the price of nickel in 1967 increased the construction costs of a chlorobutyl plant by 20 per cent. Early warning of price increases could have enabled management to search for other lower-cost metals that could have been substituted for nickel, and to review the profitability of the plant under the new cost structure.

Of course, the difference between detecting potential cost increases and controlling them must be stressed. An internal audit or internal consulting group can help management by reviewing the organization and the methods and systems of analysis and control.

In an inflationary environment, projected costs and returns often prove faulty. The divergence reflects a poor and frequently biased information and forecasting base, and a lack of control and detection of cost increases or price changes. Abandonment decisions are the most difficult to make. In this area an independent and highly skilled corporate audit function within the comptroller's or treasurer's department can play a critical role in aiding line management to improve efficiency, and help the board to make more informed and rapid decisions.

Summary

Capital-expenditure controls in the suggested framework will be more or less formal and rigorous depending on the size of the company, the particular project and the prevailing management philosophy. In theory, line management should simply be made responsible for operations. In practice, the financial capability of management in most companies is not of a sufficiently high standard to allow this philosophy to be implemented fully. Until line managers and their staff become more skilled in financial management practices, the necessity for increased control and review remains in most companies. Evaluation and control must be present if corporate profitability is to reach projected levels. As the relative size of capital projects has increased, the principles discussed have become more important.

Notes

1   Ray Ball and Phillip Brown, 'An Empirical Evaluation of Accounting Income Numbers', *Journal of Accounting Research*, vol. 6, Autumn 1968, pp. 159–178.
2   R. S. Kaplan and R. Roll, 'Investor Evaluation of Accounting Information: Some Empirical Evidence', *Journal of Business*, 43, April 1972, pp. 225–257.

PART THREE
CAPITAL STRUCTURE

12

Equity and debt capital for public companies

This chapter examines the different sources of long-term funds for an existing public company and describes the relative advantages of equity, preference shares and debt.

Equity capital – ordinary shares

Ordinary shares represent the funds supplied to a business by its owners. If the company is a private one, the shareholders usually consist of a few people who effectively exercise control. The shares cannot be sold on the Stock Exchange, thus restricting most owners' ability to sell all or part of their company and raise substantial amounts of capital. When a company is a public one, the value of its shares is quoted on the Stock Exchange and the shareholders may number many thousands. They may change frequently, as current holders sell their shares to other investors and consequently they exercise only indirect control over the management of the business by electing a board of directors that is responsible for the day-to-day decisions.

A shareholder is interested primarily in the returns he receives on his capital. This return may take two forms: cash dividends and capital gains. A shareholder has no legal or contractual entitlement to receive a dividend. The directors may decide to reduce or not to give a dividend, when recent operations have shown little or no profit, or when the company is short of funds to finance its investment programme. A company in the UK cannot buy and sell its own shares, unlike corporations in the USA, although it may hold shares in other companies. In addition to dividends, shareholders hope to obtain capital gains through an appreciation in the price of their shares. Capital gains are an important part of the shareholders' return, but neither the company's cash flow nor its profits benefits directly from share price fluctuations. However, the directors do well to watch the price carefully, for a falling share price relative to the market and industry often signals shareholders' dissatisfaction with the company's progress and future cash flow prospects.

Par value

Shares are always given a par value in the UK. This is the nominal value at which the shares are carried on a company's books. If the company sells shares for a sum greater than par value, the difference is known as a *share premium*, which is shown on the balance sheet separately from other reserves and cannot be used to pay dividends.

At one time when a company first offered shares to the public, they were priced at their par value. Over time, as the company's earnings grew and the price of the shares rose their par value would remain constant rendering it irrelevant to their real value; further issues of shares in the company would then be made at a price in excess of their par value and totally unrelated to it.

Nowadays, companies tend to issue shares with a par value well below the issue price. They feel that the par value should be a common one – 25p and £1 are popular levels – but this has no connection with the value of the company or the market price of the shares. In some parts of the United States the irrelevance of par values has been recognized and companies are permitted to issue shares of no par value, but at present this is not possible in the UK. The concept of the par value of shares is not an important one today.

Authorized and issued capital

In the registered documents of a company, the memorandum and articles of association, the analyst will find shares which the company may issue. Usually companies issue less than the authorized maximum, to allow some 'elbow-room' in financing. From time to time the company may request its shareholders to increase the authorized share capital, and this can be done at an annual general meeting or at an extraordinary general meeting. The par value multiplied by the number of shares actually issued is called the issued capital.

Consider, as an example, a company with the following shares:

Authorized share capital
1,000,000 shares at 25p each = £250,000
Issued share capital
500,000 shares at 25p each = £125,000

500,000 shares have been issued with a par value of 25 pence each, the company is, therefore, able to issue a further 500,000 shares. If it wishes to issue more than 500,000, it must request its shareholders to increase the authorized share capital. Suppose the company's shares stand at £1 in the stock market, and the company wishes to raise a further £1 million from shareholders through an issue of ordinary shares. To achieve this 1,000,000 new shares at £1 must be issued, which will require an increase in the authorised share capital of 500,000 shares.

Voting rights

Ordinary shares usually carry voting rights which entitle the owner to vote at general meetings, in this way influencing the management of the company. Some shares are, however, specifically designated 'non-voting' and, although sharing in the profits of the company and viewed legally as owners, the non-voting shareholders cannot vote at general meetings and cannot have any direct influence on the company's affairs. The existence of non-voting shares usually means that the voting control of the company rests in relatively few hands, and this can be of critical importance in a bid situation.

Dividends

These are cash payments to shareholders. When audited accounts are published, the company may declare a dividend and this is subject to the shareholders' approval at the annual general meeting; the dividend is paid subsequent to their approval. In a bad year, a company may wish to pay a larger dividend than total earnings allow. The difference must be paid from reserves, which represent accrued profits from previous years.

General meetings

General meetings must be held every year for the presentation of the company's accounts, and shareholders may attend and vote on a variety of matters, including the election of directors, approval and ratification of the proposed dividend, and sometimes for an increase in authorized capital. An extraordinary general meeting is unusual, and tends to occur in a crisis situation, either when, for one reason or another, the company is doing very badly, or when an acquisition or merger is in progress and the company requires immediate shareholder sanction by way of an increase in the authorized capital.

Financial ratios

Dividend yield and dividend cover

The financial press often comments on the dividend yield of a company. This is the ratio of the current dividend in monetary terms to the current share price, expressed as a percentage. Thus, if a company paid a dividend

of 5p on every share, and the current share price was £1, the dividend yield
would be 5 per cent.

Dividends are usually expressed as a percentage of the par value of the
shares and this can cause confusion with the dividend yield. If, in the
previous example, the par value of the share was 25p, the company would
declare a dividend of 20 per cent. The reader should note the difference
between the *dividend rate* of 20 per cent and the dividend yield of 5 per cent;
the former is related to the par value of the share, the latter to its market
price.

The dividend *cover* is the number of times the dividend could have been
paid from current after-tax profits (the ratio of earnings to dividends paid).
Thus in the example above, if a 5p dividend was paid from earnings after
tax, totalling 12.5p per share, the dividend would be covered 2½ times. If
interest is paid to preference shareholders, divided cover is computed after
deduction of this payment from earnings.

PE ratio

The price-earnings ratio (PE) is the ratio of current after-tax earnings to the
current share price. A PE of 15 implies that it will take the company 15
years, at the present earnings level, to earn profits per share equal to the
current share price. This can be highly misleading, because a company's
share price has a high PE ratio if its growth prospects are high. Thus a
company that is on a PE of 15 may be expected to earn profits per share
equal to the current share price in much less than 15 years. The implications
of this ratio will be discussed in greater detail in later chapters.

Share issues to existing shareholders

Companies may issue shares to their existing shareholders in a variety of
ways. The most common are outlined below.

Split issues

In making a split a company replaces existing shares with a large number of
shares at a lower par value. This is usually undertaken when the share price
is relatively high and the company believes that trading in the share would
be improved by a smaller unit price. Thus, in, say, a 10-for-1 split, the
company replaces each existing share by ten new ones. If the old shares had
a par value of £1, each new share will have a par value of 10p. The theory
that a high price is detrimental to trading has not been proved in practice
and a split affects neither the earnings of a company, nor its value.
American research[1] has shown that share prices do not improve as a
result of a split; rather such an improvement is associated with dividend
and earnings increases which accompany share splits (or bonus issues).

Scrip or bonus issues

A *bonus* issue is a way of changing the method of reporting shareholders' funds in the balance sheet. The number of issued shares is increased by capitalizing reserves. Apart from accounting considerations, bonus issues are viewed favourably by the market only in so far as they are a manifestation of management's optimism in the future. A bonus or scrip does not change the earning power of the company. When shareholders receive 1-for-1 scrip, they may say they own twice as many shares in the company than previously, but they should also realize that earnings per share have been halved and the value of the company has not been altered.

Rights issues

The most common way of raising further equity capital is by means of a rights issue to existing shareholders. In such an issue, every shareholder receives a certain number of rights in proportion to his present holding of shares. Each right entitles its owner to purchase shares in the company, usually at a discount on the current market price. The right will specify the number of shares that may be purchased, the purchase price and the expiration date.

Two alternatives are open to the holder of rights: to exercise the rights and purchase additional shares, or to sell the rights. A date (date of record) is set when the rights become unattached (from the shares previously held) or issued and on that date all holders of the company's stock become eligible for the rights issue. Shares which sell with rights attached are known as cum rights; when the rights are detached, the shares are sold ex rights. Once the date of record is passed, the rights can be bought and sold separately up to the time they are converted into shares.

It is relatively simple to calculate the theoretical price of rights, the difference in cost between the shares the rights can buy at the rights price and the current market price. For example, if a company's shares stand at £1 and a rights issue is announced in which the holder of a right is entitled to buy 1 share for 50p and 1 right is allotted for every 4 shares already held, the price of the ordinary shares will fall to around 90p, all other things being equal. This is computed as follows:

4 existing shares at £1	£4
Cost of taking up 1 right at 50p	0.50
5 shares	£4.50
Value of each share	£0.90

Therefore, the value of each right is 40p (90p–50p)

If an existing shareholder is not to lose money, the price of the ordinary shares must not fall below 90p. It may remain above 90p if the rights issue provides further information and shareholders believe the new money is being reinvested profitably. If the price of the ordinary shares falls to 90p, the value of the unconverted right will be 40p as shown. When payment of 50p per share is made, the new share will stand at 90p like all the other ordinary shares. New shares – that is, those obtained by exercising the rights – may command a slight premium over the old shares because shareholders do not pay stamp duty on the sale of the rights. Normally arbitrage ensures that the actual price of the rights is close to the theoretical value.

When companies have to raise equity capital they find rights issues attractive because issue expenses are low and further capital is offered to existing shareholders who favour the company in terms of their risk and returns preferences. Thus existing shareholders are more likely to subscribe to a rights issue, assuming they have sufficient funds available, than an equivalent body of outside investors.

Two main factors are involved in determining the terms of a rights issue: the number of shares to be issued and the discount offered on the current market price. The greater the discount, the more shares must be issued to obtain the same amount of capital. Where existing shareholders are involved, the size of the discount on the current market price is irrelevant, as the increased number of shares will be matched by an increase in individual holdings. Thus, whether the issue basis is one-for-four or a one-for-two, each shareholder's proportional ownership of the company's earnings stream remains unchanged. Of course, if a rights issue price is pitched too high and the market price of the shares falls below this value, then shareholders will refuse to take up their rights as they could increase their holding in the company more cheaply by buying shares in the market.

Private placings

In a private placing, financial institutions subscribe to an issue of shares. It is a relatively cheap method of issuing equity, but problems may arise with the concentration of ownership and the dissatisfaction of existing shareholders. As a placing is made to a few persons or institutions, they will tend to take relatively large amounts of shares, and, with a widely dispersed shareholding, these blocks may be a source of disproportionate power to their owners. Existing shareholders may also be unhappy with a private placing if the purchase price is significantly below the market price and they may resent the fact that they are not given the opportunity to purchase on similar terms. This dissent does not normally become severe enough to be a serious deterrent, but it should be considered if the company is giving any sizeable discount on the shares being placed.

Equity capital – preference shares

A preference share is similar to an ordinary share, but carries specific rights that do not belong to ordinary shareholders. Usually the preference dividend is fixed as a percentage of the par value of the share and the company can only avoid payments of the preference dividend if it does not declare an ordinary dividend. In addition, in a liquidation, the preference shareholders must usually be paid in full prior to the ordinary shareholders.

Cumulative and non-cumulative

All previously omitted cumulative preference dividends must be paid as well as the current preference dividend prior to the declaration of an ordinary dividend. Non-cumulative preference capital does not carry this right and in such cases payment of an ordinary dividend is not dependent on payment of previous preference dividends.

Preferred ordinary/participating preference

These shares carry an additional feature in that the holders are not only entitled to their fixed dividend, but also to a share in future profits above a specific level. Usually this right is bought at the expense of a lower fixed dividend.

Redeemable and irredeemable preference capital

Ordinary share capital is irredeemable, unless the company is liquidated, or decides on a repayment of capital. However, some preference capital is redeemable: on or after some specified date, the company must offer to buy back all the shares it has issued. Obviously redeemable shares are more secure than non-redeemable shares and, in return for this lower risk, redeemable shares tend to carry a lower dividend.

Conversion

Sometimes preference capital will carry a conversion option, giving the owner the option of converting his preference shares into ordinary shares after a stated date or for a particular period. Convertibles are discussed in more detail on pages 177–8. Most of the advantages and disadvantages of convertible loan stocks apply to preference convertibles as well.

Cost of preference capital

In general, preference capital provides lower returns to shareholders than equity because it is less risky. For a shareholder, preference shares offer greater security than ordinary shares but a lower return. For a company, preference capital tends to have many of the characteristics of debt, except that interest payments are made from after-tax instead of pre-tax profits.

After the 1965 Finance Act, many companies retired their preference capital and substituted debenture or loan stock carrying a higher interest charge. As the interest on loan stock is tax-deductible (unlike preference dividends), the after-tax cost is lower. A conversion of this type requires the consent of preference shareholders at a general meeting.

Debt capital

Debt capital is a composite term for those funds loaned to the company for a period of years. The company pays periodic interest on the debt and repays the original sum borrowed when it reaches maturity. The original sum is called the principal.

The company has a legal obligation to meet interest charges when due and cannot defer them except by agreement with the debt holders or their trustees. This legal obligation means that debt financing is more risky than equity financing, as in a poor year the company will not be able to pass interest charges without the risk of the debt holders' trustees petitioning for the liquidation of the company. The cost of debt to a company is reduced as interest payments are tax-deductible, and hence can be paid from before-tax earnings. For example, if a company pays 9% on a debenture, and corporation tax is 50%, the effective cost of debt to the company is 4.5%, $[9\% \times (1-0.5)]$. However, repayments of principal are not tax-deductible.

From the lender's point of view, the return on his loan is less risky than on equity, as he has legal guarantees on his interest payments and a prior claim to the company's assets in a liquidation. Thus the debt holder receives greater security than a preference or ordinary shareholder on both his interest payments and principal.

Debentures

All loans carry legal security in that they rank ahead of shareholders' funds in a liquidation, but secured loans – that is, debentures – are ranked above other loans. There are two types of debenture, those which are secured against specified assets, and which are known as *mortgage debentures*, and, more commonly, those which carry a floating charge over all the company's assets. Only if default occurs does the charge become specific to particular assets. The floating charge is more flexible to a company since it is allowed to dispose of any asset without reference to the debenture holders.

Debentures are secured, ranking the holders above other lenders, but a *subordinated* debenture is one which is ranked below other debentures. On liquidation, other debentures would have to be repaid in full before the subordinated debenture holders receive any payment, although they would rank above other unsecured lenders.

If the debenture carries a call option, the company can, at its discretion, repay the debenture before the maturity date is reached. This gives the company some safeguard against changes in interest rates. It may be that interest rates will fall significantly during the life of a debenture and the company would be paying high interest rates at a time when it could borrow money more cheaply. If the discrepancy is wide enough and the stock has a call option attached, the company would repay the debenture early and issue a similar amount of debt at a lower interest rate. Assuming all other things are equal, the following points can be made:

1   Secured debentures will carry a lower rate than unsecured debentures, because their security decreases the holder's risk.
2   Subordinated debentures will carry a higher rate than non-subordinated debentures, because of increased risk.
3   Debentures with call options will carry a higher rate than those without, because the debenture holder's downside risk is unaltered by a call option, but his upside potential is decreased, and hence he will require an increased rate in compensation.

Debenture holders are represented by a trustee – for example, a commercial bank – who has a legal duty to protect them. In fact the trustee is limited in his negotiating powers should default occur, and may only call in a receiver to manage the company's affairs to protect the rights of debenture holders.

Unsecured loan stock

This is very similar to debenture stock, except that it is unsecured and therefore is ranked below all debentures in a liquidation. The main advantage of unsecured loan stock for the company is that it is issued on the basis of the company's earnings, whereas debentures are regulated by the value of a company's assets and there are legal limitations on the amount of debentures a company may issue. If a company feels that it would like more debt than its asset base allows, then it will issue unsecured loan stock. Investors will consider the company's ability to generate sufficient earnings to repay the loan rather than its position in the event of liquidation. Consequently, unsecured stocks usually carry a higher interest rate or coupon.

Convertibles

A convertible debenture or loan stock carries all the rights of non-convertible stock, but in addition entitles holders to convert into ordinary shares of the company at a specified time. Until and unless converted, convertibles are exactly the same as debenture and loan stocks, carrying an interest rate and the legal rights of the relevant securities. At or after its due conversion date, a convertible can, at the holder's option, be exchanged for ordinary stock at a specified price. The advantages of convertibles are:

1   The convertible feature is attractive to investors who hope for capital gains and this often allows the company to place a lower coupon rate on the stock.
2   A convertible, while unconverted, can be treated as a loan for tax purposes, and therefore the interest charges are tax-deductible. Also, as a convertible usually pays a lower interest charge than an equivalent debenture, earnings per (ordinary) share will be greater than under pure debt financing.

The balance of cost and advantage depends on the company's view of the future. The conversion price should be set with the future likely price in mind, but not so high that investors attach no immediate value to convertibility.

There are two possible disadvantages to convertibles:

1   Earnings dilution on conversion. The tax advantages discussed above assume that the company really wishes to issue equity and uses the convertible as a suitable substitute. If, however, the company wishes to issue debt, but attaches conversion rights to make the issue more attractive, it will incur earnings dilution on conversion. If the earnings of the company grow more rapidly than anticipated, the convertible proves more costly.
2   Financial analysts may view the company in the worst of both possible lights. They may treat the convertible as debt when assessing the company's level of, or proportion of, debt in the capital structure. They may also treat the convertible as already having been converted when projecting earnings per share.

To the investor, the attractions of convertibles lie in their flexibility. If the company does well, he can convert and participate in that prosperity to a greater degree than if he held debt. On the other hand, if the company does poorly, he can retain his convertibles and obtain a high fixed income with the prospect of eventual capital repayment provided things do not get so bad that the company goes out of business. This accounts for the lower interest rate on convertibles compared with debentures.

Warrants

A warrant 'is nothing but a call option sold by the company'. Like convertibles, warrants are sometimes used as 'sweeteners' for loan or debenture stock issues and they carry the right to purchase ordinary stock in the company at a specified price after a particular date, or for a period of time. If the warrants are not detachable they cannot be bought and sold separately from the loan stock or debenture; if detachable, they may be traded separately. One difference between warrants and convertibles is that the former, if exercised, require further cash to be paid to the company, whereas the latter provide a straight exchange of one form of capital for another.

To the investor, warrants often prove an attractive alternative method of investment to the corresponding ordinary share. First consider the position when the conversion date or period has been reached (there is usually some time between the date when warrants first become convertible and the date when all unconverted warrants automatically become cancelled). Under these circumstances the theoretical price or intrinsic value of the warrant would be the difference between the current share price and the warrant conversion price, assuming the former to be greater. Thus if the current share price was 150p and the warrant conversion price 100p, the value of the warrant would be 50p, if conversion was required immediately. However, prior to conversion, the price of the warrant is above this price, because of the effects of gearing. Consider an ordinary share selling at 150p, for which there are outstanding warrants which may be converted into ordinary shares on a one-for-one basis at 140p. The value of the warrant immediately before conversion will be 10p:

$$150p - 140p = 10p$$

If the market price of the ordinary share were to rise by 5p, a $3\frac{1}{3}$ per cent rise, the value of the warrant should rise to 15p:

$$155p - 140p = 15p$$

Thus a $3\frac{1}{3}$ per cent rise in the share price could lead to a 50 per cent rise in the market price of the warrant. The potential value of the option to convert increases, the more distant is the conversion date. It will also increase with the risk of the security.

The gearing of a warrant is defined as the market price of the share divided by the value of the warrant on immediate conversion (that is, market price of warrant minus fixed conversion price). The lower the conversion price relative to the market price the lower the gearing element.

So far the analysis has assumed that the warrant has immediate convertibility. In practice, warrants tend to be issued with conversion dates well into the future, so that for some years a market in the warrant exists without holders having the option to convert at once into the ordinary share. In such circumstances, an investor must consider not only the gearing, but the growth rate in earnings and dividends implied by the current warrant price discounted by the equity shareholders' required rate of return. Furthermore, changes in the expected dividend payout ratio must be considered, since an unanticipated increase in the payout ratio will reduce expected earnings growth and therefore the capital appreciation of the ordinary shares. This will reduce the conversion value of the warrant.

Short-term debt

Short-term debt covers several sources of finance, including bank overdrafts, creditors, deferred tax payments and short-term bills. It is usually required to finance only part of a company's need for working capital.

Some types of short-term debt are treated as long-term funds. If the net requirement for working capital is permanent, then it should be financed by long-term and not short-term funds. For example, many companies treat bank overdrafts as long-term financing, when in fact the loan can be recalled at short notice.

Short-term funds may be used as a convenient bridge between successive long-term fund-raising operations. Just before such an operation, bank balances and other short-term debts are often very large, but after the funds have been raised, the company is able to pay off the short-term debts it has run up to cover its position. Viewed as a bridging mechanism, short-term debt can perform a useful function in maintaining a balanced capital structure.

Summary

Specific factors associated with particular types of capital issue have been discussed in this chapter. There are some common factors which tend to affect several types of issue. Generally these factors are associated with the timing of a particular issue; making the issue at the correct time with due regard to market factors is important. For all types of equity issues, including convertibles and warrants, it is advantageous to make the issue when earnings prospects are good. The price tends to reflect general market confidence in the company and at a high price the market will tend to be more willing to subscribe to particular issues.

Note

1   E. F. Fama, L. Fisher, M. C. Jensen and R. Roll, 'The adjustment of stock prices to new information', *International Economic Review*, vol. 10 (February 1969), pp. 1–21.

Further reading

W. J. Baumol, B. G. Malkiel and R. E. Quandt, 'The valuation of convertible securities', *Quarterly Journal of Economics*, vol. 80 February 1966, pp. 48–59.

F. Black, 'Fact and Fantasy in the Use of Options', *Financial Analysts Journal* 31, pp. 36–72.

F. Black and M. Scholes, 'The Pricing of Options and Corporate Liabilities', *Journal of Political Economy*, 1973, pp. 163–75.

E. F. Brigham, 'An analysis of convertible debentures: theory and some empirical evidence', *Journal of Finance*, vol. 21, March 1966, pp. 35–54.

G. H. Evans, Jr, 'The theoretical value of a stock right', *Journal of Finance*, vol. 10, March 1955, pp. 55–61.

D. Galai, 'Pricing of Options and the Efficiency of the Chicago Board Options Exchange', unpublished PhD dissertation, University of Chicago, Chicago, Illinois, 1975.

J. R. Nelson, 'Price effects in rights offerings', *Journal of Finance*, vol. 20, December 1965, pp. 647–50.

P. A. Samuelson, 'Rational theory of warrant pricing', *Industrial Management Review*, vol. 6, no. 2, Spring 1965, pp. 13–32.

C. W. Smith, Option Pricing: A review, *Journal of Financial Economics*, Vol. 3, 1976, Nos. 1/2.

R. L. Weil, Jr, J. E. Segall and D. Green, 'Premiums on convertible bonds', *Journal of Finance*, vol. 23, June 1968, pp. 445–63.

13

Methods of raising public funds for private companies

An expanding private company that has reached a certain size may decide to obtain public status. This may arise because of its needs for long-term funds which cannot be provided by the existing owners or by their banks. In addition, the existing owners may wish to acquire other companies for shares rather than for cash and, unless the shares can be traded publicly, such acquisitions prove difficult to consummate. Finally, the shares may be more highly valued when they are publicly traded, and thus the owners may experience an increase in the value of their shareholdings and their wealth on attaining public status.

This chapter examines the differences between public and private companies and describes the various ways in which a private company can transform itself into a public one.

Private companies

The essential difference between private and public companies is that a private company does not enjoy the public trading of its equity capital and therefore does not have access to public funds. For this reason private companies tend to be smaller than public companies, some notable exceptions being Littlewoods and Laker Airways.

When a private company does go public the number of shareholders increases substantially and the original owners find their powers of ownership reduced in consequence. However, the increase in the number of shareholders makes it easier for the company to raise substantial amounts of equity because shareholdings are correspondingly smaller, and holders are more likely to be able to take up their allotment of shares.

The absence of a stock exchange quotation for the shares of a private company and their consequent lack of marketability often prevent management and outsiders estimating an accurate value for the company and tend to reduce its worth compared with companies in the same industry that enjoy public status.

New issue market

A decision to transform a private company into a public one has important implications for the management and structure of the company. The change from a small company, managed by one or two people, to a larger company requiring more substantial management often requires a reorientation of thinking. It is important to appreciate that going public is not a mechanical exercise but may require substantial resources of management's time and effort to restructure the company.

The mechanics of making a public issue can appear deceptively simple. In essence, the company, through its brokers, offers to the public a specified amount of equity captial at a price. Members of the public who wish to participate subscribe for whatever portion they wish and the shares are allotted among the subscribers. However, in practice, going public is a complicated business and takes a substantial length of time from the initial decision to the final issue; the minimum period is normally one year.

The first stage in the process of going public is an approach to the new issue specialists. A merchant bank or issuing house will study the present state of the company, its past growth rate and its potential and advise on the feasibility of a public issue. Assuming that both parties agree to go ahead, the next step will be to reorganize the company from a private concern into one suitable for public participation. The capital structure has to be rationalized, the management team may need strengthening and assets may require revaluation. This process also enables the company to comply with stock exchange regulations.

While all this is going on, the amount and method of issue must be decided. The methods of issue available are discussed. They vary to some extent with the amount raised which must be related to available investment opportunities within the company and the value of existing assets.

The company should also consider its capital mix after the issue and how it might try to improve that mix. The idea of a target capital structure will be discussed in more detail later, but it is simply the structure which the management believe is optimum given the risk characteristics of the company (that is, its attitude to fixed interest commitments) and its projected earnings stream.

The target capital structure is a medium term rather than a short term objective because of the nature of the processes involved. The equity issue must be thought of as a rational move towards that objective, fitting into a viable long term financial strategy, rather than an isolated once-and-for-all event.

As the issue date moves nearer, the company's advisers formally request a stock exchange quotation. In theory any share can be bought and sold by different persons without the intervention of third parties, but in practice the meeting place where such transactions are usually made is the stock exchange. If a company wants its shares to be traded on the exchange, it must obtain a quotation from the Stock Exchange Council. If a new company wishes to apply for a quotation – that is, allow its shares to be bought and sold on the exchange – it must meet the stringent criteria laid down by the council. These include fully audited accounts for the previous five years, and constraints on the amount of capital to be issued. Part of the work done in reorganizing the company will be for the purposes of meeting these stock exchange rules. In this way the rights of the individual investor are protected.

Further details still need to be resolved, such as the issue price of shares, the choice of underwriters and requirements for short term debt before the issue. Of greater importance is the timing of the issue. The company may be halfway through its financial year and it must predict earnings for the remaining part of the year. The value placed upon the company's after-tax earnings will be influenced by that forecast.

The state of the market will also affect the price of the shares at flotation. If markets are unsettled and weak, it may be advisable to postpone the issue. All that can be said here is that the final decision and the flotation price should be made as late as possible to take into account the state of the market.

Appendices I and II outline the work involved in issuing shares of a company to the public for the first time and give a typical time-table.

Methods of making new issues

There are various ways in which the company can make the issue, and the particular method depends on circumstances, the amount to be raised and the costs.

Private placing

In a private placing, shares in the company are distributed by a merchant bank or issuing house to private clients, usually institutional investors. This method does not directly involve a public issue, since a public market does not exist in the shares. However, it is often a useful intermediary step towards going public – the institutional investors improve confidence in the company. This is the least costly method of raising equity capital and tends to be used for small issues. It is also possible to use a private placing, not as an intermediary to a public issue, but as a substitute for one. In this case, a market must be established in the shares, and this can be accomplished by the next method.

Stock exchange introduction

When a private company has a large body of shareholders, it may decide to establish a market in the shares without going through the mechanics of making an issue. Where the shareholding body is at least 50 strong, the company can apply for a stock exchange introduction. Criteria similar to any public issue are applied and, if the application is successful, the company's shares can be bought and sold on the exchange after publicising the issue on a chosen date.

Stock exchange placing

This method is similar to a private placing, in that shares are placed with institutions, but after the issue a proportion is offered to the general public. This means that a stock exchange quotation must be sought and that a market in the shares is established subsequently. The Exchange does not favour placings as it wishes a wide market to be established in the shares and is concerned that the institutional investors and the subscribing public should enjoy the same status and privileges. However, the exchange accepts that a placing is a relatively cheap form of fund raising and is prepared to allow the use of such a method when the amount of the issue is small, usually less than £500,000 and when the public is offered at least 25 per cent of the total issue. Because of its cost advantages, a stock exchange placing is favoured by companies for relatively small new issues.

Public issue by prospectus

In this type of issue, all the equity offered for sale is sold to the general public. The issue must be well advertised and at a price that looks certain to ensure full subscription. The issue is accompanied by a prospectus in which the company sets out its recent financial record in detail, highlights its past growth and future potential and states the terms of the issue. With this information, investors are able to make judgements about the attractiveness of the price of the shares. The costs of this type of issue are high, but less so for larger companies, which frequently use this method.

The 'stag', or short term speculator, often plays a role in this type of issue. When making an issue, the company will wish to have it fully subscribed – that is, sell all the shares at the issue price. The issue may be underwritten – in other words, if any under subscription takes place, the underwriters will purchase the outstanding shares which have not been taken up by the general public. Merchant banks and other financial institutions associated with the issue do not wish it to be undersubscribed. This means establishing an issue price that takes account of the company's growth prospects, current earnings and asset base but is somewhat lower than the shares can be expected to command in a free market to ensure that all shares offered are applied for. The merchant bank must also set a price some days prior to the subscription date. In this interval the market may fall or rise and thereby change the attractions of the issue. Thus new issues are often underpriced as a precaution against failure, so encouraging the stags. Stagging can by symptomatic of an underpriced issue which tends to be costly for the company, in that a low price reduces the issue proceeds and the wealth of the original owners.

Offer for sale

An offer for sale is similar to a public issue by prospectus, but in this case the issuing house or merchant bank involved buys all the shares for sale and then offers them to the general public at a slight premium. This route is often convenient when the company making the issue is relatively unknown to the market. By buying the shares in the first place, the issuing house effectively attaches its name and reputation to the shares and this tends to enhance public confidence in the issue. Here too, the issue price tends to be on the low side, offering opportunities to the stag.

Tender

The tender is a mechanism used to avoid the problem of under- or over-pricing that takes place with public issues and offers for sale. Instead of setting an issue price, tenders are invited at or above a minimum price. From all the tenders it receives, the company sets a price which clears the entire issue, offering shares to all who have tendered above this price. To ensure the tender is cleared, the final issue price is set below the highest tender price. This method aims to obtain the maximum proceeds for the company and thus minimize the difference between the issue price and the share price after initial dealings commence.

At least one factor works against this; many subscribers to new issues are looking for capital gains, even if they are not stags; and they will subscribe at a price near to what they consider should be the offer price, rather than the ultimate market price. Stags can still operate if they assume the tender price will be at a discount on the eventual market price. They do so by tendering at an inflated price, relying on others to tender lower, so that they will be assured of an allotment at a lower price. However a company unwilling to cooperate with stags and also wishing to prevent large individual shareholdings may be unwilling to allot tenders in full. Althoug such factors tend to reduce the final price paid for the shares, several issuin houses feel that this method obtains a price above that achieved by an off for sale or issue by prospectus.

Choice of method of going public

A company must weigh up the costs of issue and the suitability of particul methods. Many companies prefer to use a merchant bank rather than brokerage firm or issuing house. Management should beware of aut matically choosing one kind of institution or another merely on th grounds of prestige. A wide variety of institutions should be approached for advice on the method of issue. In this way management will gain further insight into the advantages and disadvantages of using specific methods and institutions.

Costs of issues

Issue costs include administrative costs arising from the issue and underpricing. Administrative costs vary with the size of the issue.

Merrett, Howe and Newbould[1] found that issues below £100,000 are extremely costly and concluded that if possible a company seeking to make an issue below this amount should delay until it requires more finance and use instead the ICFC or a similar finance institution specializing in long term finance for private companies.

Between £100,000 and about £300,000 a stock exchange placing is the cheapest method. A £250,000 placing, for example, would typically cost (at 1976 prices) 14 per cent of the amount raised.[2] An offer for sale costs correspondingly more at these levels, but the differential is reduced with the size of the issue. Thus a £1 million offer for sale will cost about £80,000, or 8 per cent of the issue proceeds. The costs decline to about 4 per cent with issues in excess of £2.0 millions. It is only with issues of such a size or greater that the costs of an offer for sale are close to those of a placing. Some evidence of the relationship between issue size and costs is shown in Figure 13:1.

Public issues tend on average to cost less than an offer for sale and they are the usual vehicle for very large issues, where percentage costs are low. Tenders also appear to be less costly than offers, though at present only limited data are available.

Evidence on the discount between offer price and prices in first dealings is inconclusive and varies with each company. Tenders are designed to reduce the premium achieved on first dealings and in certain circumstances they appear to have done so. In others, the tender price was still substantially below the market price after initial dealings. Apart from tenders, the company sets the issue price, and hence the premium reflects the reliability of the estimate of future market price made usually by a merchant bank, perhaps ten days prior to first dealings, and the movements in the market during that period.

Tactics before going public

Several tactical decisions need to be made when making a public offering. It is now usual to have a minimum pre-tax profit of £400,000 before going public. Recent profit growth should have been favourable, and some indications are needed that the growth will be maintained for the foreseeable future. Assets should be revalued, so that the company provides the maximum information about its value. It has been shown by Sharpe and Walker,[3] in an Australian study, that asset revaluations can provide new information to investors and consequently increase share price.

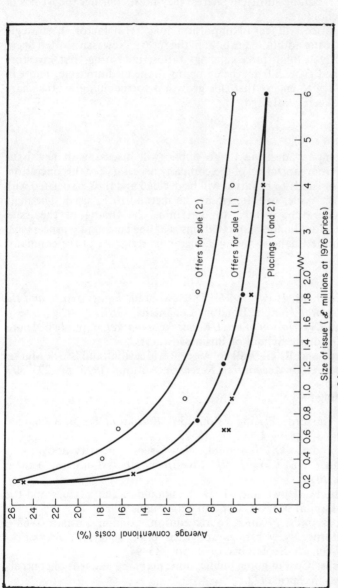

Figure 13.1   Conventional costs of issue

Sources:
(1) Fielding, Newson-Smith (1972). Based on 59 issues during 1969. Represented by ° and x.
(2) Merrett, Howe and Newbould (1967). Based on 391 issues during 1959–63. Represented by ° and x.

Thought should be given to the general state of the market, and the mood over new issues. Obviously, no one can predict the state of the market before the planned issue, but some flexibility should be allowed for moving the issue date backward or forward, depending on market developments. Once the issue has been made, the private company has changed into a very different animal, the public company. Even if the original owners stay in command by retaining sufficient shares, they must consider the wishes of the new shareholders.

The share price will be an important long term factor in strategic decisions requiring additional capital in the future. New issues often begin life with relatively high price-earnings ratios, indicating that investors expect sustained growth from the company in the medium term. Those in control must try to ensure that this growth is forthcoming, or the share price will be severely affected.

Summary

A private company desiring to go public will discuss with new issue specialists the reorganization of the company necessary for this operation. The amount of funds to be raised will be decided and this, associated with the costs of the issue, will determine the method to be used. The main tactical consideration is then to determine the timing of the issue. Management should understand that this is a time consuming process that involves both the financial and organizational structure of the company.

Notes

1 A. J. Merrett, M. Howe and G. D. Newbould, *Equity Issues and the London Capital Market*, London: Longmans, 1967.
2 E. Dimson, *Description of the UK new issue market*, unpublished note, London Graduate School of Business Studies.
3 I. G. Sharpe and R. G. Walker 'Asset Revaluations and Stock Market Prices', *Journal of Accounting Research*, Autumn, 1975. pp. 293-309.

Further reading

Sir Timothy Harford, 'Pricing a flotation', *Journal of Business Finance*, vol. 1, no. 1, Spring 1969, pp. 17-23.
M. E. Lehr and G. D. Newbould, 'New issues – activity and pricing performance 1964 to 1967', *The investment Analyst*, no. 18, October 1967, pp. 20-3.
A. J. Merrett, M. Howe and G. D. Newbould, Equity Issues and the London Capital Market, London: Longmans, 1967.
F. W. Paish, *Business Finance*, fourth edition, London: Pitman, 1968.
J. C. Van Horne, 'New listings and their price behavior', *Journal of Finance*, vol. 25, September 1970, pp. 783-94.
M. H. W. Wells, 'Cost of going public: time, planning and loss of control', *The Times*, 5 April 1972.

Appendix 13:1

Critical path of the work of an issuing house in connection with a flotation

Only the main steps are shown. An issue may involve the production of up to fifty documents. The time span can vary from two to nine months and is typically four months. No time scale is shown here but Appendix 13.2 gives a specimen timetable. Reproduced by permission of Industrial and Commercial Finance Corporation Ltd. (Appendix 13.1 continues on pp.190–2.)

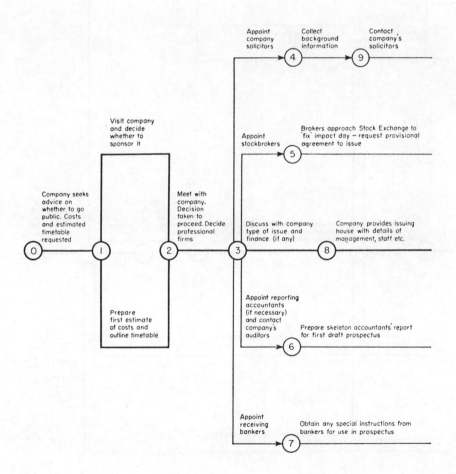

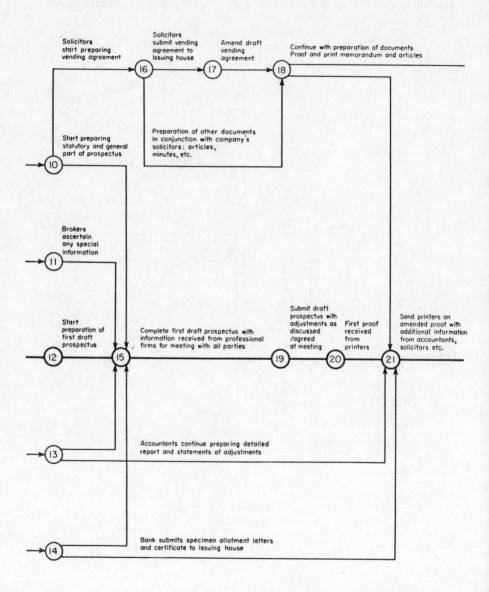

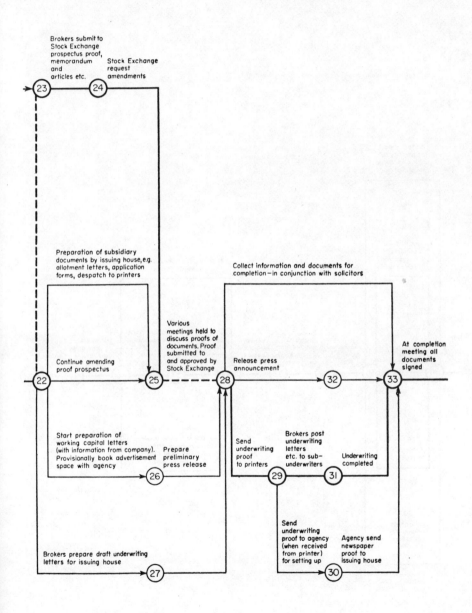

Brokers submit to
Stock Exchange
prospectus proof,
memorandum
and
articles etc.

Stock Exchange
request
amendments

(23)   (24)

Preparation of subsidiary
documents by issuing house, e.g.
allotment letters, application
forms, despatch to printers

Collect information and documents for
completion – in conjunction with solicitors

Various
meetings held to
discuss proofs of
documents. Proof
submitted to
and approved by
Stock Exchange

At completion
meeting all
documents
signed

Continue amending
proof prospectus

Release press
announcement

(22)   (25)   (28)   (32)   (33)

Start preparation of
working capital letters
(with information from company).
Provisionally book advertisement
space with agency

Prepare
preliminary
press release

Send
underwriting
proof
to printers

Brokers post
underwriting
letters
etc. to sub-
underwriters

Underwriting
completed

(26)   (29)   (31)

Send
underwriting
proof to agency
(when received
from printer)
for setting up

Agency send
newspaper
proof to
issuing house

Brokers prepare draft underwriting
letters for issuing house

(27)   (30)

continued

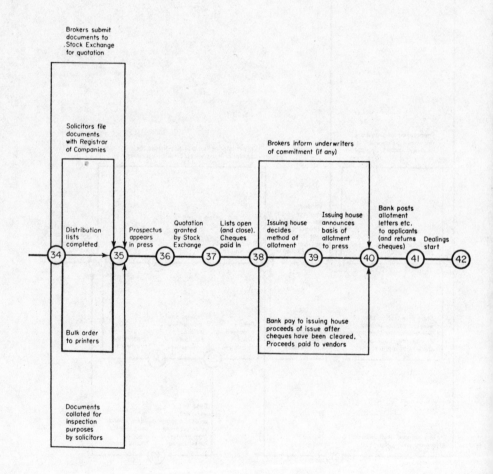

Appendix 13:2

Typical timetable for a flotation

Reproduced by permission of Industrial and Commercial Finance
Corporation Ltd

No. of weeks to opening of subscription lists	Date	Action
−16	Thursday 23 May	Meeting between directors of the company and the issuing house to discuss strategy and timing of a flotation. Reporting accountants and brokers instructed by the issuing house
−11	Friday 28 June	Meeting between directors of the company, the issuing house, reporting accountants, solicitors and brokers to discuss the flotation in the light of a first draft of the ten-year profit record and to consider a proposed timetable for the flotation
−9	Wednesday 10 July	First draft of the narrative section of the prospectus discussed by the company, the issuing house and solicitors
	Friday 12 July	First draft of prospectus to printers
−8	Wednesday 17 July	Meeting for company, issuing house, solicitors, reporting accountants, auditors, brokers to discuss first proof of prospectus. Second proof of prospectus incorporating a draft accountants' report to Stock Exchange for comments
−6	Thursday 1 August	Meeting for company, issuing house, solicitors, accountants, brokers to consider second proof of prospectus with Stock Exchange comments

No. of weeks to opening of subscription lists	Date		Action
–4	Monday	12 August	Meeting for company, issuing house, solicitors, accountants, brokers to consider third proof of prospectus and first proofs of application form, allotment letter and letter of acceptance
–3	Tuesday	20 August	Meeting for company, issuing house, solicitors, accountants, brokers to discuss further proofs of documents
–2	Thursday	29 August	Meeting for directors of company, issuing house, solicitors, accountants, brokers to prepare underwriting proofs and fix price subject to amendment on Monday morning
	Monday	2 September	Underwriting proof to printers, showing price
	Tuesday	3 September	Brokers post underwriting letters and proof to sub-underwriters
	Wednesday	4 September	Impact day
–1	Thursday	5 September	Advance notice of offer for sale appears in press. Completion meeting for all available directors of company (powers of attorney to be available for any absent directors), issuing house, solicitors, accountants, brokers. Capitalization issue effected. Contracts signed. Solicitors file documents with Registrar of Companies. Brokers deliver documents to Stock Exchange. Bulk order for offer document given to printers.
	Monday	9 September	Offer for sale advertised in press and distributed to banks

No. of weeks to opening of sub- scription lists	Date		
	Wednesday	11 September	Quotation granted by Stock Exchange
0	Thursday	12 September	Subscription lists open (10.00 a.m.) and close. (Striking price fixed if issue by tender)
	Friday	13 September	Subscribers' cheques paid into bank
	Wednesday	18 September	Letters of acceptance posted
+1	Thursday	19 September	Dealings in shares start on Stock Exchange
+4	Thursday	10 October	Last day for splitting
+4½	Monday	14 October	Last day for renunciation
+8½	Monday	11 November	Share certificates ready

14

The theory of capital structure

The use of debt in financing a firm's investment programme involves two kinds of financial risk: the risk that the firm will become insolvent and the risk that results from an increase in the variability of the earnings and dividend stream. The increase in earnings variability is due to the characteristics of debt; that is the interest payments constitute fixed charges which must be met by the company if it is to remain in business. Thus, the cost of such debt includes not only the explicit costs – the interest charges – but also a hidden or an implicit cost. This implicit cost derives from the increase in earnings variability and the consequent increase in the shareholders' required rate of return per £ of equity.

Consider the example of company X which has 100 shares outstanding. They are priced at £10 each on the stock market. Earnings are £100 for period 1, and there are no corporate or personal taxes (Figure 14:1).

Figure 14:1   Earnings of company X

Number of shares	100
Earnings before interest and taxes	£100
Earnings per share	£1

The company wishes to embark on a major investment costing £1,000 and expects to double earnings from £100 to £200 in perpetuity. It has a choice of financing the project's cost by an issue of 100 shares, or by issuing £1,000 of 8 per cent loan stock. Given the firm's forecast, earnings per share under the different methods of financing would be as in Figure 14:2.

Figure 14:2   Comparison between equity and debt financing for company X

	Equity financing	Debt financing
Number of shares	200	100
Debentures	—	£1,000
Earnings before interest	£200	£200
Interest charges	—	£80
	£200	£120
	£200	£120
Earnings per share	£1	£1.20

It appears that shareholders are significantly better off by using loan stock than by the issue of shares. If earnings from existing investments increase further, the interest charges will take a *decreasing* proportion of earnings and further improve the attractions of debt financing. However, if earnings do not reach management's expectations, then debt financing will take an increased share of the company's profits and earnings per share could be less than that prevailing under all-equity financing. For example, if profits reach only £120, earnings per share will be lower under debt financing (Figure 14:3). We have illustrated this effect graphically in Figure 14:4. Below a certain level of income, earnings per share will fall under the debt-financing alternative. The increased volatility of earnings caused by debt financing suggests that shareholders require increasing rates of return per pound of equity in order to compensate them for the change in risk.

Figure 14:3   Comparison between equity and debt financing at lower profit level

	Equity financing	Debt financing
Number of shares	200	100
Debentures	—	£1,000
Earnings before interest	£120	£120
Interest charges	—	£80
	£120	£40
	£120	£40
Earnings per share	60p	40p

Figure 14.4   Source of the implicit cost of debt

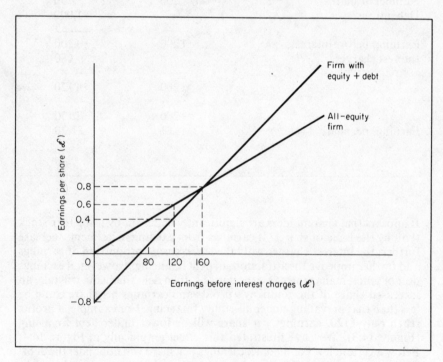

The question arises as to how we can quantify the increased risk of debt finance. We shall use the symbols and example of E. Solomon[1].

Initially, assume the following conditions:

1   There is no income or corporation tax.
2   Changes in capital structure can be effected immediately and there are no transaction costs.
3   The firm pays out all earnings in the form of dividends. The earnings are constant and continue in perpetuity.
4   The earnings streams of the two firms to be examined are the same in terms of business risk in the eyes of their shareholders.
5   Both business risk and the risk-free rate are constant over time.

The following three rates are used in the subsequent examples: the cost of debt

$$k_i = \frac{\text{annual interest charges}}{\text{market value of the debt}}$$

This assumes the debt is perpetual and consequently the cost is the straight interest rate or yield.

Similarly, the cost of equity is equal to the earnings yield:

$$k_c = \frac{\text{earnings available to shareholders}}{\text{market value of the ordinary shares}}$$

and therefore the weighted average cost of capital is,

$$k_o = \frac{\text{net operating earnings}}{\text{total market value of the firm (equity + debt)}}$$

This term k_o is a function of earnings before deduction of interest as a ratio of the total market value (debt and equity).

What are the effects on k_e and k_o of varying the amount of debt in the capital structure? Two approaches have been proposed by Durand[2]. The first is the net income approach.

Net income approach

Assume that firm A has a total capital requirement of £11,500. It has £3,000 in debt at 5 per cent interest, the expected annual operating earnings are £1,000, and the cost of equity, k_e, is 10 per cent. Under these conditions the value of the firm is £11,500 (Figure 14:5).

Now assume that another firm, B, which has the same capital requirements, earnings stream, and risk characteristics, uses £6,000 of 5 per cent debt finance; the difference of £3,000 is reflected in a consequent decrease in the amount of equity capital required (Figure 14:6).

Figure 14:5   Market value of firm A

Net operating earnings	£1,000
Interest	150
Earnings available to ordinary shareholders	£850
Equity capitalization rate (equivalent to P/E of 10), k_e	10%
Market value of the ordinary shares	£8,500
Market value of debt	3,000
Total market value of the firm	£11,500

Figure 14:6   Market value of firm B

Net operating earnings	£1,000
Interest	300
Earnings available to ordinary shareholders	£700
Equity capitalization rate, k_e	10%
Market value of the ordinary shares	£7,000
Market value of debt	6,000
Total market value of the firm	£13,000

For the first firm the weighted average cost of capital is 8.7 per cent ($k_o = 1,000/11,500 = 8.7\%$); for the second it is lower at 7.7 per cent ($k_o = 1,000/13,000 = 7.7\%$).

If firm A has 850 shares outstanding, the price of the ordinary shares would be £10 (£8,500/850). The firm B has only 550 shares outstanding (it has 300 shares – valued at £3,000 – less than A because it is using an extra £3,000 of debt) and therefore their market price is £12.73 (£7,000/550). It appears that firm B has been able to utilize low-cost debt finance and increase earnings per share, and, assuming that k_e is constant, reduce the weighted average cost of capital and increase the value of the company. (Figure 14:7).

Figure 14:7   Net income approach

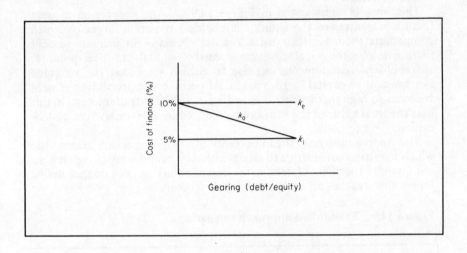

Clearly a firm would employ all debt under these assumptions.

The traditionalists' view of debt does not support this position, although it agrees fundamentally that the use of low-cost debt can change the market value of the firm. Traditionalists argue that, while firm B can achieve greater earnings per share and a high valuation through debt financing, this value will not be as high as that suggested by the net income approach because shareholders' required rate of return, k_e, rises when substantial amounts of debt are introduced into the capital structure. Take firm B again and assume that k_e rises from 10 per cent to 12½ per cent (Figure 14:8).

Figure 14:8   Market value of firm B if k_e rises to 12½ per cent

Net operating earnings	£1,000
Interest	300
Earnings available to shareholders	£700
Equity capitalization rate (equivalent to P/E of 8), k_e	12½%
Market value of ordinary shares	£5,600
Market value of debt	6,000
Total market value of the firm	£11,600

With 550 shares outstanding, the share price of the ordinary shares would be £10.18. Clearly, if k_e was below 12½ per cent, the share price would be greater.

This view is summarized in Figure 14.9. As the proportion of debt finance increases, so the equity shareholders require a larger return to compensate them for their increased risk. Initially an increase in debt finance lowers the weighted average cost of capital but after point *Y*, shareholders' requirements increase to such a level that the weighted average cost of capital k_o rises again. At point *X*, the proportion of debt becomes so high that lenders demand an increased rate of interest. In this case the total value of the firm can be reduced by an excessive use of debt capital.

This approach stresses the importance of an optimum capital structure which the firm should strive to attain, although proponents of the view do not quantify the effect of debt on the cost of equity, k_e, nor do they define how a firm reaches an optimum capital structure.

Figure 14:9   Traditional approach to gearing

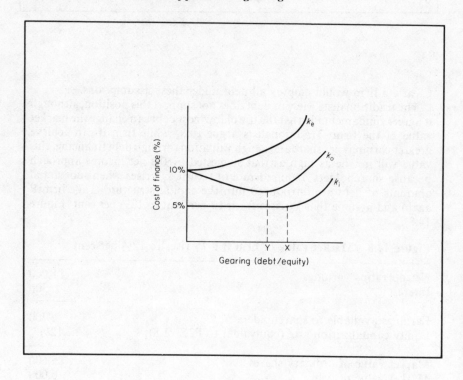

Net operating income approach

This approach, frequently associated with Modigliani and Miller (M-M), suggests that the method of financing will not affect the overall valuation of the firm. If debt is used, any benefits in its low explicit cost will be wholly and exactly offset by an increase in the shareholders' required rate of return, k_e (Figure 14:10). It is clear from this approach that the market price of the ordinary shares will not be changed by different methods of financing because the shareholders will be indifferent to this.

Figure 14:10   Net operating income approach

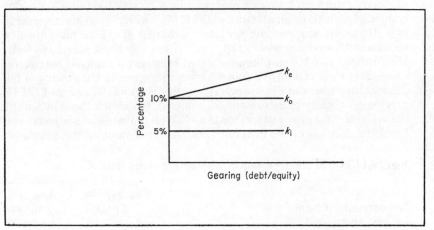

Modigliani and Miller have offered important theoretical support for this approach[3]. They make a number of important assumptions:

1 Capital markets are efficient so that information flows freely and perfectly to all investors, who are considered to act rationally. In addition, there are zero transaction costs.
2 There are no corporate income taxes (an assumption to be relaxed subsequently).
3 The investor or an investment institution is able to borrow at the same interest rate as the company, given the same asset base.
4 There are no bankruptcy costs.

Modigliani and Miller contend that changing the capital structure cannot affect shareholders' wealth. They examine two firms within a risk class – that is, with identical business risk. Modligliani and Miller argue that even if the capital structure of the two firms is different, the presence of arbitrage will ensure the values of the two firms remain equal.

Consider the two firms described in Figure 14:11[4]. Company A is totally ungeared while company B has £30,000 in 5 per cent debentures.

The valuation of the two firms is different. However, Modigliani and Miller conclude that the situation cannot continue, for arbitrage will equate the values of the two firms. They argue that investors in company B will be able to obtain the same monetary return by investing in company A, without any increase in financial risk, and will accomplish this with a smaller investment outlay. In order to do this, they will sell their shares in B, driving the share price down, and purchase those in A, pushing the share price up. Suppose an investor owned 1 per cent of company B, with a market value of £772.72. Modigliani and Miller argue that he would sell his shares at that price, borrow £300 at 5 per cent, which is equivalent to 1 per cent of B's debt capital, and buy 1 per cent of A's shares for £1,000. His monetary return on his new investment in A totals £100 (10% × £1,000) compared with his original return of £85 (11% × £772.72) on his investment in B. However, he must now pay interest charges of £15, so his monetary return on A's shares is now exactly equal to that obtained previously in B. His financial risk has not been increased because his personal borrowing constitutes 1 per cent of A's debt which is equivalent to the gearing of his original investment in B. However, his outlay is only £700 against £772.72 previously. Clearly investors will sell shares in B and buy those in A until the weighted average rates of return (k_o) are equated. As a result the financing decision of the firm does not affect the value of the company.

Figure 14:11   Market valuation with and without debt

	Company A	Company B
Net operating income	£10,000	£10,000
Interest on debt		1,500
Earnings available to ordinary shareholders	10,000	8,500
Equity capitalization rate	0.10	0.11
Market value of the shares	100,000	77,272
Market value of debt		30,000
	100,000	107,272
Implied overall capitalization rate (k_o)	10%	9.3%
Ratio of debt to equity	0	38.8%

The Modigliani-Miller thesis relies heavily on the ability of the investor or his agent to borrow and engage in this arbitrage process. Providing a group of investors can and does engage in this process, the thesis holds. Some investment trusts are allowed to use debt and can borrow at the corporate rate. However, transaction costs may impede the arbitrage process.

We have explained how, under specific assumptions, the valuation of the firm will not vary with changes in capital structure on a pre-tax basis. However, in an article in 1963[5], M-M agreed that if interest on debt was deductible for tax purposes and if the tax deduction could not be obtained by shareholders, then an advantage is conferred on debt financing. How does this advantage affect the value of the company? Let us assume that a company expects annual earnings totalling X in perpetuity and pays interest on riskless debt at a rate i and that the debt is perpetual. The corporate tax rate is T and the amount of debt borrowed in D. The value of the company is simply

$$V = \frac{X}{R} + TD$$

where R is the shareholders' required rate of return (ungeared) and,

$$TD = \sum_{t=1}^{\infty} \frac{T(i\,D_t)}{(1+i)^t}$$

$$= \frac{Ti\,D}{i}$$

$$= TD$$

The introduction of taxes and the tax deductibility of interest payment changes the attitudes of proponents of all three views towards debt financing. For simplicity we shall examine the implications of taxes on the NOI Approach and the M-M proposition only.

Under M-M's assumptions the advantage of debt financing is dependent only on the tax rate and the amount or proportion of debt in the capital structure. The implication is that the advantage of debt increases linearly with changes in the debt to equity ratio, and therefore management will be encouraged to increase debt to 99.9% of the firm's capital structure! Although management would not care to take this course of action because of the risk and consequent costs of bankruptcy the fact is that most banks would not permit such high levels of gearing. It is too simple to put such limitations on debt capacity down to financial conservatism. It appears that there is an inverse relationship between risk and gearing in the financing of real assets. There are therefore other reasons for such limitations:

1   Shareholders may not be able to borrow at the same interest rate as the companies in which they invest. Therefore the arbitrage process will not go as far as Modigliani and Miller suggest. However, this is not an important criticism, as the shareholder can obtain personal gearing by investing in investment trusts which hold shares in other companies. Investment trusts borrow on behalf of shareholders and can do so at competitive rates. Thus these trusts will ensure the effectiveness of the arbitrage process.
2   Lenders may not be prepared to finance a company's investment programme totally by debt, even at relatively high rates of interest

because of the cost of monitoring the loan.

3   Even if it is in the shareholders' interests to finance their investments entirely by debt, it may not be in the interests of the management and employees. Management may be unwilling to take a substantial risk of loss and liquidation even if the prospective returns to shareholders warrant such risks. This is simply because of the personal impact of liquidation.

The above analysis assumes that none of the tax benefit (TD) can be obtained by the shareholder or his financial intermediary through home-made borrowing. The UK now operates an imputation tax system where the firm acts in part as an agent for the revenue authorities in collecting shareholders' taxes. The effect of the system is to substantially eliminate the double taxation of earnings and dividends. The Corporation Tax rate T (52 per cent) is deemed to include a shareholders' tax on dividends at the standard rate of 35 per cent. Thus for the corporation with net operating income X and paying interest I the total tax paid by company and shareholders is,

$$(X-I)T$$

if shareholders pay the standard rate of tax. For simplicity, assume that all earnings are paid out as dividends. Now, what taxes would the shareholders pay if they purchase the shares of an ungeared company with the same operating income and borrow the money to do so? Let us assume again that the investors' marginal tax rate is equal to the standard rate of 35% and that all earnings are distributed. The total tax paid by the company and shareholders is

$$XT - .35I$$

where it is assumed the investors can borrow at the same rate as the company and that interest charges are deductible from their income for tax purposes. Thus the difference in taxes between corporate and home-made leverage is simply,

$$I(T - .35)$$

With a corporate tax rate of 52% the advantage of debt financing under the UK system is only 17 per cent. If we assume that a firm can raise debt finance equivalent to one half of the present value of the project, then the advantage of debt is equivalent to an additional 8½ per cent of the project's present value. This advantage of debt financing does not change significantly with alterations in the shareholder's marginal tax rate. We have, of course, assumed that the shareholder can borrow and obtain a tax deduction on the interest charges. This is not a necessary assumption if financial intermediaries, such as investment trusts, are able to obtain the same tax deduction. Clearly, if the shareholder or his financial intermediary *cannot* obtain those tax benefits on interest charges, then the advantage of debt financing is much higher, that is IT (Interest charge × Tax Rate).

Conclusion

It is important to appreciate that the cost of debt is lower than the cost of equity because the interest is tax-deductible. This suggests that the manager should use as much debt finance as possible. It must be recognized that often he will not wish to take such risks, or transaction costs will not allow him to. With these qualifications in mind, we turn to a method of examining the risk and returns of accepting an investment programme and financing it with a given combination of debt and equity that may satisfy management's risk preferences.

Notes

1   E. Solomon, *The Theory of Financial Management*, New York: Columbia University Press, 1963 chs 8–9.
2   D. Durand, 'The cost of debt and equity funds for the business', in *Management of Corporate Capital*, edited by E. Solomon, New York: Free Press, 1959.
3   F. Modigliani and M. H. Miller, 'The cost of capital, corporation finance and the theory of investment', *American Economic Review*, vol. 48, June 1958, pp. 261–97. Reprinted in *Foundations for Financial Management: A Book of Readings*, edited by J. Van Horne, Homewood, Ill: Irwin, 1966, pp. 367–405.
4   M. H. Miller and F. Modigliani, The cost of capital, Corporation Finance and the Theory of Investment: Reply' *American Economic Review* (Sep. 1959) pp. 656–668.
5   F. Modigliani and M. H. Miller, 'Corporate Income Taxes and the Cost of Capital: A Correction', *American Economic Review*, 53, June 1963, pp. 433–43.

15

Determining the level of debt and equity in the capital structure

The theory of capital structure has been described. This chapter looks at the relationship and relative advantages of different types of capital. It explains a number of frequently-used financial ratios for calculating debt capacity and their usefulness. Finally, it shows the importance of conducting sensitivity analysis in order to highlight the impact of changes in estimated revenues and costs on the firm's ability to service the burden of debt.

Cost relationships

An examination of the relative explicit costs of various forms of capital gives the following ranking, with the cheapest first:

1 Debt
2 Preference capital
3 Ordinary capital

Despite the above ranking, a detailed survey[1] highlighted two interesting features.

1 The average dividend yield on ordinary shares was approximately 4½

per cent, whereas the average return on debentures was approximately 7½ per cent.

2 Preference capital showed a 7 per cent return whereas debt gave 7½ per cent.

Superficially, the first suggests that ordinary shares give a lower return than debt. The explanation lies in the full composition of the shareholders' return. Not only does the shareholder receive a dividend payment, but his shares may be expected to appreciate in value over time, providing capital gains; the final return is a composite of the dividend yield and the capital gains from an increasing share price. However, debentures are eventually repaid at or near par, and so capital appreciation in debentures is very limited, assuming interest rates do not change. Thus, in calculating the full return to the different shareholders, the capital-growth element provides the ordinary shareholder with a better return than the debenture-stock holder receives. The latter is compensated by the lower risk characteristics of debentures, compared with the ordinary shares of the same company.

The second phenomenon noted was that preference capital showed a 7 per cent return, whereas debt gave 7½ per cent. This again appears to contradict earlier analysis of the ranking of cost. There are basically three reasons why market forces in preference shares produce this phenomenon.

First, there is some potential capital appreciation involved in convertible preference shares. Conversion takes place when the price of the ordinary share exceeds the conversion price.

Not all preference shares are convertible, but enough to cause some distortion in a composite average figure, which is the basis of the survey.

Second, preference shares are also liable to some capital appreciation, even if they are not convertible into equity. Investors may buy hoping that their holding will be converted into debt on favourable exchange terms. Tax aspects have encouraged firms to retire preference shares and issue debt, and in so doing the company usually increases the coupon rate on the new debt compared to the old preference stock. As long as this increase is not too large, the company will still be better off in after-tax terms.

Third, some institutional investors obtain a higher return on preference shares than debt; in practice the risk characteristics of the two are similar, but preference dividends are paid from after-tax income, this being known as franked income (when received by institutions or companies) whereas debt interest is serviced from pre-tax funds. Institutional investors who pay their own corporation tax can claim relief on franked income to avoid double taxation, and thus the effective return on holdings of preference shares is substantially greater than on a debenture holding. This factor has encouraged certain institutional investors to hold preference shares.

Choice of capital structure

In discussions on capital structure, attention is normally focused on the balance between debt capital and equity capital, as this usually accounts for a major proportion of total corporate funds. In Chapter 14 it was shown that in pre-tax terms debt is not cheaper than equity, but that after tax it has a lower cost.

Given Modigliani and Miller's assumptions, this lower cost implies that the firm should borrow as much as is possible. We mentioned in the previous chapter a number of reasons why banks would not usually lend a high proportion of debt to firms, and indeed why the firm would not wish to borrow an excessive amount. The bank is confronted with significant costs of monitoring its customer's affairs when large amounts of debt are borrowed. As the risk of bankruptcy increases so does the cost of monitoring. One suspects at some point these transaction costs become so great that they exceed the tax benefits of debt. Similarly, the costs of bankruptcy are significant to managers and employees of the company and even if the bankruptcy risk is compensated by high expected returns, the consequent personal costs of liquidation may deter management from borrowing all they can.

Debt capacity

Various methods for calculating the debt capacity of a particular company are used by banks and these are outlined below. They are not mutually exclusive.

Traditional debt ratios

The most widely used ratio is the debt to equity ratio based usually on the book (accounting) value of assets and liabilities in the balance sheet. One computes the amount of debt (usually the nominal value in the balance sheet) and divides by the net worth or shareholders' equity. The net worth is the difference between the total assets and liabilities of a company.

Balance sheet as at 31 December 1976

Bank Overdraft	75	Fixed Assets	100
Net Worth	75	Current Assets	50
	150		150

It can be seen in the above balance sheet, that the debt to equity ratio is 1 to 1 or 100 per cent. An alternative is to compute the debt to debt plus equity ratio, which, in this example would be 50 per cent. Lenders prefer this ratio because it relates the loan to the value of real or tangible assets in the balance sheet. It is frequently stated that the ratio ignores the earning power of the company and its ability to repay interest and principal. This is true to some extent, but then the banker may wish to base his loan on the break-up or liquidation value of the company. He reasons that the cash flow stream of the company is often unique to the existing management; if earnings deteriorate the value of such goodwill approaches zero. The banker requires assets that have alternative uses to the existing ones. Alternative uses for the assets and a reasonable secondary market provide the critical reason why banks do not often accept the value of intangible assets in lending decisions; they are not easily transferred to another party and their value is difficult to assess.

The bank usually bases the debt ratio on the book value of assets, and it will usually try to obtain an up-to-date value for the tangible assets. Many financial analysts wonder why the bank does not use the market value of the firm in computing the debt to equity ratio. This assumes that the shares are quoted on the stock exchange. However, the market value of such shares reflects the profitability of existing investments and future growth opportunities. Thus there is a goodwill element in share price. Frequently the bank will not wish to lend funds on future investments which are but a twinkle in the eye of management.[2] They wish to lend on current investment opportunities and the value of tangible assets appears a reasonable rule of thumb.

We do not wish to give the impression that banks will not lend on cash flow forecasts. Rather, we wish to emphasise the difference between the economic value of an asset reflecting the unique source of the cash flows and the liquidation value which represents the price of the asset in alternative uses. The proportion a bank will lend of the market value of the assets depends upon the risk of the asset. By risk we mean the possibility that the value of the asset will vary from one period to another. For example, if the asset is risk free, then a bank should be prepared to lend 100 per cent of the value of the asset. If the lender defaults the bank can sell the asset at a certain price without fear of loss. However, if the asset's price can be expected to vary over time, then a bank will lend a sum less than the full value of the asset. How much less is a function of the asset's risk and the costs of frequently valuing the asset. The banks have developed, through experience, various debt to equity ratios for assets of different classes of risk. The borrower must also appreciate that the debt ratios used by the bank often appear conservative. The reason is simply that the higher the risk of the loan the more monitoring or control is required. Further, increased monitoring requires a more sophisticated or analytical lending officer. Thus there are good reasons, those of transaction costs, to limit borrowing below a level that often appears permissible to the borrower.

A second ratio used by banks is interest cover which reflects the company's ability to pay interest charges out of current reported earnings.

$$\text{Interest cover} = \frac{\text{Earnings before interest and taxes (EBIT)}}{\text{Interest charges}}$$

Inevitably, such a ratio provides only a rule of thumb. It is generally accepted that for a manufacturing company a ratio of four and above is acceptable. However, this ratio varies with the industrial sector. The drawbacks to such a ratio are easy to see. It is based usually on reported earnings rather than cash flow. The firm's ability to repay its interest charges is determined by its current and expected cash flows rather than the operating profits reported in each accounting period. It is also difficult to define precisely the right cover as this should be related to both current and future expected cash flows and the risk attached to those earnings. Clearly, if the cash flows are certain then a cover of no more than one is required. Indeed, in a particular period cash flows may be permitted to be less than one (interest charges would be carried forward) providing future cash flows compensate for deficits in previous years. Even if cash flows are risky over time, lenders may be willing to accept that the cover will be low (even less than one) in some years and high in others.

Finally, interest cover, by definition, does not include the repayment of the principal. It must be expected that the earnings from the investment will repay the loan and the repayment term should be equal to or less than the life of the firm's investment set. In addition, the pattern of net cash flows may determine the size and timing of the repayments.

$$\frac{\text{interest} + \text{annual repayment}}{\text{cover}} = \frac{\text{EBIT}}{\text{interest} + \text{annual repayment} \times \frac{1}{(\text{I-T})}}$$

where T = corporation tax rate

This ratio informs us how many times interest charges and annual repayment of principal are covered by current earnings before interest and taxes. As loan repayments are not tax deductible they are paid out of after-tax profits. Thus, they must be grossed-up to be made consistent with the interest component of this ratio.

It is widely accepted that such a ratio should exceed two for a manufacturing company, but once again the timing of earnings in terms of the trade cycle and the specific risk of the industry must be taken into account. Clearly, during a recession, firms in particular industries may be making losses due to their high fixed costs and the sensitivity of sales to the general economic climate. In this sense the firm has a high level of operating gearing or leverage. The bank must take a view over the life of the investment rather than estimate cover for a particular year.

This ratio is based upon earnings rather than cash flow. Industries where the level of fixed costs is high will probably make substantial depreciation provisions. This reduces reported profits but does not reduce cash flow. In prosperous times capital expenditures are made for both replacement and expansion and these may be greater or less than the depreciation provision. One would expect them to be greater at the top of the trade cycle and less near the bottom. On reflection one could adjust this ratio, adding back depreciation and subtracting capital expenditures.

$$\text{Interest} + \text{repayment cover} = \frac{\text{EBIT} + \text{depreciation} - \text{capital expenditure}}{\text{interest} + \text{repayment} \times \dfrac{1}{(1-T)}}$$

One may then ask why not adjust this ratio for changes in working capital levels or dividend disbursements? Once we make such adjustments we are simply arriving at a cash flow based calculation. Thus we would show the surplus or deficit in cash each period after payment of interest and principal. It may be argued that even if the repayment of principal is not made until the end of the loan period an annual amount could be substituted assuming the loan was repayable over the life of the investment set.

Even if we can obtain or construct the expected cash flow profile, we have not yet decided how risky the company is, the rate of interest to charge on the loan and the kind of covenants or restrictions to incorporate into the loan agreement. Of course we can develop further rules of thumb. Initially the cash flow must cover interest and repayments over the life of the loan by a satisfactory margin. To some extent we can test for the necessary margin through sensitivity analysis. We can construct a number of scenarios and see what happens to net cash flows under reasonably pessimistic assumptions. This may help to-identify how risky the loan is and the interest rate that should be charged. In addition it also serves to reinforce the need for properly constructed covenants in any loan agreement that will enable the bank to recall its loan or apply further restrictions when the company's profits deteriorate. Such covenants also permit the bank to obtain financial information and monitor financial performance. In addition, where performance deteriorates beyond a certain point the loan may be renegotiated or recalled. Such clauses may prevent the company from making dividend distributions or capital expenditures without the permission of the bank.

Financial ratios and prediction of failure

Companies and lenders use financial ratios to decide the maximum amount of debt they should carry and as a predictor of financial distress. We have listed a number of reasons why these ratios are of limited value. W. H. Beaver in several pieces of empirical work,[3], has tested the proposition that these rules reflect underlying events that affect the solvency position of the company and that they can be used as surrogates for the probability of failure. He constructed a sample of failed and non-failed firms and tested the predictive powers of a group of ratios in forecasting financial distress. He found that most of the ratios tested were not good predictors of financial failure, including the current ratio and the acid test. However, he found that three ratios (Figure 15.1) had a high predictive power. But, as Beaver states 'this result does not imply that the market is ignoring the data nor that one can beat the market by using the financial ratios.'

Figure 15.1   Market prices, financial ratios, prediction of failure

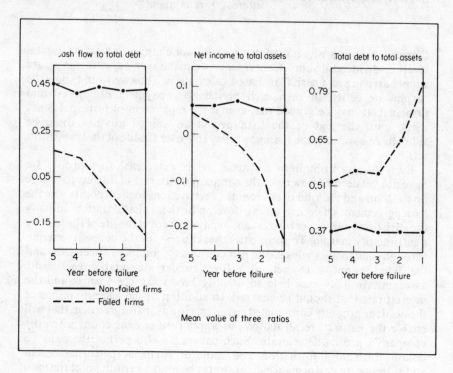

Financial planning

If a company raises debt, it should be able to invest the funds and earn a return. Forecasts of earnings must include the return on the invested funds arising from the financing in the projected earnings stream.

In explaining and utilizing gearing and the coverage ratios so far one important aspect has been neglected: the sensitivity of these measures to changes in sales volume and revenue and costs.

In Figure 15:2 a company has predicted earnings per share, average coverage ratios and sources and uses of funds on the basis of specific forecasts of sales prices and costs. The company proposes to raise debt finance based on these forecasts.

Figure 15:2   Forecast of financial position

	1973	1974	1975	1976	1977	1978
Earnings per share (£)	4.5	5.2	6.4	7.3	8.7	9.8
Interest cover	10.3	12.1	15.4	19.0	22.3	25.1
Interest plus loan repayments	6.1	6.9	8.1	9.3	10.6	11.5
Annual sources less uses (£ million)	34.8	–15.3	–20.0	–2.0	2.9	7.5
Cumulative sources less uses (£ million)	34.8	19.5	–0.5	–2.5	0.4	7.9

How would variations in sales volume and costs affect the forecast coverage ratios and sources and uses of funds? The following assumptions are made:

1   Any changes in sales and cost projection take place after 1974.
2   The dividend payout ratio remains constant.
3   One-quarter of the costs are fixed and three-quarters are variable.
4   Annual repayments calculations include profits before deduction of depreciation.
5   Any cumulative funds-flow deficit is financed with 6 per cent short-term debt.

Figure 15:3 shows how decreases in sales volume of 5 and 10 per cent would affect the earnings per share, coverage ratio and sources and uses of funds.

A decline in sales volume of 5 per cent has a relatively limited effect on earnings per share and debt coverage. This is due to the high variable element in the cost structure. Nor does it lead to a serious cash crisis. Likewise a 10 per cent fall in sales does not significantly worsen the cash position.

Figure 15:4 shows the effect of a 15 per cent increase in cost levels. It is apparent that an increase in operating costs presents serious problems to the company. Earnings per share fall heavily; interest cover disappears because of losses; and cash outflows exceed cash inflows. Management must ask itself if such an increase in operating costs is likely to occur, other things being equal, and, if so, what level of debt can be accepted. It may decide, in view of the risks, to finance its investment programme entirely by equity or by a mixture of debt and equity. Thus it is important, if not a prerequisite, in estimating debt capacity to subject projections of profits to a comprehensive sensitivity analysis of the important variables.

Figure 15:3   Effect on forecasts in Figure 15:2 of decreases in sales volume

	1973	1974	1975	1976	1977	1978
5% decrease in sales volume						
Earnings per share (£)	4.5	5.2	5.4	6.2	7.4	8.4
Interest cover	10.3	12.1	13.2	16.3	19.3	21.8
Interest plus loan						
repayment	6.1	6.9	8.0	9.2	10.5	11.4
Annual sources less uses						
(£ million)	34.8	−15.3	−21.0	−3.1	1.7	6.2
Cumulative sources less uses						
(£ million)	34.8	19.5	−1.5	−4.6	−2.9	3.3
10% decrease in sales volume						
Earnings per share (£)	4.5	5.2	4.5	5.1	6.2	7.1
Interest cover	10.3	12.1	11.0	13.6	16.3	18.4
Interest plus loan						
repayment	6.1	6.9	7.9	9.0	10.3	11.2
Annual sources less uses						
(£ million)	34.8	−15.3	−22.0	−4.2	0.5	4.8
Cumulative sources less uses						
(£ million)	34.8	19.5	−2.5	−6.7	−6.2	−1.4

Figure 15:4   Effect on forecasts in Figure 15:2 of a 15 per cent increase in costs

	1973	1974	1975	1976	1977	1978
Earnings per share (£)	4.5	5.2	−1.1	−1.2	−0.4	−0.4
Interest cover	10.3	12.1	neg	neg	neg	neg
Interest plus loan						
repayment	6.1	6.9	2.7	3.1	4.0	4.2
Annual sources less uses						
(£ million)	34.8	−15.3	−27.5	−10.5	−6.1	−2.6
Cumulative sources less uses						
(£ million)	34.8	19.5	−8.0	−18.5	−24.6	−27.2

*Although in some years interest cover disappears, interest plus sinking fund cover can still be more than 1, because profits are included before deduction of depreciation.

Such a sensitivity analysis must reflect discrete economic scenarios of the future. The specific assumptions behind the changes in the economy, industry and firm must be stated. Such changes may affect the firm's products in isolation or other competing firms in the same industry; it is important to distinguish between relative and unique changes in the prices of the firm's inputs and outputs.

Summary

The amount of debt a company should employ in the financing of its investment programme is a function of both internal and external factors. They include both the magnitude of the asset base and the level of the earnings stream; they will define the ability of the company to meet its interest charges and debt repayments. However, the acceptable ratio of earnings to the level of debt is also a function of the risk preferences of the management and of the company's earnings stream. Historical data and sensitivity analysis on important variables in the cost and revenue stream will aid the company and the lender to achieve a perspective in deciding how much debt the company should employ given their risk preferences.

Notes

1   K. Midgley and R. G. Burns, *Business Finance and the Capital Market*, London: Macmillan, 1969.

Yields in February 1977

Consols 2½%	12.22%
20-year Government securities	11.61%
Commercial and Industrial Preference shares	13.26%
Ordinary Shares (All-share Index)	5.81%

2   S. C. Myers, 'Determinants of Corporate Borrowing', *Working Paper*, 875-76, Sloan School of Managements, MIT, September 1976.
3   W. H. Beaver, 'Market Prices, Financial Ratios and the Prediction of Failure', *Journal of Accounting Research*, 6 (Autumn 1968), pp. 179-92.

Further reading

E. Altman, 'Corporate Bankruptcy Potential, Stockholder Returns, and Share Valuation', *Journal of Finance*, 24 (December 1969), pp. 887-900.
G. Donaldson, 'New Framework For Corporate Debt Policy', *Harvard Business Review*, (March-April 1962).
G. Donaldson, 'Strategy for financial emergencies', *Harvard Business Review*, vol.47, no. 6, (November-December 1969) pp. 71-9.

16

Valuation of the firm and cost of capital

A company has various sources of finance, including equity capital and debt capital. This chapter examines a simple model of company valuation and explains the concept of the cost of capital of the firm.

Valuation of the firm

The shareholders' return from an equity holding in a particular company is equal to the discounted sum of the dividends received and the capital gains realised on the sale of the shares. This can be expressed using a simple model which assumes that the shareholder pays P_0 for a share now, holds it for five years and receives a dividend D annually. If he sells the share at the end of year 5, the expected rate of return for the shareholder would be found by solving for r in the following equation:

$$P_0 = \sum_{t=1}^{5} \frac{D_t}{(1+r)^t} + \frac{P_5}{(1+r)^5} \qquad (16.1)$$

where the Greek capital letter sigma, Σ, means the sum of.

Thus if the shareholder predicted the dividends the market expected for the next five years and the price in year 5, he would be able to find the annual compound rate of return, r, that would be received on his investment, P_0

As the reader will recognize, r is merely the internal rate of return on the investment.

Suppose now that the shareholder holds the share in perpetuity or, as we shall express it, to infinity (represented by the sign ∞). Then the expected rate of return, r, is given by:

$$P_0 = \sum_{t=1}^{\infty} \frac{D_t}{(1+r)^t} \qquad (16.2)$$

Although an investor who holds his stock for a short period may be primarily interested in capital gains rather than dividends, the person to whom he expects to sell the stock will be assumed to be making his purchase for the dividends and capital gains he expects to receive.

Since companies give their shareholders a return in the form of a dividend, the price of a share will be a function of expected dividends. The capital gains the shareholder expects as part of his return are a function of the expected growth in dividends, over time, which is reflected in a rise in share price over time.

The price of a share is determined in the marketplace by the expectations of buyers and sellers. A particular investor expects a return, r, but this may be different from the market's or marginal investor's required rate of return or discount rate for the expected dividend stream. If k_e denotes the market's required rate of return or discount rate given the current share price P_o, and the expected dividend stream, D, then equation 16.2 may now be rewritten as follows:

$$P_0 = \sum_{t=1}^{\infty} \frac{D_t}{(1+k_e)^t} \qquad (16.3)$$

So far, no assumptions have been made about the size of dividends. As many companies reinvest part of their earnings, they may be assumed to increase dividends at a constant growth rate, g. Thus equation 16.3 may be rewritten:

$$P_0 = \sum_{t=1}^{\infty} \frac{D_0(1+g)^t}{(1+k_e)^t} \qquad (16.4)$$

In this equation dividends are growing by a constant annual percentage to infinity. This model assumes that dividends grow perpetually at one rate. If this is correct, and k_e is greater than g, then it can be shown that

$$P_0 = \frac{D_0(1+g)}{k_e - g}$$
$$= \frac{D_1}{k_e - g} \quad \text{where } D_1 = D_0\,(1+g) \qquad (16.5)$$

If k_e is less than g, then the price of the stock will be infinite; this is clearly unrealistic. With this simple formulation, a company's share price can be determined if the current dividend per share, the expected growth in dividends, and the marginal investor's required rate of return are known.

Assume that a company pays a current dividend amounting to 50p, and that an investor believes it will grow at 5 per cent per year in perpetuity. If the investor's required rate of return is 10 per cent then:

$$P_O = \frac{0.5}{0.10 - 0.05}$$

$$P_O = £10$$

The previous model can be adjusted to incorporate a period of rapid growth followed by a period of normal growth. Assume a company's period of rapid growth, g_1, lasts for 5 years, and thereafter the rate is much lower, g_2, the equation will be:

$$P_O = \sum_{t=1}^{5} \frac{D_0(1 + g_1)^t}{(1 + k_e)^t} + \sum_{t=6}^{\infty} \frac{D_5(1 + g_2)^{t-5}}{(1 + k_e)^t} \qquad (16.6)$$

This model has been described by B. G. Malkiel as being particularly applicable to rapidly growing companies. It may easily be adjusted to take into account both corporation and personal income taxes.

These models have described the value of the firm in terms of the dividend stream. This value could have been expressed similarly in terms of earnings or free cash flow; the value of the company would not be different under either specification. However, it is important to appreciate that the value of the firm consists of two types of assets: existing investments and growth opportunities. The share price of a company, or a value imputed to the firm if it is unquoted, is equal to future cash flows from the current set of investments plus some value for the firm's ability to find profitable new projects. The shareholder is buying in part an option on the profits of investment opportunities which have not yet been undertaken or possibly even planned. Why is it important to distinguish between these two types of investments? Clearly, one is riskier than the other. Intuitively, investors recognize that growth firms in the same industry are higher risk than non-growth firms. The reason is simply that the value of a growth firm reflects in part some future investment opportunities which are by their very nature high risk. Valuing such future investment opportunities is beyond the scope of current theory. However, it is a useful device to separate the cash flows from these two types of investments and accept that the cash flows from future investments are of a higher risk; consequently, a higher discount rate should be used to estimate their net present value.

Cost of capital

Cost of capital may be defined as the minimum return an investor would be willing to accept for investing funds in a particular project. This concept of a required rate of return applies just as much to the purchase of loan stock in a company as it does to the purchase of equity. The rate of return will depend on the form the investment takes (loan, equity, preferred stock, convertible etc.) and the risk attached to the particular company.

Investors' required rate of return

An investor in loan stock will require a return for surrendering the use of his money for a particular period and an added amount for the risk that the company may default on interest payments or repayment of the loan stock. This explains the difference between yields on government and corporate loans. The difference is due to the possibility, however small, that a firm will go bankrupt and put the investor's capital at risk.

Equally, an investor's required rate of return for a share will be determined in part by the return that could be achieved in other forms of investment and by the risk inherent in the particular business or firm. An investor could hardly be expected to require a lower after-tax return on a blue-chip share if he could obtain a higher return on the fixed-interest securities of the same company where the risks of losing money are significantly lower. In this context, returns include dividend payments and expected capital gains.

The minimum rate of return that an investor will accept for a particular investment can differ from that which he hopes to receive. He may invest with the hope of making a 15 per cent return after tax, but he may still invest if he requires only 12 per cent. In this case his cost of capital or minimum required rate of return will be 12 per cent. Of course, if a large proportion of investors expect 15 per cent and their required rate of return is only 12 per cent new investors will buy the particular security and bid up the price. If the price rises, then the rate of return falls, and this process will continue until the rate of return reaches 12 per cent. This is analogous to movements in the price of a bond. If an irredeemable bond is issued at £100, with a coupon rate of £8 per £100, and the market price remains at £100, then the yield is 8 per cent. One could express this in another way, and say that the bondholder's required rate of return on this investment is 8 per cent. However, suppose interest rates on other bonds of similar risk changed, and the investor's required rate rose to 9 per cent. Then the price must fall to increase the bond yield from 8 to 9 per cent. In other words, the price would fall to about £89.

It is important to appreciate that the price of these securities is determined in a highly competitive market, where knowledgeable buyers and sellers compete with one another. It is against this background that economists have found that such a market exhibits a high degree of efficiency. Evidence suggests that unless an investor has important information unavailable to analysts or specialists, the price ruling in the market should be taken as the fair or competitive one. It is tempting to claim that a security is undervalued, or even overvalued. In a competitive market such a statement should be treated with scepticism unless the individual has insider information or he is an 'angel of prophecy'.

Cost of equity capital

A company will use several sources of capital for financing its investment programme: equity, debt, preference stock and convertibles. This section reviews the cost of new equity. New equity is distinguished from retained earnings (that is, the portion of earnings not distributed to shareholders) which will be discussed later.

The cost of equity is defined as the minimum rate of return required by the equity investors or shareholders, or the minimum rate of return that a company must earn on an investment to leave the current share price unchanged (assuming it has no debt capital). The cost of equity is a function of three elements: the riskless rate of interest, business risk and financial risk.

The riskless rate

The riskless rate is essentially compensation to investors for giving up the use of their money for a period of time. This rate can be represented by the Treasury bill rate (3- or 6-month government securities) which was approximately 13 per cent early in 1977 (or 9 per cent after tax, assuming a personal tax rate of 35 per cent for investors). The principle here is that an investor surrendering money for a period of time will require a minimum return before any risks will be considered. One pound now is obviously worth more than one pound three months hence, and it is this concept of time value of money that is the essence of the riskless rate. This rate reflects expectations as to the rate of inflation, and, as inflation has increased, so have interest rates and consequently shareholders' required rates of return.

Business risk

The second important element in a firm's cost of capital is business risk. This is the risk that earnings will be volatile due to changes in the firm's markets, the industry and the economy at large.

If we take a mining company as an example, a number of risks are immediately apparent. Funds invested in exploration might not yield sufficient quantities of ore to justify commercial development. Development costs, usually spread over a period of years, might change due to inflation or difficulties encountered in developing the mine. Even when the mine is developed, the price of the metal could be different from that expected. In addition, many minerals are mined in developing countries where political instability might pose the threat of sudden changes in royalty and tax agreements and the possibility of outright expropriation. These risks appear formidable and all are embraced by the concept of business risk. It is understandable that an investor in such an enterprise should require a premium for the high risk compared to either fixed-interest securities, or, for example, a share in a long-established retail store which has a history of stable earnings.

A study by Brealey and Dimson[1] estimated the premium for risk received by shareholders at 9.1 per cent. The average rate of shareholders' personal taxes at the margin is not known with any degree of accuracy. However, if we assume it is around 35 per cent, then we can estimate a risk premium of around 6 per cent after both corporate and personal taxes. Given a risk-free rate of interest of 9 per cent after taxes, we can obtain a total cost of equity of 15 per cent for the average firm on the London Stock Exchange.

Inevitably, these results are subject to a number of qualifications. The risk premium was computed using past share price and dividend data for the period 1919–72. We are assuming that over the long term shareholders have received what they have expected. In addition, we have averaged risk over time. It is possible that the risk premium changed significantly in 1972 but this will have had little effect on the results reported by Dimson and Brealey. Secondly, we have assumed a personal tax rate of 35 per cent. There is some reason to believe that the market may be dominated by institutions and individuals with lower tax rates; a lower tax rate than 35 per cent would increase our estimate for both the risk free rate of interest and the risk premium. Finally, the risk premium reflects financial risk as well as business risk. However, since the proportion of debt in the capital structure for the average company was only around 15 per cent the risk premium may be taken as reflecting the financial risk of the average firm.

Of course, the cost of equity will not be the same for every company. As we showed in an earlier chapter, firms that have a higher risk than the average will have a higher cost of equity capital, simply because shareholders expect greater returns for more risk.

Finally, the cost of equity is a useful guide for estimating the discount rate for an individual project; but it is only a guide. If the firm consisted of only one type of project the discount rate for the firm might be exactly right for the project. However, a firm frequently consists of projects of differing risk and the cost of equity for the firm is simply an average of the discount rate of the individual projects, weighted by their present values. A discussion of project risk and the choice of discount rate is to be found in Chapter 7.

Cost of debt capital

Debt may be contracted in a number of forms: overdrafts, short, medium and long term. The cost of debt or of a bond is the interest paid and this is usually termed the 'coupon'.

The cost of a bond will not be the straight coupon rate if the bond is issued below par. For example, the cost of a 9 per cent bond issued at £95, which is to be redeemed for £100 in the future, is 9½ per cent approximately. The cost will be affected by the date of maturity and the frequency of interest payments. This rate may be called the 'explicit' or direct cost of debt. The explicit cost is a function of interest rates prevailing, the life of the bond, and the status and the risk profile of the borrower.

Prevailing interest rates are influenced by a multitude of factors both national and international. Not only have they increased over the years, but fluctuations have been substantial. The life of the debt is important, since usually the longer the maturity of the bond, the higher the interest rate. The status or risk characteristic of the borrower will also affect the interest rate paid. Risk here is related to the possibility of default.

Bonds also have an implicit cost, discussed under the cost of equity and which is represented by financial risk. This cost is the increase in the shareholders' required rate of return due to the presence of debt in the capital structure. Thus the cost of debt can be more than simply the interest rate paid to the holders of loan stock.

Cost of retained earnings

It should be apparent to both managers and investors that retained earnings carry a cost. If a firm is unable to reinvest earnings profitably, they should be distributed to shareholders. The cost of retained earnings is the shareholders' required rate of return, k_e, adjusted for the personal taxes the shareholder would have to pay if the earnings were distributed. E. Solomon[2] has argued that the company is able to reinvest retained earnings in the securities of other companies with the same risk profile as the original company. This concept of reinvestment in external securities suggests that the cost of retained earnings is the same as new equity. For simplicity, transaction costs have been ignored; if they were included the cost of new equity would increase relative to retained earnings.

Weighted average cost of capital

The capital budget of a firm is financed by both debt and equity; and the cost of capital to the firm, or the required rate of return to be earned on the total capital budget, is a function of the costs of finance employed and the relative proportions of each used. As an example, consider a company whose existing capital structure is given in Figure 16.1. The capital structure is based on the market value of the equity and the long-term debt outstanding, and not on the book value.

Figure 16.1 Weighted average cost of capital

Source of finance	Amount	Cost after taxes	Weighted cost
Share capitalization	£10 million	15%	10%
Long-term debt	£5 million	8.3%	2.7%
			12.7%

One might say that the weighted average cost of capital of the firm was 12.7 per cent. The cost of debt was arrived at by deducting 1.7 per cent from the 10 per cent interest rate on loan stock. The 1.7 per cent corresponds to the tax advantage to debt that cannot be obtained by shareholders; the tax advantage of debt is discussed in Chapter 14. The cost of equity was estimated using the methodology outlined in Chapter 7. Thus the company must earn 12.7 per cent on all its assets to secure a 15 per cent return for the equity shareholders. The firm's cost of capital, or the minimum return it must earn from its investment, is less than the required rate of return of its equity shareholders, because of the presence of lower-cost sources of finance in the capital structure. The low cost of debt is entirely due to the tax subsidy provided by the government.

It is important not to associate a specific source of finance with a particular project; the mere fact that the company has exhausted existing funds and raises debt to finance a project does not mean the incremental cost of capital is the cost of debt. Suppose another project had to be financed by equity, or that the timing of the projects were reversed. It is clear a project could be made profitable or unprofitable depending on the time of the year. Obviously, leaving aside the different risk characteristics of individual projects, the weighted average cost of capital must apply to all projects in the capital budget, and it must be based upon a target capital structure. When account is taken of a project's risk characteristics, the discount rate may be above or below the weighted average cost of capital. Indeed, if the project is entirely risk-free then the minimum required rate of return for the project will be the risk-free rate. The average cost of each source of finance should not be confused with the expected return required for an individual project with a specific risk. This is of course the central theme of Chapter 7.

Project life and the weighted average cost of capital (WACC)

If we assume that a company consists only of projects within one risk classification and that the cash flows of those projects are perpetuities, then the WACC can be used as the appropriate discount rate. That is, using our previous example, we would discount the project's after tax cash flows (but always without deducting interest charges) at 13 per cent. We have, however, made an important qualification; that is, that the project's cash flows are constant through time and that the project is infinite (i.e. a perpetuity). Suppose a project has a finite life and the cash flows are not constant over time? It should be apparent that the present value of the tax benefits of debt depend upon the pattern of cash flows over time and the project life, as well as the risk of the investment opportunity. The WACC assumes that the value of the tax benefits is constant over its entire life.

Stewart Myers[3] proposes that the tax benefits from corporate debt should be estimated and discounted separately from the operating earnings stream of the project. The tax benefits are computed each period during the project's life and their size is determined in part by the magnitude of the present value of the operating stream in each future period and the proportion of debt that can be raised.

This formulation explicitly recognises

1 That the tax benefits are a function of the life of the specific project. The usual weighted average cost of capital formulation assumes perpetuities.
2 That projects have different debt capacities and therefore different tax benefits per £ of present value cash flow.
3 That debt capacity and therefore tax benefits are not constant throughout the project's life, since the present value of the project declines with time and the cash flows are not constant through time.

The example in Figure 16:2 demonstrates how the tax benefits can be derived from the operating cash flow stream of the project. In period one, for example, the present value of the net operating cash flows total £100. The discount rate used is based upon an all-equity financed project. Given the particular amount of debt that can be raised on the value of the project for one period, the tax benefit is derived. Thus, at the beginning of period one the present value of the net operating cash flows is £100. It is possible to raise £50 (of one year debt) on the basis of that present value. The interest charges on that debt total £7.5 for the year and since the tax advantage to debt is 17 per cent (explained in Chapter 14), the value of the financing advantage is £1.27. The tax benefit is estimated for the second period on the basis of the present value of the future cash flows in periods two, three and four. This process is repeated for each of the remaining periods. The tax benefits are subsequently discounted at the pre-tax interest rate.

Figure 16:2 Estimation of the present value of a project's tax benefits from debt financing

Period	1	2	3	4
Net operating cash flows	23	46	23	23
Present value of the project in a period	100	80	40	20
Proportion of debt in the capital structure	.5	.5	.5	.5
Interest rate	.15	.15	.15	.15
Tax rate advantage to corporate gearing (T*)	.17	.17	.17	.17
Value of the tax benefit	1.27	1.02	.51	.25

Present value of the tax benefits $= 2.33$[2]

1 The present value of the project is obtained by discounting the net operating cash flows at a rate that reflects all-equity financing.
2 This is only a close approximation because the additional tax benefits create debt capacity, and therefore could increase the present value of the tax benefits.

Summary

In this chapter, we have discussed a commonly used valuation model. In addition, we have described how the cost of equity for the average firm can be estimated. The tax subsidy for debt finance confers an advantage on this source of financing compared with equity financing. Debt financing does lower the cost of finance for a project and this advantage can either be incorporated into the discount rate (estimating the WACC) or into the project's cash flows. If the project has a finite life and uneven cash flows over time, we would recommend the use of Myers' adjusted present value approach.

Notes

1 R. Brealey and E. Dimson, 'The Excess Return on U.K. Equities: 1919–1975', Unpublished Manuscript, London Graduate School of Business Studies, 1976
2 E. Solomon, 'Measuring a Company's Cost of Capital', *Journal of Finance*, vol. 28, October 1955, pp. 240–52.
3 S. C. Myers, 'Interactions of Corporate Financing and Investment Decisions — Implications for Capital Budgeting', *Journal of Finance*, March 1974, pp. 1–25.

Further reading

D. Durand, 'Growth stocks and the Petersburg paradox', *Journal of Finance*, vol. 12, September 1957, pp. 348–63.
E. F. Fama, 'Efficient Capital Markets: a Review of Theory and Empirical Work', *Journal of Finance*, May 1970.
M. A. King, 'Taxation and the Cost of Capital', *Review of Economic Studies*, January 1974.
R. C. Stapleton and C. M. Burke, 'Taxes, The Cost of Capital and the Theory of Investment.' A Generalisation to the Imputation System of Dividend Taxation. *Economic Journal*, December, 1975.
James C. Van Horne, *Financial Management and Policy*, fourth edition, Englewood Cliffs NJ: Prentice-Hall, 1977.

17
Dividend policy

This chapter examines the role of a company's dividend policy. Initially it is concerned with the dividend payout ratio, which determines the level of retentions and thus the contribution of shareholders' funds to the investment programme of the firm. We then discuss the evidence for determining whether dividends are weighted differently from retentions in the mind of the shareholder and how companies should pursue a rational dividend policy.

Dividend payout ratio

A company should reinvest its earnings if the prospective returns are greater than its shareholders' cost of capital or required rate of return. Changes in dividend policy should reflect the company's investment opportunities. However, dividend policy can change in this way only if shareholders are indifferent to distinctions between dividends and capital gains.

If capital markets are competitive, and there are no taxes, no transaction or flotation costs, then investors would be indifferent to the level of dividend payout[1] (for a proof see Supplement 17:1). Any reduction in dividends would lead to a greater reinvestment of retained earnings and an equivalent increase in capital gains. Company operations in this situation would not be affected by the dividend payout ratio, because if retentions were insufficient to finance the company's investment programme, a rights issue could be made. If the dividend paid was insufficient for the shareholder's income requirements, then he could sell a proportion of his holding to compensate for inadequate income. Similarly, if the dividend paid was in excess of his income requirements, he could reinvest the surplus in the company's shares. This argument has been given rigorous support by Modigliani and Miller[1]. They claimed that in a competitive capital market shareholders could always reinvest surplus income or sell part of their capital in order to consume. Whether such income was received in the form of dividends or capital gains *was mere packaging*.

It has been argued that, under conditions of uncertainty,[2] the shareholder is not indifferent to the split between dividends and retentions (the profitable reinvestment of retained earnings increases the share price). This is because dividends are more certain than capital gains. It is believed that shareholders prefer to reduce uncertainty and hence are prepared to pay a higher price for a share that offers a greater current dividend compared to one of the same risk class that offers a lower dividend. Thus the rate of return required by shareholders would rise with the percentage of earnings retained, or, put another way, a shareholder would prefer a company that pays high dividends to one that pays low dividends, other things being equal. On this basis the cost of retentions would increase, the greater the retention rate.

Associated with this argument is the fact that dividends have an effect on share price because they communicate information about the company's profitability. If a company has had a stable dividend payment policy and this policy is altered, shareholders could interpret this as a change in management's expectations of the future and the share price may adjust accordingly; for example, a reduction may be construed by the shareholders as indicating management's pessimistic view of the future, rather than greater investment opportunities. If there is stability in dividend payment, investors may rely upon dividends as predictors of what is to come[3]. However, it can be argued strongly that management should be able to persuade shareholders that lower dividends – that is, greater retentions – will lead to a more profitable investment policy and will benefit future earnings and dividends. If shareholders accept this, the share price will not fall as a result of such a change in dividend policy.

Under the UK tax rules before April 1973, the rate of capital gains tax for individuals was a maximum 30 per cent but a shareholder's income-tax rate could be much greater than 30 per cent. Shareholders with a high marginal tax rate would prefer low dividend payout and high capital gains. Moreover, if income is provided in the form of capital gains, tax is deferred until the shareholder actually sells his securities. Thus, there is a strong bias in favour of capital gains as opposed to dividends, and this bias favours the retention of earnings[4]. Under these circumstances, the choice between the shareholder reinvesting a part of his dividends and the company distributing a lower proportion of earnings is of consequence; the differential in tax rates may encourage companies to retain and invest more. It should be noted that since April 1973, under the imputation system, although there is less bias between capital gains and dividends, capital gains will still be favoured by taxpayers with high marginal tax rates because the tax liability is postponed until the shares or securities are sold.

A survey of the proportion of income received as dividends *vis-à-vis* capital gains in the USA showed a tendency for people with high incomes to get a much higher proportion of their income from capital gains than those with low incomes, suggesting that people with high incomes tend to favour shares with a low dividend payout ratio (see Figure 17:1).

The introduction of flotation costs would give a company a preference for retentions. If a company's dividends are such that it has to go to the capital market to raise funds, then for each £1 paid out as dividend, the company will receive less than £1 through external financing because of flotation costs. Furthermore, the smaller the size of the issue, the greater the flotation costs as a percentage of the funds raised.

The preference for retentions is reversed if transaction costs are involved in the sale of shares. If dividends are insufficient to provide for a shareholder's income requirements, then he will have to sell a proportion of his holding. On the sale of these shares, he will have to pay brokerage fees, stamp duty, etc. For a small sale, the brokerage fee can be quite significant. These fees may make some investors more interested in dividends than in capital gains.

Figure 17:1   Dividends in 1959 in the USA as a percentage of realized long-term capital gains by income class

Adjusted gross income ($)	Dividends as a percentage of net long-term capital gains (%)
Under 10,000	376
10,000–50,000	223
50,000–100,000	186
100,000–200,000	144
200,000–500,000	85
500,000–1,000,000	61
Over 1,000,000	70
All incomes	186

Source: R. A. Brealey, *Security Prices in a Competitive Market*

Empirical studies

If dividends are relevant then there will be an optimum policy that will maximize shareholders' wealth. In the simple model of the previous section, a shareholder would be indifferent as between dividends and retentions. However, a preference for current income, and the occurrence of transaction costs, favour dividends, whereas the differential tax rates for capital gains and flotation costs favour retentions. Obviously no straightforward statement can be made, as there are reasons for preferences either way and it is necessary to examine the empirical evidence.

Most studies on share price movements suggest that the dividend payout does affect the value of the firm. Graham and Dodd[5] concluded that a dollar of dividends has four times the average impact on share price as a dollar of retained earnings. Several other studies[6] have shown that the impact of dividends on share price is greater than that of retentions, although the size and difference varies considerably from industry to industry and from year to year. However, surveys of investors' opinions suggest the reverse. Friend and Parker[7] found that investors who say a change in corporate earnings would influence their investment decision outnumbered by 3:1 those who would be influenced by a change in dividends. In a later survey Merrill Lynch[8] found that not only did the majority of the respondents place capital appreciation at the head of their list of objectives, but the emphasis placed upon it varied according to their income.

The evidence of the effect of dividends and retentions on share price is inconclusive.

Distribution of company profits

The connection between changes in dividend rate and changes in the share price should become somewhat clearer if the factors that lead to a company altering its dividend could be identified. Many reasons are given by companies for profit appropriation. What factors motivate a board to pay out a particular dividend? Why not more or less or none at all?

A study by Dobrovolsky[9] established:

1 A clear pattern of corporate preference for profit retention.
2 A time lag in the response of dividends to a change in profits.
3 Some differences between the policies of large corporations as opposed to medium- and small-sized corporations.

Similar conclusions were drawn in a later study by Florence[10].

How does management decide a payout policy? Some help on the question was provided by a series of interviews with the management of 28 companies[11] which reviewed established rules of behaviour that govern the amount of profit paid out as dividend. They were as follows:

1 Dividends are always considered in terms of annual periods.
2 Given the financial results of the company and the existing circumstances, the board first asks itself if the existing dividend should be changed. Thus, built into the decision-making process is a heavy reliance on what has been done before, especially last year.

3 If the answer to 2 is negative, then an amount equal to last year's dividend is paid and the decision process is complete. If, however, it is thought desirable to change the dividend, the board then addresses itself to how much this should be. Here management seeks to avoid making any changes in dividend rates which might have to be reversed in a year or two.

The company's first concern was with regard to the absolute amount of earnings to be distributed rather than the proportion which should be retained for financial investments. Two-thirds of the companies said they had a target payout ratio. However, the interviews provided no indication of how this was determined. The fact that the present dividend was made with reference to the previous year's dividend implied that boards feel that shareholders prefer reasonably stable income and react adversely to dividend reduction.

According to the survey, companies adopt a target payout ratio that they apply to current earnings. If dividends were adjusted each year to attain this target level, the payment would be the target ratio times the current earnings, and the difference in dividend would be this figure less the previous year's dividend.

$$\text{dividend change} = \text{target ratio} \times \text{earnings} - \text{previous dividend}$$

However, the interviews suggested that companies adopted only a proportion of this indicated change, thus incorporating a safety factor. Therefore:

$$\text{dividend change} = \text{safety factor (target ratio} \times \text{earnings} - \text{previous dividend)}$$

In addition, there may be a tendency for dividends to drift upwards even when earnings are stable, so that:

$$\text{dividend change} = \text{annual drift} + \text{safety factor} \times \text{(target ratio} \times \text{earnings} - \text{previous dividend)}$$

Recently R. A. Brealey[12] fitted US data to this equation. When the equation was fitted to 1920–41 data, it was found to be successful in explaining a large part of the movements in dividends during this period and the values for annual drift, the safety factor and target payment were all plausible. However, for 1942–60 data, an unreasonably high target ratio was obtained. The explanation suggested for this outcome was that increased depreciation allowances had encouraged companies to raise the target payout ratios during this period.

Summary

Evidence from empirical studies that dividends are considered more important than retentions is inconclusive.

If shareholders do have a preference for dividends, then this must be balanced against the company's investment opportunities.

In the final analysis the company should seek to ascertain the opinions of shareholders and this may aid management in determining shareholders' needs and their reaction to a change in policy.

Supplement 17:1 In perfectly competitive capital markets, the level of dividends does not affect investors

The Modigliani-Miller hypothesis is that the effect of dividend payments on shareholders' wealth is offset exactly by other means of financing. This is based on the following assumptions:

1 Perfect capital markets in which all investors are rational.
2 An absence of flotation costs.
3 Transaction costs are zero.
4 No taxes.
5 A given investment policy for the company.
6 Absolute certainty by every investor as to future investments and profits of the company.

When a firm has made a decision to invest it must decide whether to pay for the investment by retaining earnings or to pay dividends and sell new shares to the amount of these dividends to finance the investment (or a combination of the two). Modigliani and Miller's suggestion is that the sum of the discounted value per share, after the dividend has been paid and external financing has been carried out, is the same as the discounted value before payment of the dividend.

The market price of a share at time 0 is defined as equal to the present value of the dividend paid at the end of the year plus the price of the share at the end of the year. Therefore,

$$P_0 = \frac{1}{1+r}(D_1 + P_1)$$

(17.1)

Where:

D_1 = dividend at the end of the year
P_1 = share price at the end of the year
r = discount rate for capitalization of the firm
P_0 = market price per share at time 0.

If n is the number of shares at time 0, and m is the number of additional new shares sold at time 1 for P_1, then:

$$n\mathrm{P}_0 = \frac{1}{1+r}(nD_1 + nP_1)$$

which may be written

$$n\mathrm{P}_0 = \frac{1}{1+r}\left[nD_1 + (n+m)\mathrm{P}_1 - m\mathrm{P}_1\right] \tag{17.2}$$

The total amount of new shares is:

$$mP_1 = I - (X - nD_1) \tag{17.3}$$

Where I = total new investments during period 1
X = total new profit of firm for the period.

Substituting for mP_1 from equation 17.3 into equation 17.2:

$$n\mathrm{P}_0 = \frac{1}{(1+r)}\left[(n+m)P_1 - I + X\right] \tag{17.4}$$

Since D_1 does not appear in equation 17.4 and since X, I, $(n+m)P_1$ and r are assumed to be independent of D, Modigliani and Miller conclude that the current value of the firm is independent of its dividend policy – that is, shareholders are indifferent to distributions and retentions.

Notes

1   M. H. Miller and F. Modigliani, 'Dividend policy, growth, and the valuation of shares', *Journal of Business*, vol. 34, 1961, pp. 411–33. Reprinted in *Foundations for Financial Management: A Book of Readings*, edited by J. Van Horne, Homewood, Ill: Irwin, 1966, pp. 481–513.
2   M. J. Gordon, 'Dividends, earnings and stock prices', *Review of Economics and Statistics*, vol. 41, May 1959, pp. 99–105; J. Lintner, 'Optimal dividends and corporate growth under uncertainty', *Quarterly Journal of Economics*, vol. 78, February 1964, pp.49–95.
3   J. E. Walter, *Dividend Policy and Enterprise Valuation*, Belmont, Calif: Wadsworth, 1967.
4   E. J. Elton and M. J. Gruber, 'Marginal stockholder tax rates and the clientele effect', *Review of Economics and Statistics*, vol. 52, February 1970, pp. 68–74.
5   B. Graham and D. L. Dodd, *Security Analysis: Principles and Technique*, third edition, New York: McGraw-Hill, 1951. B. Graham, D. L. Dodd and S. Cottle, *Security Analysis: Principles and Technique*, fourth edition, New York: McGraw-Hill, 1963.

6   M. J. Gordon, in *Review of Economics and Statistics*, vol. 41, pp. 99–105.
7   I. Friend and S. Parker, 'A new slant on the stock market', *Fortune*, vol. 54, September 1956, pp. 120–4.
8   Merrill Lynch, Pierce, Fenner and Smith, *Annual Report 1959*, p. 4.
9   S. P. Dobrovolsky, *Corporate Income Retention 1915–43*, New York: National Bureau of Economic Research, 1951.
10 P. S. Florence, *Ownership, Control and Success of Large Companies; An Analysis of English Industrial Structure and Policy 1936–1951*, London: Sweet & Maxwell, 1961.
11 J. Lintner, 'Distribution of incomes of corporations among dividends, retained earnings, and taxes', *American Economic Review*, vol. 46, May 1956, pp. 97–113.
12 R. A. Brealey, *Security Prices in the Competitive Market*, Cambridge, Mass: The M.I.T. Press.

Further reading

C. A. Barker, 'Evaluation of stock dividends', *Harvard Business Review*, vol. 36, no. 4, July–August 1958, pp. 99–114.
C. A. Barker, 'Price changes of stock-dividend shares at ex-dividend dates', *Journal of Finance*, vol. 14, September 1959, pp, 373–8.
J. A. Brittain, *Corporate Dividend Policy*, Washington, DC: The Brookings Institution, 1966.
P. G. Darling, 'The influence of expectations and liquidity on dividend policy', *Journal of Political Economy*, vol. 65, June 1957, pp. 209–24.
S. P. Dobrovolsky, 'Economics of corporate internal and external financing', *Journal of Finance*, vol. 13, March 1958, pp. 35–47.
I. Friend and M. Puckett, 'Dividends and stock prices', *American Economic Review*, vol. 54, September 1964, pp. 656–82. Reprinted in *Foundations for Financial Management: A Book of Readings*, edited by J. Van Horne, Homewood, Ill: Irwin, 1966, pp. 535–61.
M. J. Gordon, 'Optimal investment and financing policy', *Journal of Finance*, vol. 18, May 1963, pp. 264–72. Reprinted in *Foundations for Financial Management: A Book of Readings*, edited by J. Van Horne, Homewood, Ill: Irwin, 1966, pp. 526–34.
A. A. Robichek and S. C. Myers, *Optimal Financing Decisions*, Englewood Cliffs, NJ: Prentice-Hall, 1965.

PART FOUR
ACQUISITIONS AND
MERGERS

18

An introduction to merger strategy and company valuation

Chapter 18 reviews the benefits of mergers to shareholders, and discusses stock market efficiency and the role of corporate strategy in acquisition appraisal. It also critically examines the traditional approach to the valuation of acquisition candidates. Chapter 19 examines more sophisticated valuation approaches. Chapter 20 discusses the financing question and the role of particular institutions.

Reasons for mergers

There are many purported reasons for mergers. Horizontal mergers – that is, the acquisition of a competitor in the same line of business – increase market share and reduce competition in one stroke, while vertical mergers – those with a supplier or customer – both strengthen the company's competitive position and may enable it to diversify. Such mergers are in some way less risky than internal projects, since they bring immediate cash flows with no gestation period, established products and an experienced management team. In addition, synergestic benefits can arise, where two firms can achieve more in combination than their individual parts. These benefits can occur, for example, through increased market power, economies of scale, combined marketing and distribution networks, reduction of administrative and other overheads and in the areas of finance, management and technology. Alternatively, mergers can be defensive, either to prevent offers from other companies for either partner, or to make the combined company less attractive for a takeover by another party. No doubt 'fashion' and 'follow my leader' play a part.

Merger analysis is complicated, as it is difficult to compare the performance of a company after a merger with the record it might have achieved without the expansion. Nevertheless, studies by Newbould[1] and Kitching[2] indicate a 'failure' rate of over 50 per cent. Why do so many mergers fail? The authors provide some generalised conclusions. Strategic factors may be over-emphasised in a merger, because by their very nature they are difficult or impossible to value. Post-merger problems, such as physically combining two separate companies, are often acute and underestimated by management. In addition, inadequate financial analysis can lead to excessive prices being paid by the acquirer, with the result that the share price falls substantially as the market perceives the worth of the company more accurately.

Recent empirical work

Recent empirical work both in the United States[3,4] and in the United Kingdom[5] has concentrated on examining the gains/losses to acquiror and acquiree shareholders and on the efficiency of the capital markets in anticipating mergers and allocating the gains between the two parties. The conclusions from these studies are summarized below:

1 Shareholders in acquired companies have enjoyed abnormal returns prior to the completion of the merger. Abnormal returns are defined in terms of dividends and capital gains after adjusting for movements in the market and industry and the risk relative to the individual securities.
2 During the same period prior to the merger, shareholders in acquiring companies do not appear to have experienced significant positive abnormal returns.
3 Stock market prices began to anticipate mergers on average about three months before the mergers were publicly announced in the UK, and as much as eight months in the US.

The first two conclusions are consistent with the hypothesis that competition among acquiring firms will cause the value of expected benefits from merging to be paid to the shareholders of the firm being acquired. In the case of the UK study which was based upon a sample of mergers in the breweries and distilleries sector during 1955-72 the results, which are summarized in Figures 18:1 and 18:2, showed shareholders in acquired companies enjoying abnormal returns averaging 23 per cent during the three-month period prior to the merger. Since the acquiring companies made a return that at least compensated them for the time value of money and the risk of the investment as shown in Figure 18:2, there were clear net gains from merging. These results are broadly in line with those of Halpern and Mandelker in the US. The third conclusion suggests that stock markets do anticipate mergers and this supports the proposition that markets respond quickly to available information.

Figure 18:1   Acquirees' abnormal returns near times of mergers

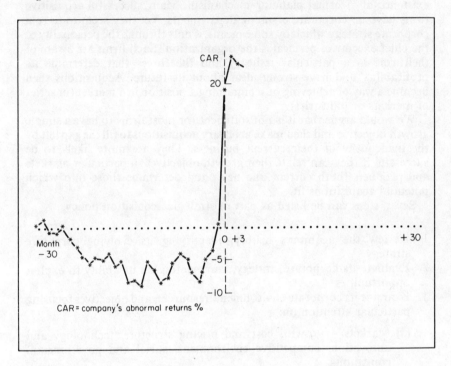

CAR= company's abnormal returns %

Figure 18:2   Acquirors' abnormal returns within 2½ years of mergers

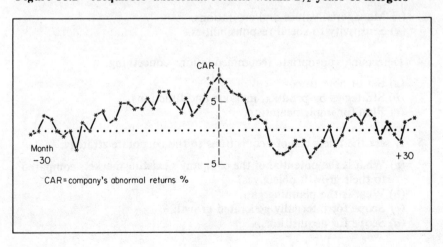

CAR= company's abnormal returns %

Role of corporate strategy

It is not our purpose here to outline the objectives of corporate planning
nor indeed to suggest that a prerequisite for successful acquisitions is the
existence of a formal planning mechanism. Many successful acquisitive
firms have no corporate planning departments. Yet they seem to have a
corporate strategy which by some means, if only through the personality of
the chief executive, permeates the organization. Such firms are aware of
their role in a particular industry and the forces that determine its
profitability and have strong ideas about its future. Acquisitions then
become a way of achieving or maintaining a position in a market (or series
of markets or industries).

We would argue that it is not sufficient for most firms to have a simple
growth objective and then make arbitrary acquisitions to fill the gap left by
the inadequacy of their current business. They are more likely to be
successful if they can relate their growth objectives to particular markets
and products (both current and new) and determine those into which
potential acquisitions fit.

Seven steps can be listed as part of strategic acquisition policy:

1   Review the acquirer's history, identifying its evolving corporate
    strategy.
2   Evaluate its corporate strategy, commenting on its ability to exploit
    opportunities.
3   Examine its corporate environment, resources, and objectives focusing
    particular attention on:

    (a) Markets – growth, cost and pricing structure; technology and
        innovation; competitive environment; social and governmental
        constraints.
    (b) The firm's resources by markets, expertise in particular functions
        etc.
    (c) Managerial values and aspirations.
    (d) Sensitivity to social responsibilities.

4   Determine appropriate recommendations concerning:

    (a) Set of objectives.
    (b) Strategies by product, markets and functions.
    (c) Plan for implementation.

5   Assess the relevance of acquisitions to the corporate strategy:

    (a) What is the potential of the company's existing markets compared
        to their growth objectives?
    (b) What is the planning gap?
    (c) Scope for internally generated growth.
    (d) Scope for acquisitions.

6 Choose and evaluate candidates for acquisition

> (a) If the acquisitions are to be outside the company's existing markets, those other markets must be examined very carefully.
> (b) Examine companies within the particular markets and provide a short list of acquisition candidates.

7 Evaluate the specific acquisition candidate focusing attention on:

> (a) Acquisition candidate's impact on acquirer's markets, products, industry competition and growth in earnings and sales.
> (b) Potential sources of synergy.
> (c) Debt capacity.
> (d) Valuation of fixed assets.
> (e) Working capital and liquidity.
> (f) Human resources.

After a rational corporate strategy has been developed, an 'acquisitions profile' can be constructed of companies that it may be desirable to acquire, based on factors such as market areas, market size and potential. Firms which fit in with this profile are valued and if it is felt that one or more of these can be acquired profitably at a realistic premium over current market price, initial approaches should be considered. The file should be updated and the share price movement of acquisition prospects reviewed periodically. Outside this list of candidates, specific merger opportunities will arise or be developed, but even these special cases should have some relevance to the corporate strategy.

It is probably worth remarking that the task of specifying corporate objectives in terms of markets and technology and the establishment of a strategy to achieve these objectives requires substantial effort and resources in terms of management time and skills if the task is to be pursued rigorously. The degree of sophistication, of course, depends on the nature of the firm and its markets and the likely returns from more detailed analysis in a situation characterized by substantial uncertainty. However, too many firms hide behind the difficulties of forecasting and planning when explaining their failure to place their acquisitions within a corporate strategy. But if the task is difficult, it is nonetheless essential to the problem of making mergers successful. Kitching's study showed that those companies which did have a carefully developed corporate strategy and acquisition policy were far more likely to make a success of acquisitions than organizations that adopted a more haphazard planning mechanism.

Valuation

Once a potential acquisition has been decided on, the next stage is valuation.

To the investor, any share bought on the stock exchange represents the right to participate in all dividend payments on that share until it is resold. Thus the benefits expected to be derived from the shareholding are the dividend payments and the potential capital gain on sale. A company's stock market valuation is a function of its present and future income stream and shareholders' perceived risk of that stream. Thus, given two companies with similar projected earnings, where one is perceived as riskier than the other, the less risky share will have a higher valuation. Risk is one part of the valuation equation. The other is the current income position and its future growth rate. Given two companies with the same risk characteristics and current income, but different perceived growth rates, the faster growing share will have a greater value because of the larger cash flows expected in later years. The growth element is in fact a vital part of valuation analysis.

The most familiar valuation tool is the PE ratio. This ratio represents the present market price divided by the present earnings per share after tax. Mathematically, the PE ratio expresses the number of years that a company would have to continue generating earnings at their present level to accumulate sufficient after-tax earnings to equal the current share price. If a company had a share price of 150p and earnings per share of 10p after tax, then the PE ratio would be 15.

$$PE \text{ ratio} = \frac{150p}{10p} = 15$$

The PE ratio, when it is inverted, produces the earnings yield – that is, the earnings divided by the share price. Therefore, a company with a PE of 20 has an earnings yield of 5 per cent. Clearly, although the present return is 5 per cent, earnings must be expected to increase, because investors could obtain more than 5 per cent after tax in a high-grade loan stock. Thus, there must be an element of expected growth in the company that will increase the earnings in the future.

It may be said, therefore, that as the PE ratio rises – or conversely, as the earnings yield falls – greater growth is expected in future earnings. Thus a company on a PE ratio of 40 is expected to produce increasing earnings per share which will accumulate to the current share price in much less than the 40 years implied by the PE ratio.

Differences in PE ratio have been explained in terms of present and future returns and risk. This is a reflection not only of the risk and growth characteristics of the company, but also the environment of the industry. Heavy-engineering companies, due to the cyclical nature of profits, are felt to be risky, and tend to have low PE's, whereas stores are generally felt to be less volatile with respect to changes in the economy and so tend to have high PEs. Within each industrial sector, different companies will have different PE ratios based on their expected performance, their particular markets within the sector and other factors. Thus risk may be thought of as a composite of sector and individual company prospects. The PE ratio therefore embodies elements of both growth and risk.

PE ratios are a relatively simple way of relating earning to a company's value; an apparently straightforward valuation approach would be to work out a notional PE based on existing earnings. This PE ratio would be related to the current income position, future growth prospects, and the risks for that particular company and the industry. If such a ratio could be developed as an effective tool of financial analysis it would be a very simple and straightforward method of valuation. However, the PE ratio is really a complex term, determined by several variables; until these are considered in more depth, together with the effect of the acquisition on the bidding company, this method of analysis will obscure more than it reveals.

Staveley Industries Ltd, with a share price in November 1971 of 125 pence, was on a PE ratio of approximately 24. However, this was very misleading, because it was based on Staveley's very low 1970/71 earnings. The market was well aware that the sale of loss-makers and the reduction in loan capital and interest charges would lead to better results in 1971/72. Thus the real or prospective PE was around 12, although the higher earnings were not immediately visible. The results announced in December 1972 confirmed this view, and the PE ratio fell to around 11 at a price of 125 pence. Two points must be borne in mind: first the earnings were reported

Figure 18:3   Accounts of prospective acquisition

Balance sheet

	£'000s		£'000s
Ordinary shares	10,000	*Fixed assets*	17,000
Reserves	12,000	*Current assets*	
Loan capital	10,000	Stocks	14,000
Minority interests	2,500	Debtors	16,000
Current liabilities		Cash	100
Creditors	5,000		
Overdrafts	7,600		
	47,100		47,100

Profit and loss account	£'000s
Trading profit for the year	3,200
Interest charges	1,460
(7% interest on loan capital	
10% interest on bank overdraft)	
Profits before tax	1,740
Taxation at 50%	870
	870
Minority interests	250
	620
Earnings per share	6.20p
Share price	62p (PE ratio 10)

after an abnormally low tax charge; on a normal tax charge the after-tax earnings would be lower and the PE ratio would rise to about 13. Second, Staveley's PE based on 1970/71 earnings was very high, but this did not indicate that the company was considered a very high-growth firm, but rather that earnings were recovering from a low base level. Indeed, the subsequent PE of around 12 at 142 pence (18 December 1972) indicated that the market then expected little growth and viewed earnings as being of low quality (high risk).

We are not suggesting that Staveley was undervalued, rather that the PE ratio on its own indicates very little. Before applying a PE ratio to earnings, a bidder should examine the balance sheet and profit and loss account of the prospective acquisition, making any appropriate adjustments. If the prospective company had the balance sheet and profit and loss account shown in Figure 18:3, what financial analysis should be carried out by the bidder?

Initially he could apply various ratios to highlight serious deficiencies or opportunities. The current ratio is 2.4:1 (£30,100/£12,600), which would appear high, although it should be remembered from Chapter 1 that a comparison should be made with the industry average. Therefore, the individual components of current assets and current liabilities must be analysed.

If sales during the year are £32,000,000 then the average age of debtors is 183 days (£16,000,000/£32,000,000 × 365). If the bidder's average age of debtors is 122 days and it is felt that the bidder's credit-control system could be applied to the acquisition then debtors might be reduced eventually by approximately £5,300,000.

The bidder should then examine the level of stocks and compare it to the sales. If the cost of goods sold is assumed to be 75 per cent of sales revenue, then the company has stocks sufficient for 7 months sales. Suppose that, after comparison with industry and company data, stocks can be reduced to £12 million.

The funds released from the reduction in debtors and stocks can be used to reduce the overdraft. On the basis of these assumptions, a revised balance sheet can be prepared (Figure 18:4).

Figure 18:4   Balance sheet after improvements in credit and stock control

	£'000s		£'000s
Ordinary shares	10,000	*Fixed assets*	17,000
Reserves	12,000	*Current assets*	
Loan capital	10,000	Stocks	12,000
Minority interests	2,500	Debtors	10,700
Current liabilities		Cash	100
Creditors	5,000		
Overdrafts	300		
	39,800		39,800

Suppose further that the potential acquirer knew that a £400,000 loss had been made by a subsidiary company and estimated that £3 million could be released on its sale or closure, how would the balance sheet and profit and loss account be affected? In Figure 18:5 it is assumed that the proceeds will equal the book value of the assets.

Figure 18:5   Balance sheet after sale of subsidiary

	£'000s		£'000s
Ordinary shares	10,000	Fixed assets	14,000
Reserves	12,000	Current assets	
Loan capital	10,000	Stocks	12,000
Minority interests	2,500	Debtors	10,700
Creditors	5,000	Cash	2,800
	39,500		39,500

The release of funds has entirely eliminated outstanding overdrafts and a cash balance of £2.8 million remains; this can be reinvested in marketable securities producing a 6 per cent return before tax (£168,000 a year). The revised profit and loss account is summarized in Figure 18:6.

Figure 18:6   Revised profit and loss account

	£'000s
Trading profit for the year	3,768
Interest charges (7% loan capital)	700
Profits before tax	3,068
Tax at 50%	1,534
	1,534
Minority interests	250
	1,284
Earnings per share	12.8p

The trading profit has increased by £568,000 owing to the closure of the loss-making subsidiary and the reduction in stocks and debtors. This, added to the reduction of bank overdrafts, has produced increased profits before tax. The result is earnings per share of 12.84p after payment of tax and minority interests.

Clearly, a potential acquirer should analyse and revise the profit and loss account and balance sheet; such revisions may provide the bidder with a useful and simple method of taking account of the potential economic benefits of a merger. The reaction of the bidder might be that the PE prior to the acquisition did not take account of the savings and increased profits perceived by the acquiror and that the PE ratio will remain constant. As will be seen in the next chapter these may be erroneous assumptions.

Such revisions can work in the opposite direction. When Associated Electrical Industries Ltd was defending itself against a takeover bid by The General Electric Company Ltd, it forecast that its 1967 profit would be £10 million. When the takeover went through GEC produced accounts which showed a loss of £4½ million for the period (Figure 18:7). The three main factors accounting for the shortfall were overvalued stocks, underestimated costs and unprofitable contracts already entered into.

Figure 18:7   Deductions made by GEC from AEI's forecast of its 1967 profits

	£ million
Shortfall in sales	0.1
Cost of sales greater than estimated	3.4
Losses of subsidiaries acquired during 1967	0.7
Write off obsolescent stock	4.3
Extra provision for losses on contracts in progress	4.4
Extra bad-debt provision	0.5
Other	1.1
	−14.5

Summary

We have outlined the general reasons for mergers and noted that some studies have suggested that although mergers on average provide gains to shareholders there is a substantial failure rate. We have proposed that a company should first decide the markets it wishes to be in, and then examine potential companies that can satisfy its objectives within these markets. Finally, we have examined a simplistic valuation approach for companies through the use of the price-earnings ratio in conjunction with a revised profit and loss account and balance sheet. Management should approach an acquisition like any other capital budgeting and this is elaborated on in the next chapter.

Notes

1   G. Newbould, Management and Merger Activity, Liverpool: Guthstead, 1970.

2 J. Kitching, 'Why do Mergers Miscarry?', *Harvard Business Review*, vol. 45, no. 6, November-December 1967, pp. 84-101.
3 P. J. Halpern, 'Empirical Estimates of the Amount and Distribution of Gains to Companies in Mergers', *Journal of Business*, October 1973, pp. 554-575.
4 G. Mandelker, 'Risk and Return: the Case of Merging Firms', *Journal of Financial Economics*, December 1974.
5 J. R. Franks, J. E. Broyles and M. J. Hecht, 'An Industry Study of the Profitability of Mergers in the UK', *Journal of Finance*, forthcoming March 1978.

Further reading

Patricia Farrant, 'The truth about mergers', *Management Today*, May 1970, pp. 120-5, 164-8.
T. F. Hogarty, 'The profitability of corporate mergers', *Journal of Business*, vol 43, July 1970, pp. 317-27.
R. Jackson, 'The consideration of economies in merger cases', *Journal of Business*, vol. 43, 1970, pp. 439-47.
E. M. Kelly, *The Profitability of Growth through Mergers*, Center for Research of the College of Business Administration, Pennsylvania State University, 1967.
W. G. Lewellen, 'A pure financial rationale for the conglomerate merger', *Journal of Finance*, vol. 26, May 1971, pp. 521-37.
W. J. Mead, 'Instantaneous merger profits as a conglomerate merger motive', *Western Economic Journal*, June 1969.
D. C. Mueller, 'A theory of conglomerate mergers', *Quarterly Journal of Economics*, vol. 83, November 1969, pp. 643-59.
S. R. Reid, *Mergers, Managers, and the Economy*, New York: McGraw-Hill, 1968.
J. M. Samuels, 'The success or failure of mergers and takeovers', *Journal of Business Policy*, vol. 1, no. 3, Spring 1971, pp.9-17.
J. F. Weston and S. K. Mansinghka, 'Tests of the efficiency performance of conglomerate firms', *Journal of Finance*, vol. 26, September 1971, pp. 919-36.

19

Acquisition valuation

This chapter critically examines various methods of acquisition valuation for quoted and unquoted companies. The first method concentrates on a comparison of the earnings per share of the combined companies with that of the acquirer alone on a present value basis. The second method is a discounted cash flow model and is based on an established normative model of share price valuation.

We first examine what we call the earnings per share accretion/dilution approach.

EPS accretion and dilution approach

The most common form of merger analysis hinges on the immediate dilution or accretion of earnings per share (EPS) and the price-earnings (PE) ratios of the two companies. As an example, consider a bidder B, who wishes to acquire a potential acquisition V by offering £3.6 million for V's shares, currently valued at £3.0 million. The characteristics of the two companies are shown in Figure 19:1.

The terms of the offer are 2 B shares for every 3 V shares, valuing the V shares at 120p. V's shareholders decide to accept the offer. If the PE of the combined company is the same as B's original PE, then the characteristics of the combined company will be as in Figure 19:2.

From the bidder's viewpoint, the deal looks attractive as an immediate

Figure 19:1   Characteristics of bidder and acquisition candidate

	B	V
Attributable profits	£1.2 million	£0.3 million
Number of issued shares	10 million	3 million
Earnings per share	12p	10p
Current P/E ratio	15	10 (12 on bid value)
Current share price	180p	100p (120p on bid value)

increase in earnings per share is achieved and, assuming the price-earnings ratio remains unaltered, B's share price rises. From the acquisition shareholders' viewpoint, total EPS has fallen (from 30p for every 3 V shares held, to 25p for every 2 subsequent B shares), but these earnings are capitalized or valued at a much higher rate, a PE ratio of 15 as opposed to 10, and a capital gain has been made. In fact, as long as the PE ratio of the combined company remains above the weighted average PE ratio of the individual companies, such a gain will be realized. This type of analysis has led to the belief that a bidder with a high PE ratio can successfully continue acquiring companies with lower PE ratios and thus experience continual increases in earnings per share.

There are two flaws in this argument, both relating to the assumptions of an unchanged PE ratio or a final PE ratio which remains above the weighted average of the PE ratio of the individual companies before the mergers. As will be shown later, the PE ratio is determined by the expected growth in future earnings and dividends and the shareholders' discount rate. Clearly any change in the PE ratio will be brought about by changes in growth expectations or the discount rate. However, expectations of future growth will be lower following the merger because B had a pre-merger PE ratio of 15 as opposed to 10 for V, and B is therefore very likely to have had a higher expected growth rate. Consequently the long term growth of the combined company (B + V) will beless than that of B before the merger as it includes the more slowly growing company V. Hence, the assumption of an unchanged PE ratio following the merger will be wrong if expectations of growth for B + V are no greater than the growth expectations of the original companies. This must be so if it is assumed that investors do not expect any synergistic effects and markets are reasonably efficient.

Figure 19:2   Characteristics of the combined company

Attributable profits	£1.5 million
Number of issued shares	12 million
Earnings per share	12.5p
Current P/E ratio	15 (B's previous)
Current market price	188p

It is generally believed that the market recognizes the long term implications of the initial accretion/dilution approach and tends to take a longer view than some investors expect; the PE ratios of a number of companies which, in recent years, have experienced repeated but temporary increases in EPS by acquiring companies with PE ratios lower than their own have fallen substantially due to lower growth expectations and/or higher required rates of return. Studies in the USA by Hogarty[1] and Weston[2] cast serious doubt on the profitability of such mergers.

To summarize, the first-year earnings per share of a merged firm may well be greater than its pre-merger earnings per share, but a proper evaluation of a merger requires an examination of the effects of growth and the shareholders' discount rate.

J. F. Weston[3] has significantly extended the accretion/dilution approach. Consider an acquisition which offers initial accretion to the acquiring company's shareholders but over the long term will result in dilution of earnings and lower growth expectations. Again the bidder is denoted by B and the prospective acquisition by V.

Figure 19:3   B's projected earnings for an initial four-year period

		Year		
	1	2	3	4
Attributable profits (£ million)	1.0	1.08	1.17	1.26
Shares (million)	10			
Earnings per share (pence)	10	10.8	11.7	12.6
PE ratio	25			
Share price	£2.50			
Expected rate of growth of earnings	8%			
Discount rate	10%			

Assume B has first-year attributable profits of £1.0 million, which are expected to grow indefinitely at about 8 per cent a year and the shareholders demand a 10 per cent return. There are 10 million shares issued and the company currently pays dividends at 50 per cent of attributable profits and is expected to continue doing so (Figure 19:3).

V is another company. Its current profits are £0.4 million, and they are expected to grow at only 3 per cent a year but the earnings are less risky than B's and the shareholders expect a 7 per cent return (Figure 19:4).

Figure 19:4   V's projected earnings for an initial four-year period

	Year			
	1	2	3	4
Attributable profits (£ million)	0.4	0.412	0.424	0.437
Shares (million)	4			
Earnings per share (pence)	10	10.3	10.6	10.9
PE ratio	12.5			
Share price	£1.25			
Expected rate of growth of earnings (g)	3%			
Discount rate (k)	7%			

To achieve the agreement of V's shareholders to the takeover, B has to offer a premium of about 30 per cent on V's current share price, and therefore bids 162p per share – that is, 2 of B's shares for every 3 of V's shares. The combined forecasts are in Figure 19:5.

Figure 19:5   BV's combined projected earnings for an initial four-year period

	Year			
	1	2	3	4
Attributable profits (£ million)	1.40	1.49	1.59	1.70
Shares(million)	12.67			
Earnings per share (pence)	11.05	11.76	12.55	13.42

To illustrate the differences in EPS over time, Figure 19:6 shows the respective graphs of B's and B+V's projected EPS.

It is clear that the disparity between the earnings per share of B and those of the combined company decreases over time. Since B is growing faster than B+V combined, at some time after year 4 the earnings per share of B+V will be lower than those of B alone.

Weston has suggested that to determine the profitability of the merger, the bidder should view the period of earnings dilution (where the earnings per share of the combined group is lower than that expected for the bidder alone) as an investment, and the earnings accretion as the return on the investment. It is then suggested that the bidder should use its own weighted average cost of capital to discount the earnings dilution and should compare it to the present value of the earnings accretion discounted at the same rate. If the difference between the present value of earnings accretion and the present value of earnings dilution is positive then the merger is a profitable one. I. H. Silberman[4] questioned Weston's use of the bidder's cost of capital claiming, as Weston subsequently agreed,[5] that the appropriate rate of discount is the weighted average discount rate of the bidder and acquisition (weighted by their projected earnings over time). Supplement 19:1 shows, however, that it is not possible to obtain an accurate weighted average discount rate in this manner.

There are other important criticisms of the earnings per share approach.

Figure 19:6 Comparison of B's projected earnings before and after acquisition

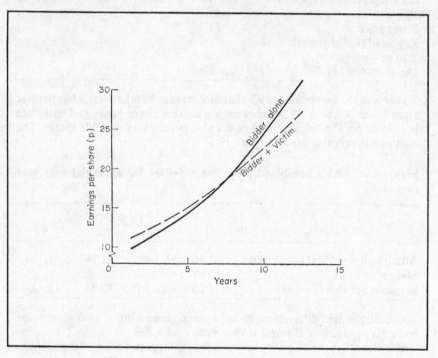

1 Weston's EPS model is based upon reported earnings rather than the cash flow generated by the acquisition. Thus he assumes that shareholders at the margin value their company on the basis of reported earnings rather than the cash flow received by them in the form of dividends. This implies that the market is deceived by the method of reporting earnings and contradicts one of the basic premises of corporate finance, that the firm maximizes the present value of cash flows in order to maximize shareholders' wealth. The unadjusted earnings per share model is inconsistent with the dividend-based discounted cash flow model.

Furthermore, there is a real danger of double counting in Weston's analysis. Part of the earnings stream is not paid out in the form of dividends but is reinvested to produce future growth. If one discounts the total earnings per share of the group, growing over time, one is assuming that depreciation provisions are adequate to finance the capital investment necessary to maintain this growth rate. Thus the analysis does not distinguish adequately between earnings that are paid out in the form of dividends and those that are retained and reinvested to produce future growth.

2   If Weston uses the weighted average cost of capital (that is, cost of debt and equity weighted by the proportion of each in the capital structure) of the bidder, there should be a strict separation of the financing and investment decisions. Therefore earnings per share should not include any financial charges – that is, interest charges should not be deducted from earnings – otherwise the method of financing the merger, with given proportions of debt and equity, will influence the trend of earnings. As a result, the profitability of the merger will alter depending on whether debt or equity is used. This basis ties a specific method of financing to a particular capital project – the acquisition – thus violating a second important rule in capital budgeting and would lead to erroneous decision-making. Also, the weighted average cost of capital has included the use of low-cost debt finance (based upon the firm's target capital structure); thus to include financing charges would constitute double counting again.

Valuation of quoted companies

It is important to distinguish between quoted and unquoted companies for valuation purposes. In an efficient or competitive capital market, the share price of a company reflects the underlying value of the existing assets and management's ability to find future investment opportunities. This may not always be correct if management does not provide financial analysts with adequate information. However, it appears reasonable, on the basis of good evidence, to assume that share values reflect the current and future earnings stream, discounted at the appropriate rate. Given this reasoning, the potential bidder should only pay a premium on the current market price of the firm if, and only if, there are improved earnings resulting from the merger. Thus, the bidder should explicitly relate the premium paid to the value of the merger benefits. This simplifies the valuation process, since it is unnecessary to go through the process of forecasting the cash flows of the entire firm and the related risks.

There is an important qualification to the previous proposition. The share price of the potential acquiree may already reflect bid prospects and therefore part of the premium on acquisition. The empirical evidence of Franks, Broyles and Hecht showed that the market began to anticipate mergers, on average, three months prior to the announcement. If the bidder fixed the price of the acquisition one week prior to the announcement, the price of the acquiree's shares might have already anticipated part of the bid premium. The bidder should estimate the price of the acquisition 'ex the bid prospects'. As a useful approximation, the analyst can compare past movements in the share price of the company with those of the market. If the company's price has risen significantly more than the market index, then the analyst must consider the implications for setting the bid price.

It is important to appreciate that the above analysis does not require the kind of complex earnings per share framework presented in the first section in this chapter. We are simply suggesting that the acquirer must evaluate explicitly the cash flow gains that will be derived from the merger and treat these opportunities as a capital budgeting proposal.

Valuation of unquoted companies

The valuation of unquoted companies proves a much more difficult task. Analysts apply a variety of valuation tools. The simplest would be to obtain the market value of the individual assets of the company. If the assets are difficult to value, then the analyst will value the earnings using the price-earnings ratio of similar companies that are quoted on the stock exchange. Inevitably, problems arise, since the risk and growth prospects of two companies are rarely identical. The third possibility is to use the growth models explained in Chapter 16 for valuing the company.

Recalling Malkiel's equation:

$$P_0 = \sum_{i=1}^{n} \frac{D_0 (1+g_1)^i}{(1+k)^i} + \frac{PE_{n+1} \times E_{n+1}}{(1+k)^n}$$

In effect, this equation states that the price of a company's share is equal to the dividend stream growing at some rate g_1 for a period of years to some horizon n, plus the value of the company in year $n+1$. That value is simply the earnings of the year multiplied by a price-earnings ratio that reflects the growth prospects of the economy.

As an example, consider a company with current operating earnings (that is, earnings before depreciation and interest but after tax) of £0.26 million with a dividend payout ratio of 0.75. Although there is development potential in the company, the precise growth rate over the next five years is not known although it can be assumed to range between 5 and 11 per cent a year. After this the company will have exhausted its unique potential and will probably grow at no more than the projected composite rate of growth in corporate profits, say 4 per cent a year. With these figures the graph in Figure 19:7 may be drawn.

It is now up to the bidder's management to identify growth more rigorously in the acquisition and to produce a more realistic price. For example, suppose further study of the acquisition's products and markets shows that growth (g_1) will be between 5 and 7 per cent a year. The required rate of return on the investment has been identified as being between 10 and 11 per cent. In these circumstances the range can be reduced to the area shown in Figure 19:8.

Figure 19:7 Malkiel growth curves
            $d = 0.75$, $g_2 = 4\%$, $n = 5$, $E_0 = £0.26$ million

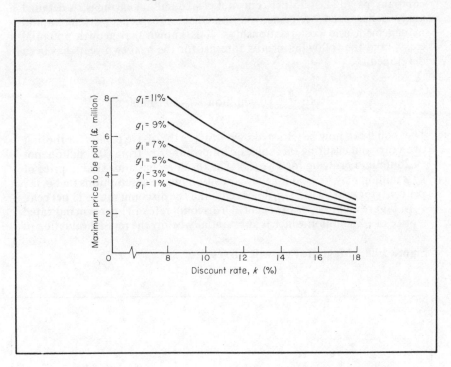

With these assumptions, the maximum price payable is £5 million. If the present market price is below this figure, a negotiating range has been set above which the bidder will not be prepared to go. In the present case, if the market valuation is £4.0 million the bidder could perhaps develop a negotiating strategy of initially bidding £4.5 million – a 12.5 per cent premium on present market price – raising it to £5 million if necessary.

As is probably apparent, the model is really a device for producing a series of cash flows which are then discounted as in any other capital-budgeting proposal. The methods used enable the decision-maker to investigate the sensitive assumptions in his model in a more critical manner compared with a simple forecast of cash flows. Using a terminal PE ratio reduces the model from an infinite series to a small number of terms. Nevertheless, this model is sometimes clumsy to use in practice, especially if the bidder has an accurate idea of early cash flows and therefore does not need to relate them to growth patterns. As the model does nothing more

than produce cash flows, it is easy to consider the cash flows in any one year
and thus refine the analysis. For example, take the previous case of a
company paying out 75 per cent of its £0.26 million earnings. A detailed
analysis has been performed of immediate prospects, working capital
management and cost relationships. It is known that growth potential
exists, and the following profits forecast for the next two years has been
developed.

Year	1	2
Profit	£0.4 million	£0.5 million

The model can now be adjusted by putting in the above profits for the first
two years and ensuring that subsequent profits grow from £0.5 million (not
£0.26 million growing for 2 years). The result is that a maximum price of
£7.3 million may be paid for the acquisition on the assumptions that g_1 is 7
per cent (for years 3 to 5), g_2 4 per cent, and the discount rate is 11 per cent.

In Figure 19:8, a g_1 of 7 per cent at a discount rate of 11 per cent indicated
a price of £4.6 million which is substantially below the revised valuation of

Figure 19:8   Magnified growth curves

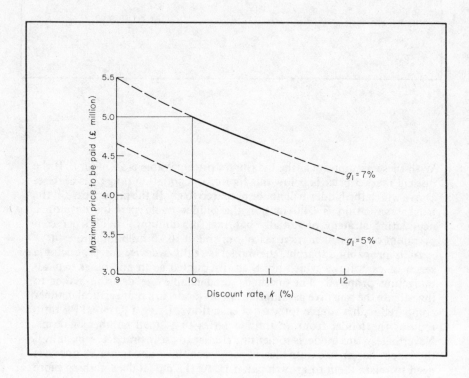

£7.3 million. This situation shows up one of the problems in any model deriving valuation from future earnings streams – that is, the sensitivity of the outcome to particular inputs. We have already discussed how changes in g_1, g_2 and k affect the final outcome, and to achieve a workable result these inputs must be defined within narrow limits. In the present case, by increasing initial cash flows, average growth has been substantially altered over the five years, as g_1 now refers only to growth in years 3 to 5. The compound average growth rate is now nearly 19 per cent for the five-year period. In practice a bidder would always have some clear idea of the likely range in the input variable and can thus reduce the range of possible prices. Nevertheless, for particular analyses, the final result may be extremely sensitive to the values of certain variables. The decision will rest inevitably upon a discerning judgement, taking into account the sensitivity analysis supplied by the analytical team. It should be clear to the reader why analysts frequently just try to value the existing assets of the firm or use PE ratios for valuing unquoted companies. More sophisticated models depend upon the accuracy of the cash flow forecasts.

Summary

This chapter has critically examined the most commonly used accretion/dilution approach, finding several problems in its application to acquisition evaluation. We have then discussed valuation of quoted and unquoted companies. Finally, we outline employment of growth models.

Supplement 19:1   It is not possible to compute a single growth rate for merged companies

We are looking for a growth rate $g^*(n)$ which is an effective growth rate to the year n for the combined earnings streams of B and V. For this purpose we propose to use the geometric mean of the weighted growth of the two companies over the period. Thus,

$$1 + g^*(n) = \left\{ \frac{e_1(1 + g_1)^n + e_2(1 + g_2)^n}{e_1 + e_2} \right\}^{1/n}$$

where we weight the growth of the two companies to year n by their corresponding initial earnings e_1 and e_2. It can be seen that this equation yields the correct total growth in earnings to year n.

$$(e_1 + e_2)(1 + g^*(n))^n = e_1(1 + g_1)^n + e_2(1 + g_2)^n$$

As time n becomes large it can also be shown that $g^*(n)$ approaches the larger of the two growth rates. For this purpose it is useful to rewrite the above equation in the following form:

$$1 + g^*(n) = (1 + g_1) \left[\frac{e_1 + e_2\{(1 + g_2)/(1 + g_1)\}^n}{e_1 + e_2} \right]^{1/n}$$

If g_1 is greater than g_2, then, as n tends to infinity,

$$\left(\frac{1+g_2}{1+g_1}\right)^n$$

approaches zero.

On the right-hand side of the equation we are left with

$$(1+g_1)\left(\frac{e_1}{e_1+e_2}\right)^{1/n}$$

The nth root of the fraction approaches unity as n tends to infinity. Thus $1 + g^*(n)$ approaches $(1 + g_1)$ as n goes to infinity if g_1 is greater than g_2.

This proof shows that as the time period n increases, the combined companies' growth rate approaches the growth rate of the faster growing company.

Thus, since the weighted average growth rate of the two companies is changing each year and approaching the growth rate of the higher growth company, one cannot represent the growth rate of the combined company by a single rate g^*. The earnings curve of the combined company is more concave than any single g^* model.

In addition, as the faster growing company dominates the other company, its own discount rate must increasingly dominate the discount rate of the combined company. To represent this by a single weighted average discount rate in the current time period is not meaningful. However, one could adjust this method to compute a time-dependent weighted average discount rate, k^*. This would yield a weighted average cost of capital for each time period.

Notes

1 T. F. Hogarty, 'The profitability of corporate mergers', *Journal of Business*, vol. 43, July 1970, pp. 317-27.
2 J. Fred Weston and Surendra K. Mansinghka, 'Tests of the efficiency performance of conglomerate firms', *Journal of Finance*, September 1971, pp.919-36.
3 J. Fred Weston, 'The determination of share exchange ratios in mergers', in *The Corporate Merger* edited by W. W. Alberts and Joel Segall, Chicago, Ill: University of Chicago Press, 1966.
4 I. H. Silberman, 'A note on merger valuation', *Journal of Finance*, June 1968.
5 J. Fred Weston, 'A reply', *Journal of Finance, June 1968*.

Further reading

J. R. Franks, R. Miles and J. Baywell, 'Critique of Merger Valuation Methods', *Journal of Business Finance and Accounting*, Vol. I, Spring 1974, pp. 35-53.

20
Financial analysis and tactical methods

In this chapter we discuss two important factors in merger analysis: first the effects of financing merger proposals on EPS, and second, the various tactical considerations firms can adopt, either to meet specific rules imposed by the City Code, or generally to improve the opportunities for acquisition. We also look at post-merger management problems.

Financing

In Chapter 19 it has been shown that the discount rate used for the evaluation of an acquisition should be based on the acquired firm's weighted average cost of capital. This argument rests on the assumption that if the bidder issues all-equity to acquire a company and substantially deviates from its optimum capital structure, it will be issuing debt for other capital projects and thus subsequently return to the desired ratio of debt to equity. The absence of suitable capital projects or the state of the capital markets could prevent further issues of debt. However, this should only be temporary, and, taking a planning horizon of three to five years, the argument stands. Thus the specific method of financing should not unduly influence the discount rate.

Although the method of financing may not be important in the long term, the use of debt or equity does alter total earnings available to the ordinary shareholder in the short term. In addition, management will wish

to examine the impact of various financing mixes on the future earnings.
This will be an important part of the financial planning process, if the
acquisition is relatively large.

Impact of financing method on EPS

Consider two companies with the characteristics shown in Figure 20:1. A
acquires B for a 30 per cent premium on market price and therefore values
B's shares at £2,080 and pays for them either by the issue of its own shares
(832 valued at £2.50 each) or by debt carrying a coupon rate of 10 per cent.
Corporation tax is assumed to be 50 per cent. The earnings per share of A
and of the combined companies are presented in Figure 20:2 on the basis of
an all-debt or all-equity offer.

The merger, under either method of financing, results in earnings
accretion immediately. However, under the all-equity alternative, earnings
per share are greater than under the debt alternative until year 4. After that
year, the debt alternative increases relative earnings per share. The
explanation follows from the fixed nature of debt costs as compared with
equity. Debt costs 10 per cent before taxes, and the cost does not alter with
the level of earnings; or, put another way, as earnings increase, interest
costs take a decreasing proportion of total earnings and the equity
shareholders take an increasing proportion. In the example, if the
management considered that the growth rate without the acquisition of B
would be higher, the all-debt offer would prove even more attractive.

Figure 20:1   Characteristics of two firms

	A	B
Total earnings (after tax)	£1,000	£160
Earnings per share	10p	4p
Number of shares	10,000	4,000
P/E ratio	25	10
Market price	£2.50	£0.40
Expected future growth in earnings	8%	4%

Figure 20:2   Earnings per share

| | Earnings per share (p) in year | | | | |
	1	2	3	4	5
A – without the merger (p)	10	10.8	11.66	12.60	13.60
A & B – under an all-equity merger (p)	10.71	11.51	12.37	13.29	14.29
A & B – under an all-debt merger (p)	10.56	11.42	12.35	13.36	14.44

The use of debt or equity must depend on the risk of the earnings stream. In addition, corporate and financial objectives may conflict. Under all-debt financing there is substantial initial earnings dilution, which may be unacceptable to the management whatever the long term benefits. This may be because the management and brokers believe that the market will reduce the bidder's share price. They will claim that dilution may affect the firm's ability to raise further finance and acquire other companies. Theoretically, we can find no justification for such conclusions. However, the issue of convertible stock to the new shareholders will partially overcome this objection; a lower interest rate is paid in return for the option to convert into ordinary shares at a later date. If in the example in Figure 20.1, 7 per cent convertible loan stock is issued, the crossover point is brought forward to year 2 (Figure 20:3).

Figure 20:3   Earnings per share with a 7 per cent convertible loan if A's growth is 8 per cent

| | Earnings per share (p) in year | | | | |
	1	2	3	4	5
A – without the merger	10	10.8	11.66	12.6	13.6
A & B – all equity	10.71	11.51	12.37	13.29	14.29
A & B – all debt	10.87	11.73	12.66	13.67	14.74

The use of the convertible increases earnings per share compared with other methods of financing. However, no account has been taken of the cost of giving the acquisition's shareholders an option to convert into ordinary shares: in practice the price of conversion is an additional cost to existing equity holders.

We have said that the particular method of financing does not affect the discount rate or required rate of return unless certain conditions hold; yet we are saying now that the company should make a decision on equity or debt, depending on the future level of earnings per share. The reader should appreciate that if A uses equity now for the acquisition, it will use debt for other capital-budgeting propositions; or, alternatively, if A finances the acquisition now with debt, it will have to raise equity for further projects. Thus, either way, earnings per share will be the same. This argument is true in the long term, but in the short term, especially when the acquisition is relatively large, the target capital structure cannot be attained so easily.

Tactical considerations

Having evaluated the acquisition and decided on the best offer mix, there are several tactical points which must be considered. There are the external limitations which are imposed by the government and the City, the Monopolies and Mergers Commission and Takeover Code, respectively.

Monopolies and Mergers Commission

The Secretary of State for Trade and Industry is able to refer any merger to the Monopolies and Mergers Commission (formerly known as the Monopolies Commission) if it involves the acquisition of gross assets in excess of £5 million or creates a potential monopoly (at least one-quarter of a particular market). The Commission then reports to the Secretary of State on whether the effects of the proposed merger will be in the public interest and what action the Secretary of State should take (including issuing an order banning the merger). The Department of Trade and Industry (DTI) may then reject or amend the recommendations on mergers, although it has until now invariably accepted the Commission's proposals. Until 1968, only five rejections were recommended by the Commission.

There are, however, several reasons for suggesting that the impact of the DTI and the Commission on the merger ambitions of companies has been greater than the number of refusals would suggest:

1   The cumulative effects of some acquisition-intensive firms have been examined by the Commission – for example, Courtaulds Ltd, whose rapid growth in man-made fibres was mainly achieved via acquisitions, examined under the cellulose fibres reference.[1]
2   Some mergers may have been prevented by the threat, latent or actual, of a merger reference.
3   At least 9 mergers have not been referred to the Commission because the DTI has extracted assurances from the companies regarding their future behaviour, for example, the takeover of United Glass Ltd by The Distillers Company Ltd.
4   Since 1969 every merger referred to the Commission has subsequently failed for one reason or another.

For prospective acquirers, there are no precise guidelines for assessing whether a merger would be rejected by the Commission or, what is more important, whether it will be referred to the Commission.[2]

The DTI has similar criteria to the Commission in assessing the advisability of a particular merger, although, for reasons of time and its role as merely a screening device, the analysis is much less in-depth. The DTI seeks to establish evidence of detriment to the public interest; and if this cannot be outweighed by the benefits to the public, then the merger will be referred or assurances sought. The public interest is usually interpreted in the light of the balance between greater market power and decreased competition and the advantages of better management, technological advance, and economies of scale, but only in so far as these advantages will be passed on to customers. Balance of payments, regional policy and redundancy considerations are also examined.

But the essence of the UK approach is that each merger is treated on its own merits, and that no rigid rules will be applied. The very small number of references and assurances and, in the past, the sympathetic attitude of the Commission towards the references suggest that the Commission has considerable difficulty in actually proving detriment to the public interest or that the criteria are liberally interpreted. Thus, government legislation on mergers does not at present impose a serious constraint on the majority of corporate acquisitions, although certain companies, especially those in a monopoly position, may find their freedom somewhat restricted.

Takeover Code

The seeds of the Takeover Code are to be found in the 1959 British Aluminium takeover battle and the City institutions' struggle throughout the early 1960s to impose some order through voluntary rules. A succession of acrimonious battles in 1967 (the bids by Aberdare Holdings Ltd and Thorn Electrical Industries Ltd for Metal Industries Ltd; the battle between Rodo Investment Trust Ltd and Courtaulds Ltd for Wilkinson & Riddell (Holdings) Ltd), in which some tactics were employed that were considered unfair to shareholders, led in 1968 to the Takeover Code being introduced with the support of the leading City institutions. It laid down certain principles for the conduct of bids. It is regularly updated to handle new circumstances, such that it now constitutes a broad and detailed list of practices, which, since 1969, the Takeover Panel and its executives have been increasingly successful in enforcing.

The Code is based on a few general principles which all parties are responsible for upholding; the spirit of the Code is as important as the rules. The principles concern the following:

1 The responsibility of the prospective acquisition's directors to their shareholders *as a whole* and the duty of the bidder to treat *all* the acquisition's shareholders equitably. This precludes oppression of minorities, creation of false share markets, and action by the directors to frustrate a bid.
2 The provision of adequate, accurate and early information, such that shareholders can make an informed choice between the alternatives.

To support these principles, 39 specific rules have been developed, which in the main concentrate on the parties' responsibilities for providing information, the documentation and mechanics of the offer and dealing in the acquisition's shares during the course of the offer. There are seven specific practice notes to handle particular situations.

Two important points are worth repeating here. First, considerable care must be exercised in the preparation of forecasts and asset valuations and the assumptions and accounting basis must be disclosed, with the assistance of a professional valuer in the case of revaluation. Second, dealings by the bidder or his associates in the acquisition's shares during the course of an offer at a price in excess of the offer price impose an obligation on the bidder to raise the offer price to the highest price paid for the shares in the market. Moreover, if the bidder or associates have acquired a total of more than 15 per cent of acquisition's shares during the previous twelve months, an offer for the rest of the shares, if it is made, must be in cash or with a cash alternative, and at a price no lower than the highest price that the bidder has paid for any of the shares previously purchased. Furthermore, if a company acquires more than 40 per cent of the voting rights of another company by whatever means, it must, within a reasonable period of time, make an unconditional offer for the rest of the equity capital in cash and at the highest price paid in the preceding year.

Merchant banks

The role of merchant banks varies from merger to merger. The takeover of a quoted company requires the assistance of a merchant bank to handle the complex legal and administrative matters, such as preparing an offer document, circulating to shareholders, recording acceptances etc. A bank will also provide advice on the form of the bid and the options one can make available to the acquiree's shareholders in the offer package, and will assist in any arrangement for underwriting the offer for cash. It may also be able to negotiate directly with any institutional shareholders, such as pension funds and insurance companies.

Their continuous experience of handling takeovers makes merchant banks an invaluable source of advice with regard to the form and manner of an offer and the probability of its acceptance. However, their role in advising bidders on the right price to pay for an acquisition and analysing the acceptability of the acquisition to the bidder's corporate strategy and managerial style is open to some doubt. These matters should be the responsibility of the bidder's management.

Timing

It is obvious that the behaviour of the prospective acquisition's share price will influence the amount which the bidder will have to pay to secure control. Moreover, if the bidder is offering his shares to effect payment, then his own share-price movements will be important. It will be advantageous to the bidder if he can make an offer when his shares are overvalued or when the acquisition's are undervalued.

Short-run movements in a company's share price reflect national, economic and industrial factors as well as the release of information by or about the company itself. If the bidder has an opinion about the factors which influence short-run movements, he will clearly be able to make a bid at the most opportune moment. This is usually when his share price is strong, and the acquisition's is weak. Ensuring that the timing is right is much easier if the bidder has a shopping list of possible acquisitions, which conform to the bidder's strategic and managerial constraints and appear likely to generate an adequate financial return at acceptable bid prices.

A small stake

There is often an advantage for a company in securing a small share-holding in other companies which are considered to be potential acquisitions. Disclosures of the stake are not necessary until it reaches 5 per cent. Such a stake offers a springboard for a future bid and provides the bidder with a defensive base from which it can counterattack against other bidders. This holding might also give the bidder a place on the acquisition's board from where it can extract further information about the acquisition. This information will assist in the decision on whether to go ahead with a complete bid, and in its timing. The Whitbread 'umbrella' of trade investments (of about 30 per cent) in a number of other brewers is a good example of small-stake tactics. Many of the original umbrella companies have been taken over completely. In the Whitbread case, however, the stakes were invariably held with the cooperation and often at the request of the companies. However, such well-known acquirers as Jessel Securities Ltd and Slater Walker Securities Ltd were accustomed to take interests in possible acquisitions as a prelude to complete takeover. J. R. Franks, in a recent paper[3], showed that if acquiring companies have superior information as to the timing of a bid and the merger benefits, they should accumulate shares prior to the bid announcement. Such information is valuable since such an acquiror will place a higher present value on the merger benefits than the market and consequently will produce trading opportunities. He showed that, under special conditions, such share accumulation could influence the date of acquisition.

Post-acquisition problems

The efficiency with which the bidder runs the acquisition is just as important as the strategic rationale for the bid. This efficiency depends in part on how the acquisition is finally absorbed into the bidder. Solutions to problems such as restructuring the acquisition, delegation and lines of control have an important effect on subsequent performance.

On the organizational side, the bidder must decide exactly what type and structure of management to impose. Should the acquisition become a new division in its entirety, or be split up and integrated with existing divisions? Should control systems be tight and restrictive or loose and informal? There is no simple answer to such questions and the bidder must analyse both his own and the acquisition's management structure before deciding on the most appropriate method of absorbing the newly acquired company. When the acquisition is of similar size to the bidder, changes will have to be made by both parties – the new company formed in such a merger is a different animal from either of its predecessors and could well require a new organizational structure.

Along with the other assets of the company, the bidder will have acquired a new management team. It may be important for the bidder to ensure that this team remains together for some time, especially when the company's activities are not comparable to those of the bidder. Changes in organizational structure will affect management attitudes and any changes should be communicated and implemented rapidly to reduce the uncertainty engendered by the merger.

As well as deciding organizational and managerial policies, the bidder must also decide what action, if any, is required to improve the overall efficiency of the acquisition. Once in control, the bidder should gather information from the various activities of the company to enable a rational post-merger policy to be adopted. Useful techniques to aid in this policy decision include an evaluation of working-capital management, determination of debt capacity and utilization, preparation of cost and profit centres for major products and divisions and decisions on any necessary disposals. The communication of such a line of actions and the results should be completed within a reasonable time to avoid any unnecessary uncertainty.

Post-audit analysis

Analysis of the subsequent performance of the acquisition against that projected in the original appraisal is useful for two reasons. First, such post-audit analysis is a control device which allows senior management a different framework from the normal budget procedures with which to evaluate performance. Second, post-audit analysis enables the project team to examine what actually happens against what was predicted. Differences between expectations and outcomes should be noted so that the team can improve the quality of further appraisals. We would suggest that post-audit analysis be conducted on an irregular basis by the corporate appraisal team, whose reports should be considered by senior management in the investment decision and operational performance area.

Summary

In this chapter we have discussed the method of financing an acquisition and its effect on EPS and the various tactical problems in considering the mechanics of a bid. These problem areas are all interrelated and require careful analysis; it is often difficult to define decision criteria, let alone structure the problem. Nevertheless, an efficient amalgamation will require a plan of how best to reorganize and absorb the acquisition; this plan can be developed only after an evaluation of the problem areas mentioned above.

Notes

1   Monopolies Commission, *A Report on the Supply of Man-made Cellulosic Fibres*, House of Commons Papers, Session 1967–68, number 263, London: HMSO, 1968.

2   A. Sutherland, *The Monopolies Commission in Action*, London: Cambridge University Press, 1969.
3   J. R. Franks. 'Insider Information and the Efficiency of the Information Market', Unpublished Paper, 1976, London Graduate School of Business Studies.

PART FIVE
GLOSSARY AND
APPENDICES

Glossary

Accounting rate of return. Average annual profits after tax and depreciation on a project or proposal expressed as a percentage of its capital outlay.

Acquisition. The purchase of a relatively small firm by a large firm.

Annual general meeting. A specified general meeting of a company which must be held once at least in every calendar year, and not more than 15 months after the last preceding general meeting.

Arbitrage. The adjustment of anomalies between value and price by a continual mechanism of buying and selling until the two are equal.

Asset base. The asset base is the total market value of the firm's assets.

Asset cover (backing). Normally used in reference to fixed-interest capital, particularly loan capital, asset cover is the multiple by which the net tangible assets of the company cover the total amount of loan capital in question.

Asset value (per share). The balance sheet figure for the net assets available for each ordinary share, calculated by ascertaining the net assets available for the ordinary shareholders and dividing it by the number of ordinary shares in issue.

Authorized nominal capital. The nominal capital of a company which is authorized by the memorandum of association. The authorized, or nominal, capital is not necessarily all issued.

Balancing allowance. On disposal of assets, if the selling price is below the written-down value of the asset, then a tax allowance, called a balancing allowance, is given on the book loss.

Balancing charge. On disposal of assets, if the selling price is above the written-down value of the asset, then the company is liable to pay tax on the book profit or difference. The amount of tax is called the balancing charge.

Bear. Someone who anticipates that prices will fall. The term used to be limited in its application to a person who sold shares he did not own, in the belief that he could buy them at a lower price when the time came for delivery.

Beta co-efficient (β). The beta co-efficient measures the sensitivity return against the market return. A beta value of one means that the investment is as risky as the market index, while a value of two indicates that the price of the security is twice as volatile or twice as risky as the market index.

Blue chip. An expression for ordinary shares of the highest investment quality.

Bull. An investor who expects that prices will rise. The term was formerly used chiefly to describe speculators who bought shares which they hoped to sell at a profit before Settlement Day when they would have to pay for them.

Call. 1. The right to demand payment of additional money due on 'partly paid' securities. 2. The option to buy a security at an agreed price at a future date.

Capital asset pricing model. The capital asset pricing model describes the way prices of individual assets are determined in efficient markets.

Capitalization (scrip or bonus) issue. An issue of shares to existing shareholders, without payment from them, normally created by the capitalization of reserves.

Capital rationing. A condition in which a company does not have the funds available to finance all its profitable projects because it is unable to generate the necessary finance internally; and it may be unable, or the timing is inopportune, to resort to the capital market.

Cash flow. The amount of money generated by a company each year from its operations.

Cash in current assets.

$$\text{cash in current assets} = \frac{\text{cash balance}}{\text{current assets}}$$

Both these figures are derived from the balance sheet.

Convertible. Description of a security which, normally at the option of the holder, can be converted into another class of security. In particular this refers to loan stocks which may be converted into ordinary shares.

Cost of capital. The minimum return an investor (company) would be willing to accept for investing funds in a particular project.

Coupon (interest) rate. The charge a company must pay for its debt expressed as a percentage of the principal sum and payable annually.

Cum. This word is used in connection with dividends, rights, etc., and indicates that shares are entitled to the distribution concerned. It is Latin for 'with'.

Cumulative. Normally descriptive of preference shares to indicate that, if the dividend is not paid out of current earnings, it ranks for payment out of future earnings – that is, accumulated unpaid preference dividends must be paid before any ordinary dividends can be paid.

Current assets. Assets which are cash or near cash, in that they may be turned into cash within one year – for example, stocks, marketable securities.

Current liabilities. Claims against a person (or body of persons, such as a company) which must be met in cash within a comparatively short period – for example, tax payments, creditors.

Current liquidity ratio.

$$\text{current liquidity ratio} = \frac{\text{net current debt} \times 365}{\text{cash earnings before tax}}$$

(from balance sheet and profit and loss account).

Current ratio.

$$\text{current ratio} = \frac{\text{current assets}}{\text{current liabilities}}$$

(from balance sheet).

Debenture. A stock issued by a company, in exchange for the loan of money, normally secured by the pledging of certain assets.

Debt. Loans to a company which carry fixed interest rates and certain legal liabilities.

Depreciation. In accountancy the application of revenue to the writing down of the cost of fixed assets in the books.

Discount: 1. The margin by which a stock or share stands below either its issue price or parity value. 2. To make allowance for future development – as in 'the price fully discounts an increase in dividend'. 3. To quantify the present value of a sum of money received at the end of a certain number of years based on a given rate of interest.

Discounted cash flow. Because of the time value of money, future cash flows are discounted to arrive at the correct sum ('present value') for a current decision.

Dividend. The portion of a company's profit which the directors decide to distribute to shareholders. It is expressed either as a percentage of the nominal (par) value of the capital to which it relates or on a per share basis.

Dividend cover. The ratio of the available earnings to the dividend distribution, which is normally quoted as a multiple – as in 'dividend cover 1.5 times'.

Dividend yield. A yield calculated by multiplying the annual dividend rate per cent by the par (nominal) value of the security and dividing by the market price.

Earnings accretion. Increase in earnings per share.

Earnings dilution. Decrease in earnings per share.

Earnings per share. The amount available for ordinary shareholders – that is, the balance of profits derived from the net surplus shown after deducting all charges, including corporation tax after allowing also for the cost of preference dividends and is the amount available for distribution to ordinary shareholders – divided by the number of issued ordinary shares.

Earnings yield. The hypothetical return which an investor would secure by investing £100 in the company's shares at their current price if all the company's latest annual profits were distributed. It is obtained by multiplying the nominal value of the shares by the percentage earnings, and dividing by the price of the shares.

Efficient market. An efficient market is one in which prices fully reflect all available, relevant information. Adjustment to new information is virtually instantaneous.

Equity capital. See 'ordinary shares'.

Ex. The opposite of 'cum': shares quoted 'ex dividend' or 'ex rights' are not entitled to participate in the forthcoming distribution. The word is the Latin preposition meaning 'without'.

Financial leases. Under a financial lease the lessee agrees to make a series of payments to the lessor for the use of equipment. The contract may not be cancelled by either side during the initial term of the lease, normally a period of several years.

Fixed assets. The assets which are continually employed in a business and which are not intended for conversion into cash in the course of normal trading – for example, buildings, plant and machinery.

Fixed interest. An interest or dividend payable per annum which is not variable.

Floating charge. A charge on assets, usually for debenture purposes, not specifically secured on particular assets until there is some default in complying with the terms of the deed creating the charge.

Franked income. Income which has already suffered corporation tax. When received by another corporation, this income does not attract further liability to corporation tax.

Funding. Raising long-term or permanent capital to repay debt.

Gearing. The relationship between fixed-interest capital and equity. An ordinary share which is 'highly geared' is one where the amount of fixed-interest capital is high compared with the equity capital.

Gilt-edged. A term usually applied to issues of British government, Dominion and Colonial government, UK corporation and certain public authority stocks, originally indicating first-class security.

Insolvency. 'Technical insolvency' occurs when a company has sufficient assets to meet all its financial obligations, but not enough time to convert those assets into cash. 'Legal insolvency' is a condition of permanent cash shortage.

Institution. A term used to indicate a class of corporate investors, particularly the insurance companies, investment trusts, unit trusts, merchant banks and pension funds.

Interest cover. The number of times the annual interest payments on a particular amount of debt are covered by earnings before interest and tax charges.

Interest and sinking fund cover. A cover similar to the interest cover but the calculation includes tax-adjusted sinking-fund payments which will on maturity be used to repay the principal sum involved.

Internal rate of return (discounted cash flow return). The discount rate which equates the present value of the cash inflow stream with the present value of the cash outflow stream.

Introduction. Securities which do not enjoy a quotation on a particular stock exchange may obtain this by means of an 'introduction' under certain circumstances, provided that the capital is already widely held and that no part of it requires to be sold immediately.

Investment grants. Cash grants paid by the government to a company for a particular investment.

Irredeemable. Having no final date of redemption.

Issued share capital. The capital for which shares have been issued; at most the same as the authorized capital, but normally less.

Issuing house. An organization which sponsors issues of stock and shares, often a merchant bank.

Liquid assets. Generally, as opposed to fixed assets, cash or assets held for the purpose of conversion into cash during the normal course of trading.

Loan. See 'Debt'.

Market price. The price of a security quoted in the market.

Maturity. When a debenture's life has run out, and repayment of the loan is due, the debenture is said to have reached maturity.

Merchant bank. A City banking house which engages in some or all of many activities such as acceptance credits, export finance, issue of securities etc.

Merger. The union of firms of similar size.

Minority interest. The equity interest in a subsidiary company which is held outside the controlling parent company.

Net present value. The net present value is the value of a project's cash flows discounted back to the present, normally at the investor's minimum required rate of return.

Nominal capital. See 'authorized capital'.

Nominal (par) value. The value printed on a share certificate – as in 'shares of £1 each'. This must not be confused with the market price.

No par value. Shares having no nominal value.

Offer for sale. In the case of a new issue the issuing house or merchant bank involved buys all the shares for sale and then offers them to the general public.

Operating lease. An operating lease differs from a financial lease, in that it allows either side to cancel the contract upon suitable notice. This cancellation clause in effect reduces the risk of obsolescence to the lessee.

Ordinary shares. The shares which have the right to participate in all the profits and assets of a company after the rights of the prior fixed charges have been satisfied.

Paid-up capital. That part of the issued capital for which the nominal value has been received by the company and on which, therefore, no further liabilities attach to the holders.

Participating. Used to describe preference shares, the holders of which are entitled not only to the fixed-interest dividend, but also to an additional distribution as described in the particulars of the issue.

Partly paid. Securities on which a liability still exists which may be called in due course. This liability results as only part of the full price is demanded at the time of issue; hence the security is only partly paid.

Payback period. The number of years taken to recover a project's initial capital outlay computed after taxes and investment incentives.

Price-earnings (P/E) ratio. The ratio of the current share price to current annual earnings per share.

Placing. Direct sale of securities by stockbrokers to their clients. This term is used either in the context of a new issue or in disposing of other securities which they are instructed to sell.

Preference shares. Those shares which have a prior claim on any profits available for dividend.

Premium. In the case of a new issue, the excess of the market price over the issue price.

Public issue by prospectus. A new issue in which all the equity offered for sale is sold to the general public.

Quick assets. That part of assets which is made up of cash and invested cash – such as government securities, other quoted investments, short-term deposits and tax reserve certificates.

Quick ratio.

$$\text{quick ratio} = \frac{\text{liquid assets}}{\text{current liabilities}}$$

Quotation. 1. Dealing price in the market. 2. In the case of securities previously unquoted, the Council of the Stock Exchange grants 'permission to deal' and 'official quotation' when it approves an application for quotation.

Redeemable. With reference to a stock, one which is repayable at some future date.

Redemption. A redeemable stock is repaid on the date of redemption.

'Retained' profits. Profits earned for the equity holders in a company which are not distributed in dividend; generally used in relation to the profits earned in any one year. Accumulated retained profits are reserves.

Rights. Any entitlement. Issues to existing shareholders on a proportionate basis as a 'rights issue'.

Risk-free rate of return (riskless rate). The risk-free rate of return is the return on an asset that is certain. This rate can be represented by the treasury bill rate (3 or 6-month government securities).

Risk premium. The risk premium on an asset is the actual return minus the riskless rate of return.

Sale and leaseback. The sale of an asset by one party to another, the latter simultaneously agreeing to lease the asset back to the seller.

Security. Assets pledged as collateral for a loan.

Share splitting. The division of shares into shares of a smaller denomination, generally done in order to reduce an unwieldy market price and to increase the number of shares in issue.

Sinking fund. A fund, normally established in connection with an issue of loan capital, to extinguish all or part of the liability over a period.

Stag. A speculator who applies for a new issue with the object of selling his allotment when dealings commence and taking a profit.

Stock dividends. Issues of dividends not in cash, but in further shares of the company.

Takeover. A company merger or acquisition.

Tax allowances. These are allowances permitting an asset to be depreciated for tax purposes.

Tender. A method of selling securities, particularly new issues, whereby applicants submit bids independently and the issue is either allocated to bidders from the highest price downwards or an issue price is selected at which subscriptions fully cover the offer.

Time value of money. £1 today is worth more than £1 next year, apart from inflation, because the former could be invested and would produce a total sum greater than £1 next year.

Turnover of cash in sales.

$$\text{turnover of cash in sales} = \frac{\text{sales per period}}{\text{initial cash balance}}$$

Undated. A security without final date of redemption is termed 'undated'.

Unfranked income. Revenue which has not suffered UK corporation tax.

Unquoted. Having no quotation on a recognized stock exchange.

Unsecured. Usually descriptive of loan capital having no specific assets earmarked as security.

Voting rights. Rights attached to share capital which permit the owners to vote at general and other meetings of the company under circumstances laid down in the memorandum of association.

Warrants. A warrant carries the right to purchase ordinary shares in a company at a specified price after a specified date or for a period of time. If warrants are 'attached' they cannot be bought and sold separately from the stock with which they were issued, if 'unattached', they may be traded subsequently apart from the stock with which they were issued.

Working capital. The surplus of current assets over current liabilities. These net current assets provide the net resources with which a company can finance day-to-day operations.

Appendix 1
Present Value of 1

Present value of 1

Year	Percentage									
	1	2	3	4	5	6	7	8	9	10
1	0.990099	0.980392	0.970874	0.961538	0.952381	0.943396	0.934579	0.925926	0.917431	0.909091
2	0.980296	0.961169	0.942596	0.924556	0.907029	0.889996	0.873439	0.857339	0.841680	0.826446
3	0.970590	0.942322	0.915142	0.888996	0.863838	0.839619	0.816298	0.793832	0.772183	0.751315
4	0.960980	0.923845	0.888487	0.854804	0.822702	0.792094	0.762895	0.735030	0.708425	0.683013
5	0.951466	0.905731	0.862609	0.821927	0.783526	0.747258	0.712986	0.680583	0.649931	0.620921
6	0.942045	0.887971	0.837484	0.790315	0.746215	0.704961	0.666342	0.630170	0.596267	0.564474
7	0.932718	0.870560	0.813092	0.759918	0.710681	0.665057	0.622750	0.583490	0.547034	0.513158
8	0.923483	0.853490	0.789409	0.730690	0.676839	0.627412	0.582009	0.540269	0.501866	0.466507
9	0.914340	0.836755	0.766417	0.702587	0.644609	0.591898	0.543934	0.500249	0.460428	0.424098
10	0.905287	0.820348	0.744094	0.675564	0.613913	0.558395	0.508349	0.463193	0.422411	0.385543
11	0.896324	0.804263	0.722421	0.649581	0.584679	0.526788	0.475093	0.428883	0.387533	0.350494
12	0.887449	0.788493	0.701380	0.624597	0.556837	0.496969	0.444012	0.397114	0.355535	0.318631
13	0.878663	0.773033	0.680951	0.600574	0.530321	0.468839	0.414964	0.367698	0.326179	0.289664
14	0.869963	0.757875	0.661118	0.577475	0.505068	0.442301	0.387817	0.340461	0.299246	0.263331
15	0.861349	0.743015	0.641862	0.555265	0.481017	0.417265	0.362446	0.315242	0.274538	0.239392
16	0.852821	0.728446	0.623167	0.533908	0.458112	0.393646	0.338735	0.291890	0.251870	0.217629
17	0.844377	0.714163	0.605016	0.513373	0.436297	0.371364	0.316574	0.270269	0.231073	0.197845
18	0.836017	0.700159	0.587395	0.493628	0.415521	0.350344	0.295864	0.250249	0.211994	0.179859
19	0.827740	0.686431	0.570286	0.474642	0.395734	0.330513	0.276508	0.231712	0.194490	0.163508
20	0.819544	0.672971	0.553676	0.456387	0.376889	0.311805	0.258419	0.214548	0.178431	0.148644
21	0.811430	0.659776	0.537549	0.438834	0.358942	0.294155	0.241513	0.198656	0.163698	0.135131
22	0.803396	0.646839	0.521893	0.421955	0.341850	0.277505	0.225713	0.183941	0.150182	0.122846

23	0.795442	0.634156	0.506692	0.405726	0.325571	0.261797	0.210947	0.170315	0.137781	0.111678
24	0.787566	0.621721	0.491934	0.390121	0.310068	0.246979	0.197147	0.157699	0.126405	0.101526
25	0.779768	0.609531	0.477606	0.375117	0.295303	0.232999	0.184249	0.146018	0.115968	0.092296
26	0.772048	0.597579	0.463695	0.360689	0.281241	0.219810	0.172195	0.135202	0.106393	0.083905
27	0.764404	0.585862	0.450189	0.346817	0.267848	0.207368	0.160930	0.125187	0.097608	0.076278
28	0.756836	0.574375	0.437077	0.333477	0.255094	0.195630	0.150402	0.115914	0.089548	0.069343
29	0.749342	0.563112	0.424346	0.320651	0.242946	0.184557	0.140563	0.107328	0.082155	0.063039
30	0.741923	0.552071	0.411987	0.308319	0.231377	0.174110	0.131367	0.099377	0.075371	0.057309
31	0.734577	0.541246	0.399987	0.296460	0.220359	0.164255	0.122773	0.092016	0.069148	0.052099
32	0.727304	0.530633	0.388337	0.285058	0.209866	0.154957	0.114741	0.085200	0.063438	0.047362
33	0.720103	0.520229	0.377026	0.274094	0.199873	0.146186	0.107235	0.078889	0.058200	0.043057
34	0.712973	0.510028	0.366045	0.263552	0.190355	0.137912	0.100219	0.073045	0.053395	0.039143
35	0.705914	0.500028	0.355383	0.253415	0.181290	0.130105	0.093663	0.067635	0.048986	0.035584
36	0.698925	0.490223	0.345032	0.243669	0.172657	0.122741	0.087535	0.062625	0.044941	0.032349
37	0.692005	0.480611	0.334983	0.234297	0.164436	0.115793	0.081809	0.057986	0.041231	0.029408
38	0.685153	0.471187	0.325226	0.225285	0.156605	0.109239	0.076457	0.053690	0.037826	0.026735
39	0.678370	0.461948	0.315754	0.216621	0.149148	0.103056	0.071455	0.049713	0.034703	0.024304
40	0.671653	0.452890	0.306557	0.208289	0.142046	0.097222	0.066780	0.046031	0.031838	0.022095
41	0.665003	0.444010	0.297628	0.200278	0.135282	0.091719	0.062412	0.042621	0.029209	0.020086
42	0.658419	0.435304	0.288959	0.192575	0.128840	0.086527	0.058329	0.039464	0.026797	0.018260
43	0.651900	0.426769	0.280543	0.185168	0.122704	0.081630	0.054513	0.036541	0.024584	0.016600
44	0.645445	0.418401	0.272372	0.178046	0.116861	0.077009	0.050946	0.033834	0.022555	0.015091
45	0.639055	0.410197	0.264439	0.171198	0.111297	0.072650	0.047613	0.031328	0.020692	0.013719
46	0.632728	0.402154	0.256737	0.164614	0.105997	0.068538	0.044499	0.029007	0.018984	0.012472
47	0.626463	0.394268	0.249259	0.158283	0.100949	0.064658	0.041587	0.026859	0.017416	0.011338
48	0.620260	0.386538	0.241999	0.152195	0.096142	0.060998	0.038867	0.024869	0.015978	0.010307
49	0.614119	0.378958	0.234950	0.146341	0.091564	0.057546	0.036324	0.023027	0.014659	0.009370
50	0.608039	0.371528	0.228107	0.140713	0.087204	0.054288	0.033948	0.021321	0.013449	0.008519

Present value of 1

| | | | | | Percentage | | | | | |
Year	11	12	13	14	15	16	17	18	19	20
1	0.900901	0.892857	0.884956	0.877193	0.869565	0.862069	0.854701	0.847458	0.840336	0.833334
2	0.811622	0.797194	0.783147	0.769468	0.756144	0.743163	0.730514	0.718184	0.706165	0.694443
3	0.731191	0.711780	0.693050	0.674972	0.657516	0.640658	0.624371	0.603631	0.593416	0.578704
4	0.658731	0.635518	0.613319	0.592080	0.571753	0.552291	0.533650	0.515789	0.498669	0.482253
5	0.593451	0.567427	0.542760	0.519369	0.497177	0.476113	0.456111	0.437109	0.419049	0.401878
6	0.534641	0.506631	0.480319	0.455587	0.432328	0.410442	0.389839	0.370432	0.352142	0.334898
7	0.481658	0.452349	0.425061	0.399637	0.375937	0.353830	0.333195	0.313925	0.295918	0.279082
8	0.433926	0.403883	0.376160	0.350559	0.326902	0.305025	0.284782	0.266038	0.248671	0.232568
9	0.390925	0.360610	0.332885	0.307508	0.284262	0.262953	0.243404	0.225456	0.208967	0.193807
10	0.352184	0.321973	0.294588	0.269744	0.247185	0.226684	0.208037	0.191064	0.175602	0.161506
11	0.317283	0.287476	0.260698	0.236617	0.214943	0.195417	0.177810	0.161919	0.147565	0.134588
12	0.285841	0.256675	0.230706	0.207559	0.186907	0.168463	0.151974	0.137220	0.124004	0.112157
13	0.257514	0.229174	0.204165	0.182069	0.162528	0.145227	0.129892	0.116288	0.104205	0.093464
14	0.231995	0.204620	0.180677	0.159710	0.141329	0.125195	0.111019	0.098549	0.087567	0.077887
15	0.209004	0.182696	0.159891	0.140096	0.122894	0.107927	0.094888	0.083516	0.073586	0.064905
16	0.188292	0.163122	0.141496	0.122892	0.106865	0.093041	0.081101	0.070776	0.061837	0.054088
17	0.169633	0.145644	0.125218	0.107800	0.092926	0.080207	0.069317	0.059980	0.051964	0.045073
18	0.152822	0.130040	0.110812	0.094561	0.080805	0.069144	0.059245	0.050830	0.043667	0.037561
19	0.137678	0.116107	0.098064	0.082948	0.070265	0.059607	0.050637	0.043077	0.036695	0.031301
20	0.124034	0.103667	0.086782	0.072762	0.061100	0.051385	0.043280	0.036506	0.030836	0.026084
21	0.111742	0.092560	0.076798	0.063826	0.053131	0.044298	0.036991	0.030937	0.025913	0.021737
22	0.100669	0.082643	0.067963	0.055988	0.046201	0.038188	0.031616	0.026218	0.021775	0.018114

23	0.090693	0.073788	0.060144	0.049112	0.040174	0.032920	0.027022	0.022218	0.018299	0.015095
24	0.081705	0.065882	0.053225	0.043081	0.034934	0.028380	0.023096	0.018829	0.015377	0.012579
25	0.073608	0.058823	0.047102	0.037790	0.030378	0.024465	0.019740	0.015957	0.012922	0.010483
26	0.066314	0.052521	0.041683	0.033149	0.026415	0.021091	0.016872	0.013523	0.010859	0.008735
27	0.059742	0.046894	0.036888	0.029078	0.022970	0.018182	0.014421	0.011460	0.009125	0.007280
28	0.053822	0.041869	0.032644	0.025507	0.019974	0.015674	0.012325	0.009712	0.007668	0.006066
29	0.048488	0.037383	0.028889	0.022375	0.017369	0.013512	0.010534	0.008230	0.006444	0.005055
30	0.043683	0.033378	0.025565	0.019627	0.015103	0.011648	0.009004	0.006975	0.005415	0.004213
31	0.039354	0.029802	0.022624	0.017217	0.013133	0.010042	0.007696	0.005911	0.004550	0.003511
32	0.035454	0.026609	0.020021	0.015102	0.011420	0.008657	0.006577	0.005009	0.003824	0.002926
33	0.031940	0.023758	0.017718	0.013248	0.009931	0.007463	0.005622	0.004245	0.003213	0.002438
34	0.028775	0.021212	0.015680	0.011621	0.008635	0.006433	0.004805	0.003598	0.002700	0.002032
35	0.025924	0.018940	0.013876	0.010194	0.007509	0.005546	0.004107	0.003049	0.002269	0.001693
36	0.023355	0.016910	0.012279	0.008942	0.006529	0.004781	0.003510	0.002584	0.001907	0.001411
37	0.021040	0.015098	0.010867	0.007844	0.005678	0.004121	0.003000	0.002190	0.001602	0.001176
38	0.018955	0.013481	0.009617	0.006880	0.004937	0.003553	0.002564	0.001856	0.001347	0.000980
39	0.017077	0.012036	0.008510	0.006035	0.004293	0.003063	0.002192	0.001573	0.001132	0.000816
40	0.015384	0.010747	0.007531	0.005294	0.003733	0.002640	0.001873	0.001333	0.000951	0.000680
41	0.013860	0.009595	0.006665	0.004644	0.003246	0.002276	0.001601	0.001129	0.000799	0.000576
42	0.012486	0.008567	0.005898	0.004074	0.002823	0.001962	0.001368	0.000957	0.000671	0.000472
43	0.011249	0.007649	0.005219	0.003573	0.002455	0.001692	0.001170	0.000811	0.000564	0.000394
44	0.010134	0.006830	0.004619	0.003135	0.002134	0.001458	0.001000	0.000687	0.000474	0.000328
45	0.009130	0.006098	0.004088	0.002750	0.001856	0.001257	0.000854	0.000583	0.000398	0.000273
46	0.008225	0.005445	0.003617	0.002412	0.001614	0.001084	0.000730	0.000494	0.000335	0.000228
47	0.007410	0.004861	0.003201	0.002116	0.001403	0.000934	0.000624	0.000418	0.000281	0.000190
48	0.006676	0.004340	0.002833	0.001856	0.001220	0.000805	0.000533	0.000355	0.000236	0.000158
49	0.006014	0.003875	0.002507	0.001628	0.001061	0.000694	0.000456	0.000300	0.000199	0.000132
50	0.005418	0.003460	0.002219	0.001428	0.000923	0.000599	0.000390	0.000255	0.000167	0.000110

Present value of 1

Percentage

Year	21	22	23	24	25	26	27	28	29	30
1	0.826446	0.819672	0.813008	0.806452	0.800000	0.793651	0.787402	0.781250	0.775194	0.769231
2	0.683013	0.671862	0.660982	0.650364	0.640000	0.629882	0.620001	0.610352	0.600925	0.591716
3	0.564474	0.550707	0.537384	0.524487	0.512000	0.499906	0.488190	0.476837	0.465834	0.455166
4	0.466507	0.451399	0.436897	0.422974	0.409600	0.396751	0.384402	0.372529	0.361111	0.350128
5	0.385543	0.369999	0.355201	0.341108	0.327680	0.314882	0.302678	0.291038	0.279931	0.269329
6	0.318631	0.303278	0.288781	0.275087	0.262144	0.249906	0.238329	0.227374	0.217001	0.207176
7	0.263331	0.248589	0.234782	0.221844	0.209715	0.198338	0.187661	0.177636	0.168218	0.159366
8	0.217629	0.203761	0.190879	0.178907	0.167772	0.157411	0.147765	0.138778	0.130401	0.122589
9	0.179859	0.167017	0.155187	0.144280	0.134218	0.124930	0.116350	0.108420	0.101086	0.094300
10	0.148644	0.136899	0.126168	0.116354	0.107374	0.099150	0.091614	0.084703	0.078362	0.072538
11	0.122846	0.112213	0.102576	0.093834	0.085899	0.078691	0.072137	0.066174	0.060745	0.055799
12	0.101526	0.091978	0.083395	0.075673	0.068719	0.062453	0.056801	0.051699	0.047089	0.042922
13	0.083905	0.075391	0.067801	0.061026	0.054976	0.049566	0.044725	0.040390	0.036503	0.033017
14	0.069343	0.061796	0.055122	0.049215	0.043980	0.039338	0.035217	0.031554	0.028297	0.025398
15	0.057309	0.050653	0.044815	0.039689	0.035184	0.031221	0.027730	0.024652	0.021936	0.019537
16	0.047362	0.041519	0.036435	0.032008	0.028147	0.024778	0.021834	0.019259	0.017005	0.015028
17	0.039143	0.034032	0.029622	0.025813	0.022518	0.019665	0.017192	0.015046	0.013182	0.011560
18	0.032349	0.027895	0.024083	0.020817	0.018014	0.015607	0.013537	0.011755	0.010218	0.008892
19	0.026735	0.022865	0.019580	0.016788	0.014412	0.012387	0.010659	0.009184	0.007921	0.006840
20	0.022095	0.018741	0.015918	0.013538	0.011529	0.009831	0.008393	0.007175	0.006141	0.005262
21	0.018260	0.015362	0.012942	0.010918	0.009223	0.007802	0.006609	0.005605	0.004760	0.004048
22	0.015091	0.012592	0.010522	0.008805	0.007379	0.006192	0.005204	0.004379	0.003690	0.003113
23	0.012472	0.010321	0.008554	0.007101	0.005903	0.004914	0.004097	0.003421	0.002860	0.002395

24	0.010307	0.008460	0.006955	0.005726	0.004722	0.003900	0.003226	0.002673	0.002217	0.001842
25	0.008519	0.006934	0.005654	0.004618	0.003778	0.003096	0.002540	0.002088	0.001719	0.001417
26	0.007040	0.005684	0.004597	0.003724	0.003022	0.002457	0.002000	0.001631	0.001333	0.001090
27	0.005818	0.004659	0.003737	0.003003	0.002418	0.001950	0.001575	0.001274	0.001033	0.000839
28	0.004809	0.003819	0.003038	0.002422	0.001934	0.001547	0.001240	0.000996	0.000801	0.000645
29	0.003974	0.003130	0.002470	0.001953	0.001547	0.001228	0.000977	0.000778	0.000621	0.000496
30	0.003284	0.002566	0.002008	0.001575	0.001238	0.000975	0.000769	0.000608	0.000481	0.000382
31	0.002714	0.002103	0.001633	0.001270	0.000990	0.000774	0.000605	0.000475	0.000373	0.000294
32	0.002243	0.001724	0.001328	0.001024	0.000792	0.000614	0.000477	0.000371	0.000289	0.000226
33	0.001854	0.001413	0.001079	0.000826	0.000634	0.000487	0.000375	0.000290	0.000224	0.000174
34	0.001532	0.001153	0.000877	0.000666	0.000507	0.000387	0.000296	0.000226	0.000174	0.000134
35	0.001266	0.000949	0.000713	0.000537	0.000406	0.000307	0.000233	0.000177	0.000135	0.000103
36	0.001046	0.000778	0.000580	0.000433	0.000325	0.000244	0.000183	0.000138	0.000104	0.791 4*
37	0.000865	0.000638	0.000472	0.000349	0.000260	0.000193	0.000144	0.000108	0.809 4*	0.608 4
38	0.000715	0.000523	0.000383	0.000282	0.000208	0.000153	0.000114	0.843 4*	0.627 4	0.468 4
39	0.000591	0.000429	0.000312	0.000227	0.000166	0.000122	0.895 4*	0.659 4	0.486 4	0.360 4
40	0.000488	0.000351	0.000253	0.000183	0.000133	0.966 4*	0.704 4	0.515 4	0.377 4	0.277 4
41	0.000403	0.000288	0.000206	0.000148	0.000106	0.767 4	0.555 4	0.402 4	0.292 4	0.213 4
42	0.000333	0.000236	0.000167	0.000119	0.851 4*	0.609 4	0.437 4	0.314 4	0.227 4	0.164 4
43	0.000276	0.000193	0.000136	0.961 4*	0.681 4	0.483 4	0.344 4	0.245 4	0.176 4	0.126 4
44	0.000228	0.000159	0.000111	0.775 4	0.544 4	0.383 4	0.271 4	0.192 4	0.136 4	0.969 4
45	0.000188	0.000130	0.900 4*	0.625 4	0.436 4	0.304 4	0.213 4	0.150 4	0.106 4	0.746 4
46	0.000156	0.000107	0.732 4	0.504 4	0.348 4	0.242 4	0.168 4	0.117 4	0.818 5	0.574 5
47	0.000129	0.873 4*	0.595 4	0.407 4	0.279 4	0.192 4	0.132 4	0.914 5	0.634 5	0.441 5
48	0.000106	0.716 4	0.484 4	0.328 4	0.223 4	0.152 4	0.104 4	0.714 5	0.492 5	0.339 5
49	0.878 4*	0.587 4	0.393 4	0.264 4	0.178 4	0.121 4	0.820 5	0.558 5	0.381 5	0.261 5
50	0.726 4	0.481 4	0.320 4	0.213 4	0.143 4	0.958 5	0.645 5	0.436 5	0.295 5	0.201 5

* The final digit is the power of 10 by which the given tabular value has to be divided.

Present value of 1

Percentage

Year	31	32	33	34	35	36	37	38	39	40
1	0.763359	0.757576	0.751880	0.746269	0.740741	0.735294	0.729927	0.724638	0.719424	0.714286
2	0.582717	0.573921	0.565323	0.556917	0.548697	0.540657	0.532793	0.525100	0.517572	0.510204
3	0.444822	0.434789	0.425055	0.415610	0.406442	0.397542	0.388900	0.380507	0.372354	0.364431
4	0.339559	0.329385	0.319590	0.310156	0.301068	0.292310	0.283869	0.275730	0.267880	0.260308
5	0.259205	0.249534	0.240293	0.231460	0.223014	0.214934	0.207204	0.199804	0.192720	0.185934
6	0.197866	0.189041	0.180672	0.172731	0.165195	0.158040	0.151243	0.144786	0.138647	0.132810
7	0.151043	0.143213	0.135843	0.128904	0.122367	0.116206	0.110397	0.104917	0.099746	0.094865
8	0.115300	0.108495	0.102138	0.096197	0.090642	0.085445	0.080582	0.076027	0.071760	0.067760
9	0.088015	0.082193	0.076795	0.071789	0.067142	0.062828	0.058819	0.055092	0.051626	0.048400
10	0.067187	0.062267	0.057741	0.053574	0.049735	0.046197	0.042933	0.039922	0.037141	0.034572
11	0.051288	0.047172	0.043414	0.039980	0.036841	0.033968	0.031338	0.028929	0.026720	0.024694
12	0.039151	0.035737	0.032642	0.029836	0.027289	0.024977	0.022875	0.020963	0.019223	0.017639
13	0.029886	0.027073	0.024543	0.022266	0.020214	0.018365	0.016697	0.015190	0.013830	0.012599
14	0.022814	0.020510	0.018453	0.016616	0.014974	0.013504	0.012187	0.011008	0.009949	0.008999
15	0.017415	0.015538	0.013875	0.012400	0.011092	0.009929	0.008896	0.007977	0.007158	0.006428
16	0.013294	0.011771	0.010432	0.009254	0.008216	0.007301	0.006493	0.005780	0.005149	0.004591
17	0.010148	0.008918	0.007844	0.006906	0.006086	0.005368	0.004740	0.004188	0.003705	0.003280
18	0.007747	0.006756	0.005898	0.005154	0.004508	0.003947	0.003460	0.003035	0.002665	0.002343
19	0.005914	0.005118	0.004434	0.003846	0.003339	0.002902	0.002525	0.002199	0.001917	0.001673
20	0.004514	0.003877	0.003334	0.002870	0.002474	0.002134	0.001843	0.001594	0.001379	0.001195
21	0.003446	0.002937	0.002507	0.002142	0.001832	0.001569	0.001345	0.001155	0.000992	0.000854
22	0.002630	0.002225	0.001885	0.001598	0.001357	0.001154	0.000982	0.000837	0.000714	0.000610
23	0.002008	0.001686	0.001417	0.001193	0.001005	0.000848	0.000717	0.000606	0.000514	0.000436

24	0.001533	0.001277	0.001066	0.000890	0.000745	0.000624	0.000523	0.000439	0.000370	0.000311
25	0.001170	0.000968	0.000801	0.000664	0.000552	0.000459	0.000382	0.000318	0.000266	0.000222
26	0.000893	0.000733	0.000602	0.000496	0.000409	0.000337	0.000279	0.000231	0.000191	0.000159
27	0.000682	0.000555	0.000453	0.000370	0.000303	0.000248	0.000203	0.000167	0.000138	0.000113
28	0.000520	0.000421	0.000341	0.000276	0.000224	0.000182	0.000149	0.000121	0.990 4*	0.810 4*
29	0.000397	0.000319	0.000256	0.000206	0.000166	0.000134	0.000108	0.878 4*	0.712 4	0.578 4
30	0.000303	0.000241	0.000193	0.000154	0.000123	0.986 4*	0.791 4*	0.636 4	0.512 4	0.413 4
31	0.000232	0.000183	0.000145	0.000115	0.911 4*	0.725 4	0.578 4	0.461 4	0.369 4	0.295 4
32	0.000177	0.000139	0.000109	0.856 4*	0.675 4	0.533 4	0.422 4	0.334 4	0.265 4	0.211 4
33	0.000135	0.000105	0.818 4*	0.639 4	0.500 4	0.392 4	0.308 4	0.242 4	0.191 4	0.151 4
34	0.000103	0.795 4*	0.615 4	0.477 4	0.370 4	0.288 4	0.225 4	0.175 4	0.137 4	0.108 4
35	0.786 4*	0.602 4	0.463 4	0.356 4	0.274 4	0.212 4	0.164 4	0.127 4	0.987 5	0.768 5
36	0.600 4	0.456 4	0.348 4	0.266 4	0.203 4	0.156 4	0.120 4	0.921 5	0.710 5	0.549 5
37	0.458 4	0.346 4	0.262 4	0.198 4	0.151 4	0.115 4	0.874 5	0.668 5	0.511 5	0.392 5
38	0.350 4	0.262 4	0.197 4	0.148 4	0.112 4	0.842 5	0.638 5	0.484 5	0.368 5	0.280 5
39	0.267 4	0.198 4	0.148 4	0.110 4	0.826 5	0.619 5	0.465 5	0.351 5	0.264 5	0.200 5
40	0.204 4	0.150 4	0.111 4	0.824 5	0.612 5	0.455 5	0.340 5	0.254 5	0.190 5	0.143 5
41	0.156 4	0.114 4	0.836 5	0.615 5	0.453 5	0.335 5	0.248 5	0.184 5	0.137 5	0.102 5
42	0.119 4	0.863 5	0.628 5	0.459 5	0.336 5	0.246 5	0.181 5	0.133 5	0.985 6	0.729 6
43	0.906 5	0.654 5	0.472 5	0.342 5	0.249 5	0.181 5	0.132 5	0.966 6	0.709 6	0.521 6
44	0.692 5	0.495 5	0.355 5	0.255 5	0.184 5	0.133 5	0.964 6	0.700 6	0.510 6	0.372 6
45	0.528 5	0.375 5	0.267 5	0.191 5	0.136 5	0.979 6	0.704 6	0.508 6	0.367 6	0.266 6
46	0.403 5	0.284 5	0.201 5	0.142 5	0.101 5	0.720 6	0.514 6	0.368 6	0.264 6	0.190 6
47	0.308 5	0.215 5	0.151 5	0.106 5	0.749 6	0.529 6	0.375 6	0.266 6	0.190 6	0.136 6
48	0.235 5	0.163 5	0.114 5	0.792 6	0.555 6	0.389 6	0.274 6	0.193 6	0.137 6	0.968 7
49	0.179 5	0.124 5	0.854 6	0.591 6	0.411 6	0.286 6	0.200 6	0.140 6	0.982 7	0.691 7
50	0.137 5	0.936 6	0.642 6	0.441 6	0.304 6	0.210 6	0.146 6	0.101 6	0.707 7	0.494 7

* The final digit is the power of 10 by which the given tabular value has to be divided.

Appendix 2
Present Value of 1 per Year

Present value of 1 per year

$$a_{n,r} = \frac{1-(1+r)^{-n}}{r}$$

Percentage

Year	1	2	3	4	5	6	7	8	9	10
1	0.990099	0.980392	0.970874	0.961538	0.952381	0.943396	0.934579	0.925926	0.917431	0.909091
2	1.97040	1.94156	1.91347	1.88609	1.85941	1.83339	1.80802	1.78326	1.75911	1.73554
3	2.94099	2.88388	2.82861	2.77509	2.27325	2.67301	2.62432	2.57710	2.53129	2.48685
4	3.90197	3.80773	3.71710	3.62990	3.54595	3.46511	3.38721	3.31213	3.23972	3.16987
5	4.85343	4.71346	4.57971	4.45182	4.32948	4.21236	4.10020	3.99271	3.88965	3.79079
6	5.79548	5.60143	5.41719	5.24214	5.07569	4.91732	4.76654	4.62288	4.48592	4.35526
7	6.72819	6.47199	6.23028	6.00205	5.78637	5.58238	5.38929	5.20637	5.03295	4.86842
8	7.65168	7.32548	7.01969	6.73274	6.46321	6.20979	5.97130	5.74664	5.53482	5.33493
9	8.56602	8.16224	7.78611	7.43533	7.10782	6.80169	6.51523	6.24689	5.99525	5.75902
10	9.47130	8.98259	8.53020	8.11090	7.72173	7.36009	7.02358	6.71008	6.41766	6.14457
11	10.3676	9.78685	9.25262	8.76048	8.30641	7.88687	7.49867	7.13896	6.80519	6.49506
12	11.2551	10.5753	9.95400	9.38507	8.86325	8.38384	7.94269	7.53608	7.16073	6.81369
13	12.1337	11.3484	10.6350	9.98565	9.39357	8.85268	8.35765	7.90378	7.48690	7.10336
14	13.0037	12.1062	11.2961	10.5631	9.89864	9.29498	8.74547	8.24424	7.78615	7.36669
15	13.8651	12.8493	11.9379	11.1184	10.3797	9.71225	9.10791	8.55948	8.06069	7.60608
16	14.7179	13.5777	12.5611	11.6523	10.8378	10.1059	9.44665	8.85137	8.31256	7.82371
17	15.5623	14.2919	13.1661	12.1657	11.2741	10.4773	9.76322	9.12164	8.54363	8.02155
18	16.3983	14.9920	13.7535	12.6593	11.6896	10.8276	10.0591	9.37189	8.75563	8.20141
19	17.2260	15.6785	14.3238	13.1339	12.0853	11.1581	10.3356	9.60360	8.95011	8.36492
20	18.0456	16.3514	14.8775	13.5903	12.4622	11.4699	10.5940	9.81815	9.12855	8.51356
21	18.8570	17.0112	15.4150	14.0292	12.8212	11.7641	10.8355	10.0168	9.29224	8.64869
22	19.6604	17.6580	15.9369	14.4511	13.1630	12.0416	11.0612	10.2007	9.44243	8.77154

23	20.4558	18.2922	16.4436	14.8568	13.4886	12.3034	11.2722	10.3711	9.58021	8.88322
24	21.2434	18.9139	16.9355	15.2470	13.7986	12.5504	11.4693	10.5288	9.70661	8.98474
25	22.0232	19.5235	17.4131	15.6221	14.0939	12.7834	11.6536	10.6748	9.82258	9.07704
26	22.7952	20.1210	17.8768	15.9828	14.3752	13.0032	11.8258	10.8100	9.92897	9.16095
27	23.5596	20.7069	18.3270	16.3296	14.6430	13.2105	11.9867	10.9352	10.0266	9.23722
28	24.3164	21.2813	18.7641	16.6631	14.8981	13.4062	12.1371	11.0511	10.1161	9.30657
29	25.0658	21.8444	19.1885	16.9837	15.1411	13.5907	12.2777	11.1584	10.1983	9.36961
30	25.8077	22.3965	19.6004	17.2920	15.3725	13.7648	12.4090	11.2578	10.2737	9.42691
31	26.5423	22.9377	20.0004	17.5885	15.5928	13.9291	12.5318	11.3498	10.3428	9.47901
32	27.2696	23.4683	20.3888	17.8736	15.8027	14.0840	12.6466	11.4350	10.4062	9.52638
33	27.9897	23.9886	20.7658	18.1476	16.0025	14.2302	12.7538	11.5139	10.4644	9.56943
34	28.7027	24.4986	21.1318	18.4112	16.1929	14.3681	12.8540	11.5869	10.5178	9.60857
35	29.4086	24.9986	21.4872	18.6646	16.3742	14.4982	12.9477	11.6546	10.5668	9.64416
36	30.1075	25.4888	21.8323	18.9083	16.5469	14.6210	13.0352	11.7172	10.6118	9.67641
37	30.7995	25.9695	22.1672	19.1426	16.7113	14.7368	13.1170	11.7752	10.6530	9.70592
38	31.4847	26.4406	22.4925	19.3679	16.8679	14.8460	13.1935	11.8289	10.6908	9.73265
39	32.1630	26.9026	22.8082	19.5845	17.0170	14.9491	13.2649	11.8786	10.7255	9.75696
40	32.8347	27.3555	23.1148	19.7928	17.1591	15.0463	13.3317	11.9246	10.7574	9.77905
41	33.4997	27.7995	23.4124	19.9931	17.2944	15.1380	13.3941	11.9672	10.7866	9.79914
42	34.1581	28.2348	23.7014	20.1856	17.4232	15.2245	13.4524	12.0067	10.8134	9.81740
43	34.8100	28.6616	23.9819	20.3708	17.5459	15.3062	13.5070	12.0432	10.8380	9.83400
44	35.4555	29.0800	24.2543	20.5488	17.6628	15.3832	13.5579	12.0771	10.8605	9.84909
45	36.0945	29.4902	24.5187	20.7200	17.7741	15.4558	13.6055	12.1084	10.8812	9.86281
46	36.7272	29.8923	24.7754	20.8847	17.8801	15.5244	13.6500	12.1374	10.9002	9.87528
47	37.3537	30.2866	25.0247	21.0429	17.9810	15.5890	13.6916	12.1643	10.9176	9.88662
48	37.9740	30.6731	25.2667	21.1951	18.0772	15.6500	13.7305	12.1891	10.9336	9.89693
49	38.5881	31.0521	25.5017	21.3415	18.1687	15.7076	13.7668	12.2122	10.9482	9.90630
50	39.1961	31.4236	25.7298	21.4822	18.2559	15.7619	13.8007	12.2335	10.9617	9.91481

$$a_{n,r} = \frac{1-(1+r)^{-n}}{r}$$

Present value of 1 per year

Percentage

Year	11	12	13	14	15	16	17	18	19	20
1	0.900901	0.892857	0.884956	0.877193	0.869565	0.862069	0.854701	0.847458	0.840336	0.833333
2	1.71252	1.69005	1.66810	1.64666	1.62571	1.60523	1.58521	1.56564	1.54650	1.52778
3	2.44371	2.40183	2.36115	2.32163	2.28323	2.24589	2.20958	2.17427	2.13992	2.10648
4	3.10245	3.03735	2.97447	2.91371	2.85498	2.79818	2.74324	2.69006	2.63859	2.58873
5	3.69590	3.60478	3.51723	3.43308	3.35216	3.27429	3.19935	3.12717	3.05763	2.99061
6	4.23054	4.11141	3.99755	3.88867	3.78448	3.68474	3.58918	3.49760	3.40978	3.32551
7	4.71220	4.56376	4.42261	4.28830	4.16042	4.03857	3.92238	3.81153	3.70570	3.60459
8	5.14612	4.96764	4.79877	4.63886	4.48732	4.34359	4.20716	4.07757	3.95437	3.83716
9	5.53705	5.32825	5.13166	4.94637	4.77158	4.60654	4.45057	4.30302	4.16333	4.03097
10	5.88923	5.65022	5.42624	5.21612	5.01877	4.83323	4.65860	4.49409	4.33893	4.19247
11	6.20652	5.93770	5.68694	5.45273	5.23371	5.02864	4.83641	4.65601	4.48650	4.32706
12	6.49236	6.19437	5.91765	5.66029	5.42062	5.19711	4.98839	4.79322	4.61050	4.43922
13	6.74987	6.42355	6.12181	5.84236	5.58315	5.34233	5.11828	4.90951	4.71471	4.53268
14	6.98187	6.62817	6.30249	6.00207	5.72448	5.46753	5.22930	5.00806	4.80228	4.61057
15	7.19087	6.81086	6.46238	6.14217	5.84737	5.57546	5.32419	5.09158	4.87586	4.67547
16	7.37916	6.97399	6.60388	6.26506	5.95423	5.66850	5.40529	5.16235	4.93770	4.72956
17	7.54879	7.11963	6.72909	6.37286	6.04716	5.74870	5.47461	5.22233	4.98966	4.77463
18	7.70162	7.24967	6.83991	6.46742	6.12797	5.81785	5.53385	5.27316	5.03333	4.81219
19	7.83929	7.36578	6.93797	6.55037	6.19823	5.87746	5.58449	5.31624	5.07003	4.84350
20	7.96333	7.46944	7.02475	6.62313	6.25933	5.92884	5.62777	5.35275	5.10086	4.86958
21	8.07507	7.56200	7.10155	6.68696	6.31246	5.97314	5.66476	5.38368	5.12677	4.89132
22	8.17574	7.64465	7.16951	6.74294	6.35866	6.01133	5.69637	5.40990	5.14855	4.90943

23	4.92453	5.16685	5.43212	5.72340	6.04425	6.39884	6.79206	7.22966	7.71843	8.26643
24	4.93710	5.18223	5.45095	5.74649	6.07263	6.43377	6.83514	7.28288	7.78432	8.34814
25	4.94759	5.19515	5.46691	5.76623	6.09709	6.46415	6.87293	7.32998	7.84314	8.42174
26	4.95632	5.20601	5.48043	5.78311	6.11818	6.49056	6.90608	7.37167	7.89566	8.48806
27	4.96360	5.21513	5.49189	5.79753	6.13636	6.51353	6.93515	7.40856	7.94255	8.54780
28	4.96967	5.22280	5.50160	5.80985	6.15204	6.53351	6.96066	7.44120	7.98442	8.60162
29	4.97472	5.22924	5.50983	5.82039	6.16555	6.55088	6.98304	7.47009	8.02181	8.65011
30	4.97894	5.23466	5.51681	5.82939	6.17720	6.56598	7.00266	7.49565	8.05518	8.69379
31	4.98245	5.23921	5.52272	5.83709	6.18724	6.57911	7.01988	7.51828	8.08499	8.73315
32	4.98537	5.24303	5.52773	5.84366	6.19590	6.59053	7.03498	7.53830	8.11159	8.76860
33	4.98781	5.24625	5.53197	5.84928	6.20336	6.60046	7.04823	7.55602	8.13535	8.80054
34	4.98984	5.24895	5.53557	5.85409	6.20979	6.60910	7.05985	7.57170	8.15656	8.82932
35	4.99154	5.25122	5.53862	5.85820	6.21534	6.61661	7.07005	7.58557	8.17550	8.85524
36	4.99295	5.25312	5.54120	5.86171	6.22012	6.62314	7.07899	7.59785	8.19241	8.87859
37	4.99412	5.25472	5.54339	5.86471	6.22424	6.62881	7.08683	7.60872	8.20751	8.89963
38	4.99510	5.25607	5.54525	5.86727	6.22779	6.63375	7.09371	7.61833	8.22099	8.91859
39	4.99592	5.25720	5.54682	5.86946	6.23086	6.63805	7.09975	7.62684	8.23303	8.93567
40	4.99660	5.25815	5.54815	5.87133	6.23350	6.64178	7.10504	7.63438	8.24378	8.95105
41	4.99717	5.25895	5.54928	5.87294	6.23577	6.64502	7.10969	7.64104	8.25337	8.96491
42	4.99764	5.25962	5.55024	5.87430	6.23774	6.64785	7.11376	7.64694	8.26194	8.97740
43	4.99803	5.26019	5.55105	5.87547	6.23943	6.65030	7.11733	7.65216	8.26959	8.98865
44	4.99836	5.26066	5.55174	5.87647	6.24089	6.65244	7.12047	7.65678	8.27642	8.99878
45	4.99863	5.26106	5.55232	5.87733	6.24214	6.65429	7.12322	7.66086	8.28252	9.00791
46	4.99886	5.26140	5.55281	5.87806	6.24323	6.65591	7.12563	7.66448	8.28796	9.01614
47	4.99905	5.26168	5.55323	5.87868	6.24416	6.65731	7.12774	7.66768	8.29282	9.02355
48	4.99921	5.26191	5.55359	5.87922	6.24497	6.65853	7.12960	7.67052	8.29716	9.03022
49	4.99934	5.26211	5.55389	5.87967	6.24566	6.65959	7.13123	7.67302	8.30104	9.03624
50	4.99945	5.26228	5.55414	5.88006	6.24626	6.66051	7.13266	7.67524	8.30450	9.04165

Present value of 1 per year

$$a_{n,r} = \frac{1-(1+r)^{-n}}{r}$$

Percentage

Year	21	22	23	24	25	26	27	28	29	30
1	0.826446	0.819672	0.813008	0.806452	0.800000	0.793651	0.787402	0.781250	0.775194	0.769231
2	1.50946	1.49153	1.47399	1.45682	1.44000	1.42353	1.40740	1.39160	1.37612	1.36095
3	2.07393	2.04224	2.01137	1.98130	1.95200	1.92344	1.89559	1.86844	1.84195	1.81611
4	2.54044	2.49364	2.44827	2.40428	2.36160	2.32019	2.27999	2.24097	2.20306	2.16624
5	2.92598	2.86364	2.80347	2.74538	2.68928	2.63507	2.58267	2.53201	2.48300	2.43557
6	3.24462	3.16692	3.09225	3.02047	2.95142	2.88498	2.82100	2.75938	2.70000	2.64275
7	3.50795	3.41551	3.32704	3.24232	3.16114	3.08331	3.00866	2.93702	2.86821	2.80211
8	3.72558	3.61927	3.51792	3.42122	3.32891	3.24073	3.15643	3.07579	2.99862	2.92470
9	3.90543	3.78628	3.67310	3.56550	3.46313	3.36566	3.27278	3.18421	3.09970	3.01900
10	4.05408	3.92318	3.79927	3.68186	3.57050	3.46481	3.36439	3.26892	3.17806	3.09154
11	4.17692	4.03540	3.90185	3.77569	3.65640	3.54350	3.43653	3.33509	3.23881	3.14734
12	4.27845	4.12737	3.98524	3.85136	3.72512	3.60595	3.49333	3.38679	3.28590	3.19026
13	4.36235	4.20277	4.05304	3.91239	3.78010	3.65552	3.53806	3.42718	3.32240	3.22328
14	4.43170	4.26456	4.10816	3.96160	3.82408	3.69485	3.57327	3.45873	3.35070	3.24867
15	4.48901	4.31522	4.15298	4.00129	3.85926	3.72607	3.60100	3.48339	3.37264	3.26821
16	4.53637	4.35673	4.18941	4.03330	3.88741	3.75085	3.62284	3.50265	3.38964	3.28324
17	4.57551	4.39077	4.21904	4.05911	3.90993	3.77052	3.64003	3.51769	3.40282	3.29480
18	4.60786	4.41866	4.24312	4.07993	3.92794	3.78613	3.65357	3.52945	3.41304	3.30369
19	4.63460	4.44152	4.26270	4.09672	3.94235	3.79851	3.66422	3.53863	3.42096	3.31053
20	4.65669	4.46027	4.27862	4.11026	3.95388	3.80834	3.67262	3.54580	3.42710	3.31579
21	4.67495	4.47563	4.29156	4.12117	3.96311	3.81615	3.67923	3.55141	3.43186	3.31984
22	4.69004	4.48822	4.30208	4.12998	3.97049	3.82234	3.68443	3.55579	3.43555	3.32296

23	4.70251	4.49854	4.31063	4.13708	3.97639	3.82725	3.68853	3.55921	3.43841	3.32535
24	4.71282	4.50700	4.31759	4.14281	3.98111	3.83115	3.69175	3.56188	3.44063	3.32719
25	4.72134	4.51393	4.32324	4.14742	3.98489	3.83425	3.69429	3.56397	3.44235	3.32861
26	4.72838	4.51962	4.32784	4.15115	3.98791	3.83670	3.69630	3.56560	3.44368	3.32970
27	4.73420	4.52428	4.33158	4.15415	3.99033	3.83865	3.69787	3.56688	3.44471	3.33054
28	4.73901	4.52810	4.33462	4.15657	3.99226	3.84020	3.69911	3.56787	3.44551	3.33118
29	4.74298	4.53123	4.33709	4.15853	3.99381	3.84143	3.70009	3.56865	3.44614	3.33168
30	4.74627	4.53379	4.33909	4.16010	3.99505	3.84240	3.70086	3.56926	3.44662	3.33206
31	4.74898	4.53590	4.34073	4.16137	3.99604	3.84318	3.70146	3.56973	3.44699	3.33235
32	4.75122	4.53762	4.34205	4.16240	3.99683	3.84379	3.70194	3.57010	3.44728	3.33258
33	4.75308	4.53903	4.34313	4.16322	3.99746	3.84428	3.70231	3.57039	3.44750	3.33275
34	4.75461	4.54019	4.34401	4.16389	3.99797	3.84467	3.70261	3.57062	3.44768	3.33289
35	4.75588	4.54114	4.34472	4.16443	3.99838	3.84497	3.70284	3.57080	3.44781	3.33299
36	4.75692	4.54192	4.34530	4.16486	3.99870	3.84522	3.70302	3.57094	3.44792	3.33307
37	4.75779	4.54256	4.34578	4.16521	3.99896	3.84541	3.70317	3.57104	3.44800	3.33313
38	4.75850	5.54308	4.34616	4.16549	3.99917	3.84556	3.70328	3.57113	3.44806	3.33318
39	4.75909	4.54351	4.34647	4.16572	3.99934	3.84569	3.70337	3.57119	3.44811	3.33321
40	4.75958	4.54386	4.34672	4.16590	3.99947	3.84578	3.70344	3.57124	3.44815	3.33324
41	4.75998	4.54415	4.34693	4.16605	3.99957	3.84586	3.70350	3.57128	3.44818	3.33326
42	4.76032	4.54438	4.34710	4.16617	3.99966	3.84592	3.70354	3.57132	3.44820	3.33328
43	4.76059	4.54458	4.34723	4.16627	3.99973	3.84597	3.70358	3.57134	3.44822	3.33329
44	4.76082	4.54473	4.34734	4.16634	3.99978	3.84601	3.70360	3.57136	3.44823	3.33330
45	4.76101	4.54486	4.34743	4.16641	3.99983	3.84604	3.70362	3.57138	3.44824	3.33331
46	4.76116	4.54497	4.34751	4.16646	3.99986	3.84606	3.70364	3.57139	3.44825	3.33331
47	4.76129	5.54506	4.34757	4.16650	3.99989	3.84608	3.70365	3.57140	3.44825	3.33332
48	4.76140	4.54513	4.34762	4.16653	3.99991	3.84610	3.70367	3.57140	3.44826	3.33332
49	4.76149	4.54519	4.34766	4.16656	3.99993	3.84611	3.70367	3.57141	3.44826	3.33332
50	4.76156	4.54524	4.34769	4.16658	3.99994	3.84612	3.70368	3.57141	3.44827	3.33333

Present value of 1 per annum

$$a_{n,r} = \frac{1-(1+r)^{-n}}{r}$$

Percentage

Year	31	32	33	34	35	36	37	38	39	40
1	0.763359	0.757576	0.751880	0.746269	0.740741	0.735294	0.729927	0.724638	0.719424	0.714286
2	1.34608	1.33150	1.31720	1.30319	1.28944	1.27595	1.26272	1.24974	1.23700	1.22449
3	1.79090	1.76629	1.74226	1.71880	1.69588	1.67349	1.65162	1.63024	1.60935	1.58892
4	2.13046	2.09567	2.06185	2.02895	1.99695	1.96580	1.93549	1.90597	1.87723	1.84923
5	2.38966	2.34521	2.30214	2.26041	2.21996	2.18074	2.14269	2.10578	2.06995	2.03516
6	2.58753	2.53425	2.48281	2.43314	2.38516	2.33878	2.29394	2.25056	2.20860	2.16797
7	2.73857	2.67746	2.61866	2.56205	2.50752	2.45498	2.40433	2.35548	2.30834	2.26284
8	2.85387	2.78595	2.72079	2.65824	2.59817	2.54043	2.48491	2.43151	2.38010	2.33060
9	2.94189	2.86815	2.79759	2.73003	2.66531	2.60326	2.54373	2.48660	2.43173	2.37900
10	3.00907	2.93041	2.85533	2.78361	2.71504	2.64945	2.58667	2.52652	2.46887	2.41357
11	3.06036	2.97759	2.89874	2.82359	2.75188	2.68342	2.61800	2.55545	2.49559	2.43826
12	3.09951	3.01332	2.93139	2.85342	2.77917	2.70840	2.64088	2.57641	2.51481	2.45590
13	3.12940	3.04040	2.95593	2.87569	2.79939	2.72676	2.65758	2.59160	2.52864	2.46850
14	3.15221	3.06091	2.97438	2.89231	2.81436	2.74027	2.66976	2.60261	2.53859	2.47750
15	3.16963	3.07644	2.98826	2.90471	2.82545	2.75020	2.67866	2.61059	2.54575	2.48393
16	3.18292	3.08822	2.99869	2.91396	2.83367	2.75750	2.68515	2.61637	2.55090	2.48852
17	3.19307	3.09713	3.00653	2.92087	2.83975	2.76287	2.68989	2.62056	2.55460	2.49180
18	3.20082	3.10389	3.01243	2.92602	2.84426	2.76681	2.69335	2.62359	2.55727	2.49414
19	3.20673	3.10901	3.01687	2.92986	2.84760	2.76972	2.69588	2.62579	2.55919	2.49582
20	3.21124	3.11288	3.02020	2.93273	2.85008	2.77185	2.69772	2.62738	2.56057	2.49701
21	3.21469	3.11582	3.02271	2.93488	2.85191	2.77342	2.69907	2.62854	2.56156	2.49787
22	3.21732	3.11805	3.02459	2.93648	2.85327	2.77457	2.70005	2.62938	2.56227	2.49848

23	2.49891	2.56279	2.62998	2.70077	2.77542	2.85427	2.93767	3.02601	3.11973	3.21933
24	2.49922	2.56316	2.63042	2.70129	2.77604	2.85502	2.93856	3.02707	3.12101	3.22086
25	2.49944	2.56342	2.63074	2.70167	2.77650	2.85557	2.93922	3.02788	3.12198	3.22203
26	2.49960	2.56361	2.63097	2.70195	2.77684	2.85598	2.93972	3.02848	3.12271	3.22293
27	2.49972	2.56375	2.63114	2.70215	2.77709	2.85628	2.94009	3.02893	3.12326	3.22361
28	2.49980	2.56385	2.63126	2.70230	2.77727	2.85650	2.94036	3.02927	3.12369	3.22413
29	2.49986	2.56392	2.63135	2.70241	2.77741	2.85667	2.94057	3.02953	3.12400	3.22452
30	2.49990	2.56397	2.63141	2.70249	2.77750	2.85679	2.94072	3.02972	3.12425	3.22483
31	2.49993	2.56401	2.63146	2.70255	2.77758	2.85688	2.94084	3.02986	3.12443	3.22506
32	2.49995	2.56403	2.63149	2.70259	2.77763	2.85695	2.94092	3.02997	3.12457	3.22524
33	2.49996	2.56405	2.63152	2.70262	2.77767	2.85700	2.94099	3.03006	3.12467	3.22537
34	2.49997	2.56407	2.63153	2.70264	2.77770	2.85704	2.94104	3.03012	3.12475	3.22547
35	2.49998	2.56408	2.63155	2.70266	2.77772	2.85706	2.94107	3.03016	3.12481	3.22555
36	2.49999	2.56408	2.63155	2.70267	2.77773	2.85708	2.94110	3.03020	3.12486	3.22561
37	2.49999	2.56409	2.63156	2.70268	2.77775	2.85710	2.94112	3.03022	3.12489	3.22566
38	2.49999	2.56409	2.63157	2.70269	2.77775	2.85711	2.94113	3.03024	3.12492	3.22569
39	2.49999	2.56410	2.63157	2.70269	2.77776	2.85712	2.94114	3.03026	3.12494	3.22572
40	2.50000	2.56410	2.63157	2.70269	2.77777	2.85713	2.94115	3.03027	3.12495	3.22574
41	2.50000	2.56410	2.63157	2.70270	2.77777	2.85713	2.94116	3.03028	3.12496	3.22576
42	2.50000	2.56410	2.63158	2.70270	2.77777	2.85713	2.94116	3.03028	3.12497	3.22577
43	2.50000	2.56410	2.63158	2.70270	2.77777	2.85714	2.94117	3.03029	3.12498	3.22578
44	2.50000	2.56410	2.63158	2.70270	2.77777	2.85714	2.94117	3.03029	3.12498	3.22578
45	2.50000	2.56410	2.63158	2.70270	2.77778	2.85714	2.94117	3.03029	3.12499	3.22579
46	2.50000	2.56410	2.63158	2.70270	2.77778	2.85714	2.94117	3.03030	3.12499	3.22579
47	2.50000	2.56410	2.63158	2.70270	2.77778	2.85714	2.94117	3.03030	3.12499	3.22580
48	2.50000	2.56410	2.63158	2.70270	2.77778	2.85714	2.94117	3.03030	3.12499	3.22580
49	2.50000	2.56410	2.63158	2.70270	2.77778	2.85714	2.94117	3.03030	3.12500	3.22580
50	2.50000	2.56410	2.63158	2.70270	2.77778	2.85714	2.94118	3.03030	3.12500	3.22580

Present value of 1 per year

$$a_{n,r} = \frac{1-(1+r)^{-n}}{r}$$

Percentage

Year	41	42	43	44	45	46	47	48	49	50
1	0.709220	0.704225	0.699301	0.694444	0.689655	0.684932	0.680272	0.675676	0.671141	0.666667
2	1.21221	1.20016	1.18832	1.17670	1.16528	1.15406	1.14304	1.13221	1.12157	1.11111
3	1.56895	1.54941	1.53030	1.51160	1.49330	1.47539	1.45785	1.44068	1.42387	1.40741
4	1.82195	1.79536	1.76944	1.74416	1.71951	1.69547	1.67201	1.64911	1.62676	1.60494
5	2.00138	1.96856	1.93667	1.90567	1.87553	1.84621	1.81769	1.78994	1.76293	1.73663
6	2.12864	2.09054	2.05361	2.01783	1.98312	1.94946	1.91680	1.88509	1.85431	1.82442
7	2.21889	2.17643	2.13540	2.09571	2.05733	2.02018	1.98422	1.94939	1.91565	1.88294
8	2.28290	2.23693	2.19258	2.14980	2.10850	2.06862	2.03008	1.99283	1.95681	1.92196
9	2.32830	2.27952	2.23258	2.18736	2.14379	2.10179	2.06128	2.02218	1.98444	1.94798
10	2.36050	2.30952	2.26054	2.21345	2.16813	2.12451	2.08250	2.04202	2.00298	1.96532
11	2.38333	2.33065	2.28010	2.23156	2.18492	2.14008	2.09694	2.05542	2.01542	1.97688
12	2.39953	2.34553	2.29378	2.24414	2.19650	2.15074	2.10676	2.06447	2.02377	1.98459
13	2.41101	2.35601	2.30334	2.25287	2.20448	2.15804	2.11344	2.07059	2.02938	1.98972
14	2.41916	2.36338	2.31003	2.25894	2.20999	2.16304	2.11799	2.07472	2.03314	1.99315
15	2.42493	2.36858	2.31470	2.26315	2.21378	2.16647	2.12108	2.07751	2.03566	1.99543
16	2.42903	2.37224	2.31798	2.26608	2.21640	2.16881	2.12318	2.07940	2.03736	1.99696
17	2.43194	2.37482	2.32026	2.26811	2.21821	2.17042	2.12462	2.08068	2.03850	1.99797
18	2.43400	2.37663	2.32186	2.26952	2.21945	2.17152	2.12559	2.08154	2.03926	1.99865
19	2.43546	2.37791	2.32298	2.27050	2.22031	2.17227	2.12625	2.08212	2.03977	1.99910
20	2.43650	2.37881	2.32376	2.27118	2.22091	2.17279	2.12670	2.08251	2.04011	1.99940
21	2.43723	2.37944	2.32431	2.27165	2.22131	2.17314	2.12701	2.08278	2.04035	1.99960
22	2.43775	2.37989	2.32469	2.27198	2.22160	2.17339	2.12722	2.08296	2.04050	1.99973

23	2.43812	2.38020	2.32496	2.27221	2.22179	2.17355	2.12736	2.08308	2.04060	1.99982
24	2.43838	2.38043	2.32515	2.27237	2.22192	2.17367	2.12745	2.08316	2.04067	1.99988
25	2.43857	2.38058	2.32528	2.27248	2.22202	2.17374	2.12752	2.08322	2.04072	1.99992
26	2.43870	2.38069	2.32537	2.27255	2.22208	2.17380	2.12756	2.08326	2.04075	1.99995
27	2.43880	2.38077	2.32543	2.27261	2.22212	2.17383	2.12759	2.08328	2.04077	1.99996
28	2.43886	2.38082	2.32548	2.27264	2.22215	2.17386	2.12762	2.08330	2.04079	1.99998
29	2.43891	2.38086	2.32551	2.27267	2.22218	2.17388	2.12763	2.08331	2.04080	1.99998
30	2.43894	2.38089	2.32553	2.27269	2.22219	2.17389	2.12764	2.08332	2.04080	1.99999
31	2.43897	2.38091	2.32555	2.27270	2.22220	2.17390	2.12765	2.08332	2.04081	1.99999
32	2.43898	2.38092	2.32556	2.27271	2.22221	2.17390	2.12765	2.08333	2.04081	2.00000
33	2.43900	2.38093	2.32556	2.27271	2.22221	2.17390	2.12765	2.08333	2.04081	2.00000
34	2.43900	2.38094	2.32557	2.27272	2.22221	2.17391	2.12766	2.08333	2.04081	2.00000
35	2.43901	2.38094	2.32557	2.27272	2.22222	2.17391	2.12766	2.08333	2.04081	2.00000
36	2.43901	2.38094	2.32558	2.27272	2.22222	2.17391	2.12766	2.08333	2.04082	2.00000
37	2.43902	2.38095	2.32558	2.27272	2.22222	2.17391	2.12766	2.08333	2.04082	2.00000
38	2.43902	2.38095	2.32558	2.27273	2.22222	2.17391	2.12766	2.08333	2.04082	2.00000
39	2.43902	2.38095	2.32558	2.27273	2.22222	2.17391	2.12766	2.08333	2.04082	2.00000
40	2.43902	2.38095	2.32558	2.27273	2.22222	2.17391	2.12766	2.08333	2.04082	2.00000
41	2.43902	2.38095	2.32558	2.27273	2.22222	2.17391	2.12766	2.08333	2.04082	2.00000
42	2.43902	2.38095	2.32558	2.27273	2.22222	2.17391	2.12766	2.08333	2.04082	2.00000
43	2.43902	2.38095	2.32558	2.27273	2.22222	2.17391	2.12766	2.08333	2.04082	2.00000
44	2.43902	2.38095	2.32558	2.27273	2.22222	2.17391	2.12766	2.08333	2.04082	2.00000
45	2.43902	2.38095	2.32558	2.27273	2.22222	2.17391	2.12766	2.08333	2.04082	2.00000
46	2.43902	2.38095	2.32558	2.27273	2.22222	2.17391	2.12766	2.08333	2.04082	2.00000
47	2.43902	2.38095	2.32558	2.27273	2.22222	2.17391	2.12766	2.08333	2.04082	2.00000
48	2.43902	2.38095	2.32558	2.27273	2.22222	2.17391	2.12766	2.08333	2.04082	2.00000
49	2.43902	2.38095	2.32558	2.27273	2.22222	2.17391	2.12766	2.08333	2.04082	2.00000
50	2.43902	2.38095	2.32558	2.27273	2.22222	2.17391	2.12766	2.08333	2.04082	2.00000

Index